LYGIA PAPE

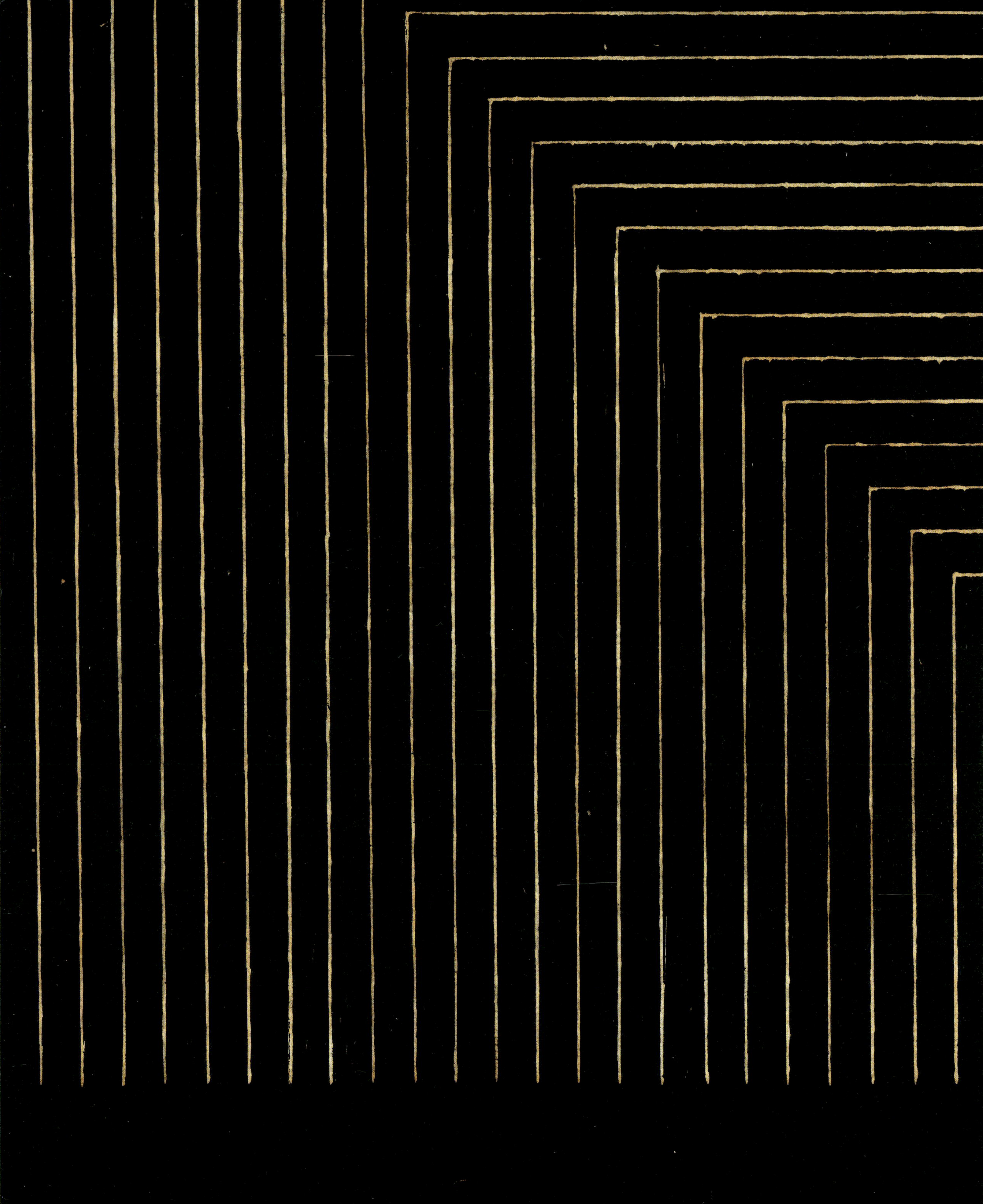

LYGIA PAPE

TECELARES

Edited by
Mark Pascale

With essays by
Adele Nelson, Mark Pascale, and
María Cristina Rivera Ramos

The Art Institute of Chicago
Distributed by Yale University Press
New Haven and London

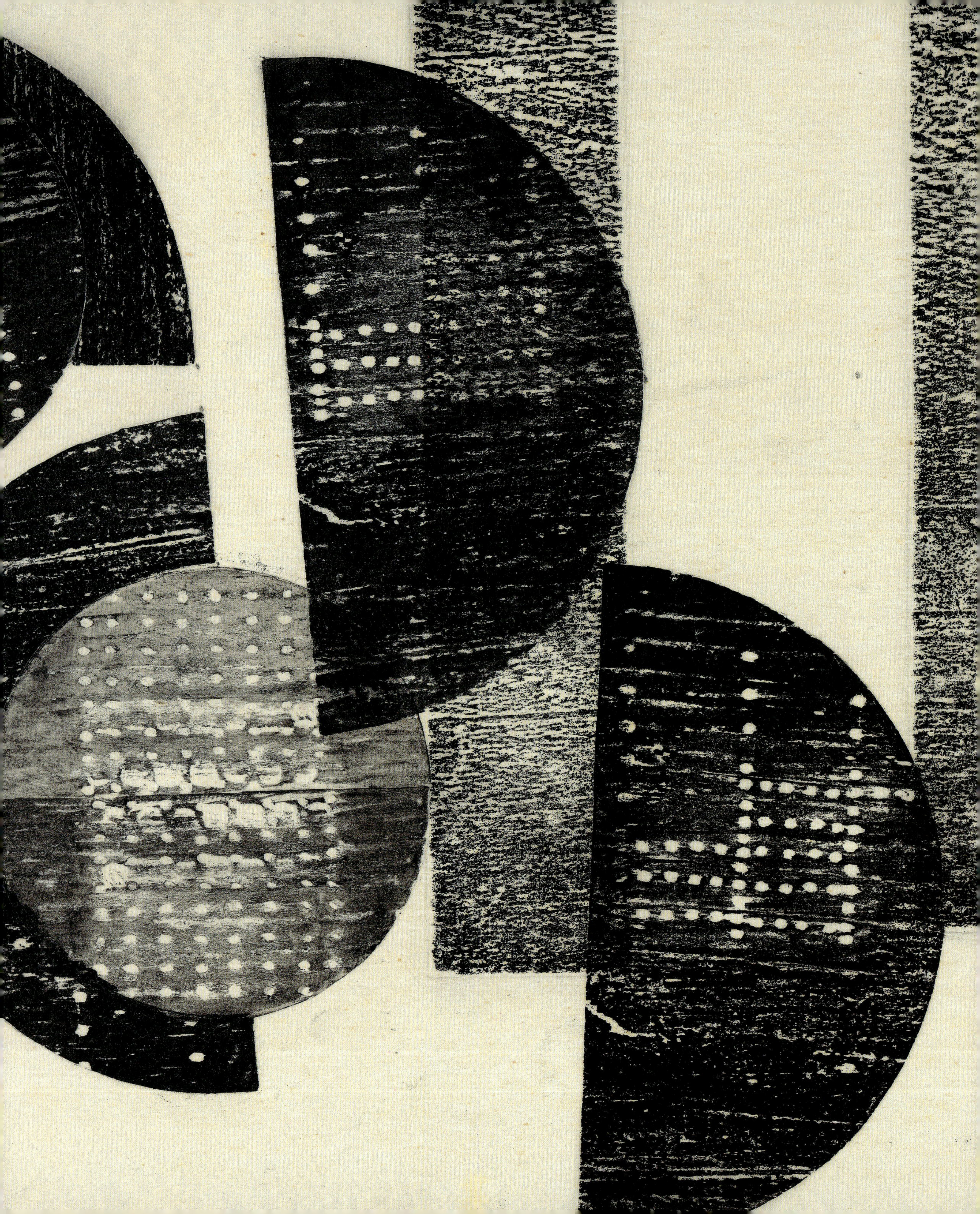

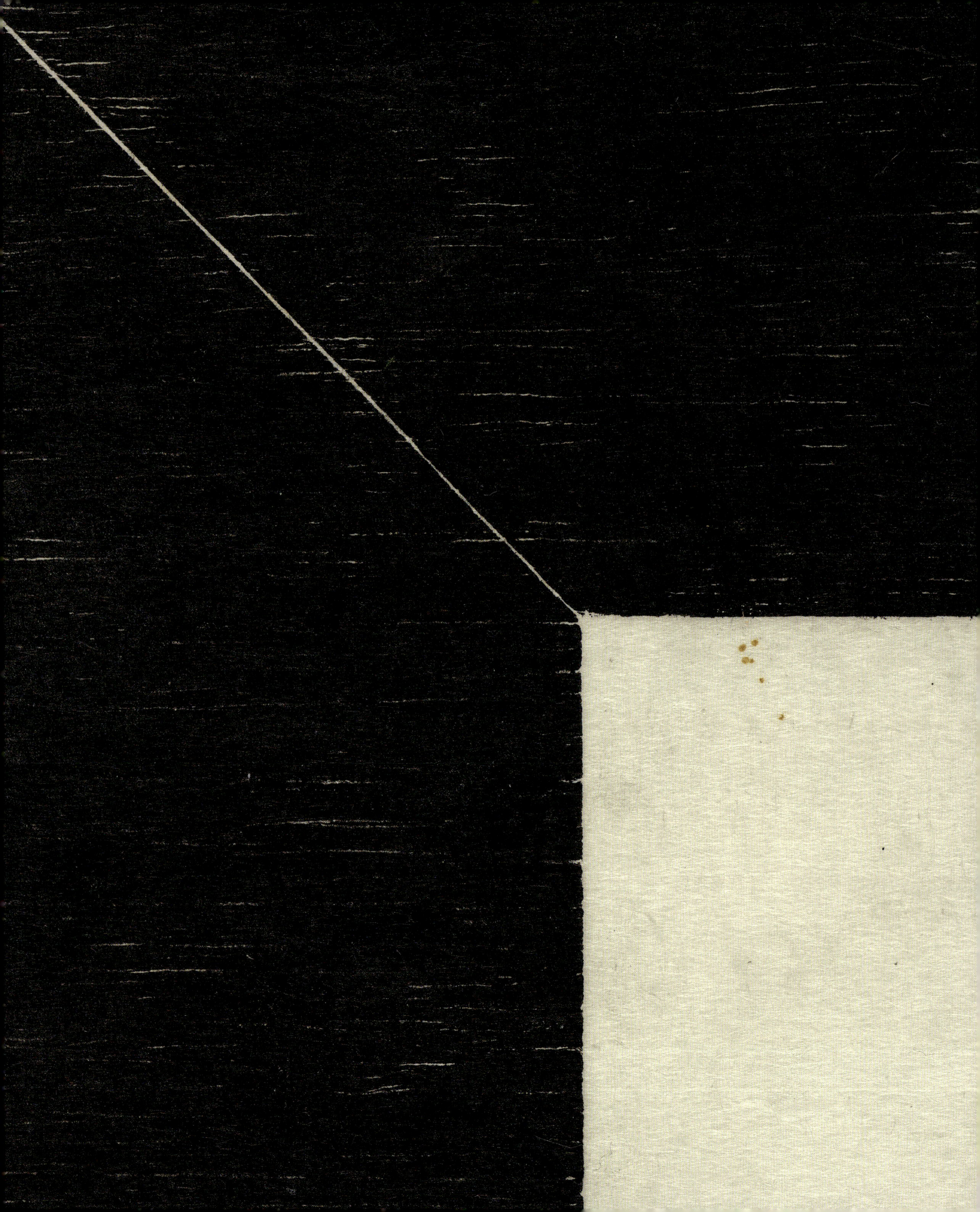

FOREWORD

Lygia Pape's early woodblock prints, composed of overlapping geometric and linear elements, embody the uniquely vibrant abstraction of Neo-Concretism, the mid-twentieth-century Brazilian art movement she cofounded. These works, which the artist later called *Tecelares* (her own coinage that translates roughly as *Weavings*), also participate in the movement's rejection of objectivity, rationalism, and pure form as artistic goals in themselves. Pape's prints eschew static shapes and mathematical logic in favor of evoking elegant movement, changing light, and pulsing rhythms. These qualities reflect her interest in developing visual languages that allow viewers to consider and experience the nature of their own existence.

Pape (Brazilian, 1927–2004) is celebrated as one of Brazil's foremost contemporary artists. Over the course of a long and illustrious career, she explored a variety of media, including film, painting, performance, poetry, and sculpture. However, Pape's woodblock prints, her earliest body of work, are comparatively less studied. This catalogue and exhibition remedy that, focusing on these prints produced exclusively between 1952 and 1960—a period during which the Brazilian press often identified her simply as *a gravadora* (the printmaker). The Tecelares are intensely experimental and modern and thus foreshadow the artistic philosophies that Pape explored throughout her life, long after she had given up printmaking.

Although recent monographic exhibitions in London, Madrid, New York, and São Paulo have drawn increased attention to this early work, *Lygia Pape: Tecelares* is unique both in its close attention to this relatively brief moment in the artist's career and in the quantity and range of work it gathers from the period. Mark Pascale, Janet and Craig Duchossois Curator of Prints and Drawings, has expertly brought together an unprecedented number of Tecelares for the exhibition—nearly one hundred, some never previously exhibited, others not seen since the artist herself showed them in the 1950s and early 1960s. His dedication to uncovering Pape's sometimes obscure processes and intentions has ensured the project's significance and produced a presentation as enlightening as it is exciting, notably advancing the Art Institute of Chicago's ongoing exploration of the art and artists of Latin America. The museum is grateful.

Crucially, *Lygia Pape: Tecelares* could not have been realized without the blessing of the artist's family. The works in the exhibition were loaned by her estate, the Projeto Lygia Pape, whose trust and cooperation were foundational to the project's success. Paula Pape, keeper of her mother's legacy as director of the Projeto, offered her enthusiastic support and hospitality in Rio de Janeiro and Lisbon and guided the project toward an ideal scholarly partner—Adele Nelson, Assistant Professor of Art History and Latin American Art at the University of Texas at Austin and Associate Director of its Center for Latin American Visual Studies. A leading authority on Pape, Adele was an indispensable consultant on the exhibition, and her deeply researched essay for the catalogue makes an undeniable case for Pape's importance to the history of modern art. María Cristina Rivera Ramos, Assistant Conservator in Paper Conservation and Science at the Art Institute, undertook a major conservation campaign on behalf of these extremely delicate works. Not only did she ensure their survival for the future, but her groundbreaking research on Pape's materials and processes also sheds new light on the artist's aesthetic and artistic aims. Finally, many thanks are also due to The Diane & Bruce Halle Foundation for their generous support of the exhibition.

Pape applied the title Tecelares to these prints decades after she created them, once she understood their importance to her later career. The term references the artist's handmade approach to printmaking as well as her regard for indigenous Brazilian craft. This conceptual interest in weaving is arguably most pronounced in her late *Ttéia* sculptures, arrangements of metal wire or string that seem to sparkle and vibrate. *Ttéia 1, B* (pl. 99) is an ethereal sculpture constructed of gold cord stretched from wall to wall to create the illusion of intersecting transparent tubes. Pape left instructions for its posthumous installation, and this exhibition marks its first public presentation. The threads—both aesthetic and ideological—that connect the artist's earliest experiments to her most mature work extend even beyond her death. For Pape, art did not exist in static representations of forms but rather in the expressive space between a work and its viewers—or "spectators," as the Neo-Concretists called them. Her artistic project thus lives on: just as the word *Tecelar* suggests the ongoing action of weaving, the relationship between her work and its spectators remains as vital as ever.

James Rondeau
President and Eloise W. Martin Director
The Art Institute of Chicago

A NOTE FROM THE PROJETO

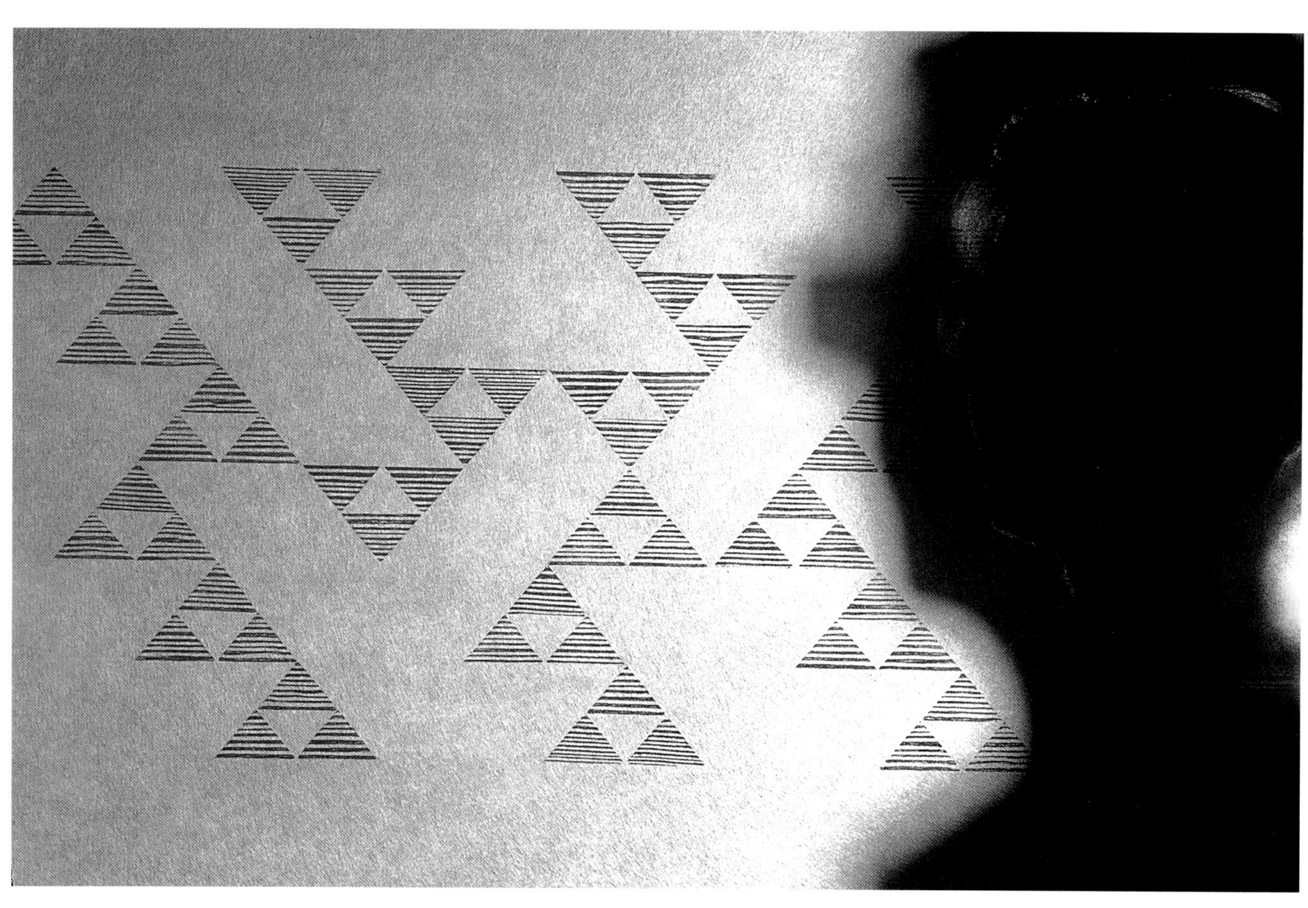

"I want to work in a poetic state, intensely."

—Lygia Pape, Rio de Janeiro, 2003

This statement could be considered a synthesis of the artist's thinking and approach over the course of more than five decades. Pape manifested her art through varied forms and materials, through construction and deconstruction, through both color and black-and-white images, through her collective as well as her individual work, through her few or many words. In short, she had no obvious direction, no preestablished rhetoric, but just the opposite. Pape sought out risk and surprise—the unusual, the unnoticed. She had an accelerated dynamic, which seemed to follow time as it, in turn, accelerated; she was quick. As the precise details of the *Tecelares* (Weavings) series demonstrate, agility was the ultimate hallmark of her expression.

For Pape, light was a fundamental element, one we can find in virtually all of her work. In one of her last pieces, *Ttéia 1, B* (pl. 99), light is the raw material. It is impossible not to associate her early print work with this late sculptural series, which shows her weaving in space what she once wove in wood. At both the beginning and the end of her career, she explored light and dark, fullness and emptiness, and the gaze of the other.

To talk about Pape is to talk about a multimedia artist who is always current, always relevant to ongoing dialogues about art and its role in the human experience. To say she was ahead of her time is an understatement. Part of a generation that profoundly changed Brazilian modernism, she has been a paradigm and a source of inspiration for many artists. This is all the more true now, following major retrospectives of her work in America, Brazil, England, Germany, and Spain in the past twenty years. Now, the Projeto Lygia Pape, together with the Art Institute of Chicago, is pleased to present—for the first time in history—an exhibition focused on the Tecelares, perhaps the most significant in the artist's career. We thank Mark Pascale for his invitation and for his expertise in meticulously selecting prints for this presentation, which includes objects never before shown to the public. Given the nineteen years of work involved in organizing and managing the Projeto, this exhibition indeed represents a great joy.

Paula Pape
Director
Projeto Lygia Pape
Rio de Janeiro

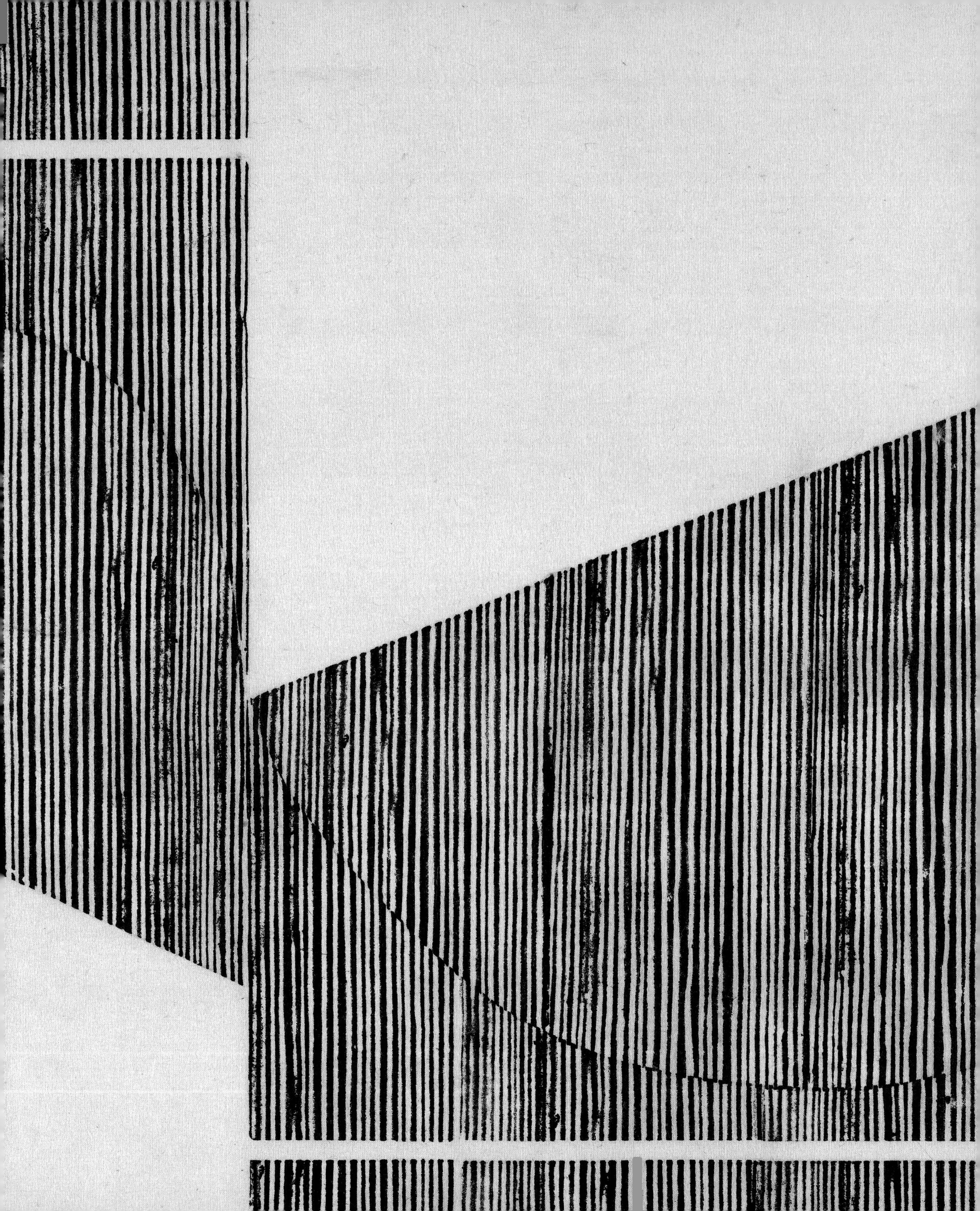

ACKNOWLEDGMENTS

Lygia Pape: Tecelares is the result of years of fruitful collaboration dedicated to highlighting this profoundly significant yet little-studied period in the artist's career. This catalogue and exhibition would not have been possible without the assistance, cooperation, and hospitality of the Projeto Lygia Pape, especially its director, Paula Pape. Ricardo and Pedro Fortes guided my investigations at the Projeto's archives in Rio de Janeiro and Lisbon and organized all records pertaining the artist's woodblock prints. António Leal served as point person between the Art Institute and the Projeto, answering innumerable questions and coordinating the delicate task of shipping the works to Chicago.

Not only did the Projeto generously loan nearly every object in the exhibition, but Paula also recommended art historian Adele Nelson as a contributor to the book. Adele's grasp of the media and institutional culture surrounding postwar Brazilian art is unparalleled, and her essay for this catalogue offers a fascinating glimpse into the ways Pape navigated this complex milieu. The greatest challenge in launching this exhibition was the poor condition of many of the prints, largely caused by the naturally hot and humid environment where they have been stored since the 1950s. María Cristina Rivera Ramos undertook the task of stabilizing and conserving the fragile works, with assistance from Mary Broadway and Gillian Marcus. The results she achieved are truly astounding. María Cristina's essay for this catalogue includes many new insights into Pape's playful and experimental approach to printmaking. Francesca Casadio and Luiz Camillo Osorio provided critical feedback on the essays.

Far-flung colleagues helped bring this project to fruition by lending advice and support. I am especially grateful to Susie Guzman, who worked directly with the Projeto, and Olivier Renaud-Clément. Both offered helpful insight as I developed an exhibition proposal as well as travel advice for my trips to Brazil.

At the Art Institute, many colleagues in Prints and Drawings, both past and present, lent their expertise, including Jay Clarke, Kevin Salatino, Douglas Druick, Suzanne McCullagh, Victoria Sancho-Lobis, and Martha Tedeschi.

The team in Publishing—led by former Vice President and Executive Director Greg Nosan, Editorial Director Lisa Meyerowitz, and Director of Production Joseph Mohan—were devoted to achieving a harmonious relationship between the book's aesthetics and content. Editor Kit Shields's encouragement, skill, and thoughtfulness brought out the best in each essay. Lauren Makholm, whose supreme organization skills are complemented by her passion and patience, shepherded the production, with assistance from Ben Bertin. Josephine Yanasak-Leszczynski intrepidly managed image rights and permissions. Sarah E. Robinson proofread the book, and Jane Friedman created the index. Amy R. Peltz, Isella Sandoval, Lisa Schrag, and Alissa Chanin-Kolaj all helped carry the project to completion. In Imaging, directed by Bonnie Rosenberg, Elyse Allen, Hayley Hinsberger, and Craig Stillwell faithfully captured these rarely seen works for a new audience. Eriksen Translations translated Portuguese text. Last but far from least, Beverly Joel of pulp, ink. distilled our excitement about this project into an engaging design that beautifully highlights the subtle details of Pape's prints.

Colleagues throughout the museum were key to the success of the exhibition. Jennifer Oberhauser coordinated the many collaborators and kept everything on track. Joyce Penn and Sara Patrello facilitated the complex shipping arrangements from Rio de Janeiro and Lisbon during a devastating world health crisis. Emily Vokt Ziemba helped catalogue the works, while Kate Howell managed the movement of objects at various stages of the project. Emily Olek ably assisted me with all aspects of the exhibition, particularly by making it possible for me to access key information during the pandemic. Nearly the entire exhibition arrived unhoused; with her sharp eye for presentation, Mardy Sears designed a framing scheme that accounted for the unconventional margins of many works. Robyn Farrell and Jason Stec assisted me in presenting video of the *Ballet Neoconcreto* (pl. 98). My colleagues in Interpretation, helmed by Emily Fry, helped develop a visitor-friendly narrative for the show, and Kit Shields edited the didactics. Sara Sukhun designed the graphics, while Michael Neault and his team in Experience Design produced exhibition and marketing materials. Letitia Pardo and Joseph Vatinno oversaw the exhibition design and installation.

I offer my sincere thanks to James Rondeau, President and Eloise W. Martin Director. It was James, then in his role as Curator of Contemporary Art, who first brought the art of postwar South America to my attention, and he has since encouraged my initiatives to broaden the permanent collection by acquiring works on paper from that period and region. This project has also benefitted from the guidance of Sarah Guernsey, Deputy Director and Senior Vice President of Curatorial Affairs; Ann Goldstein, Deputy Director and Chair and Dittmer Curator of Modern and Contemporary Art; Eve Jeffers, Chief Operating Officer; and Jennifer Oatess, Senior Director of Institutional Philanthropy.

Generous support from The Diane & Bruce Halle Foundation enabled us to achieve our ambitions for this endeavor. In addition, I have long benefited from the generosity of Janet and Craig Duchossois, whose annual funding for my travel and research covered all of my early work on the project.

Finally, I am grateful to Susan Matthews and Arthur Pascale for their patience with my absences and their emotional support.

Mark Pascale
Janet and Craig Duchossois Curator
Prints and Drawings
The Art Institute of Chicago

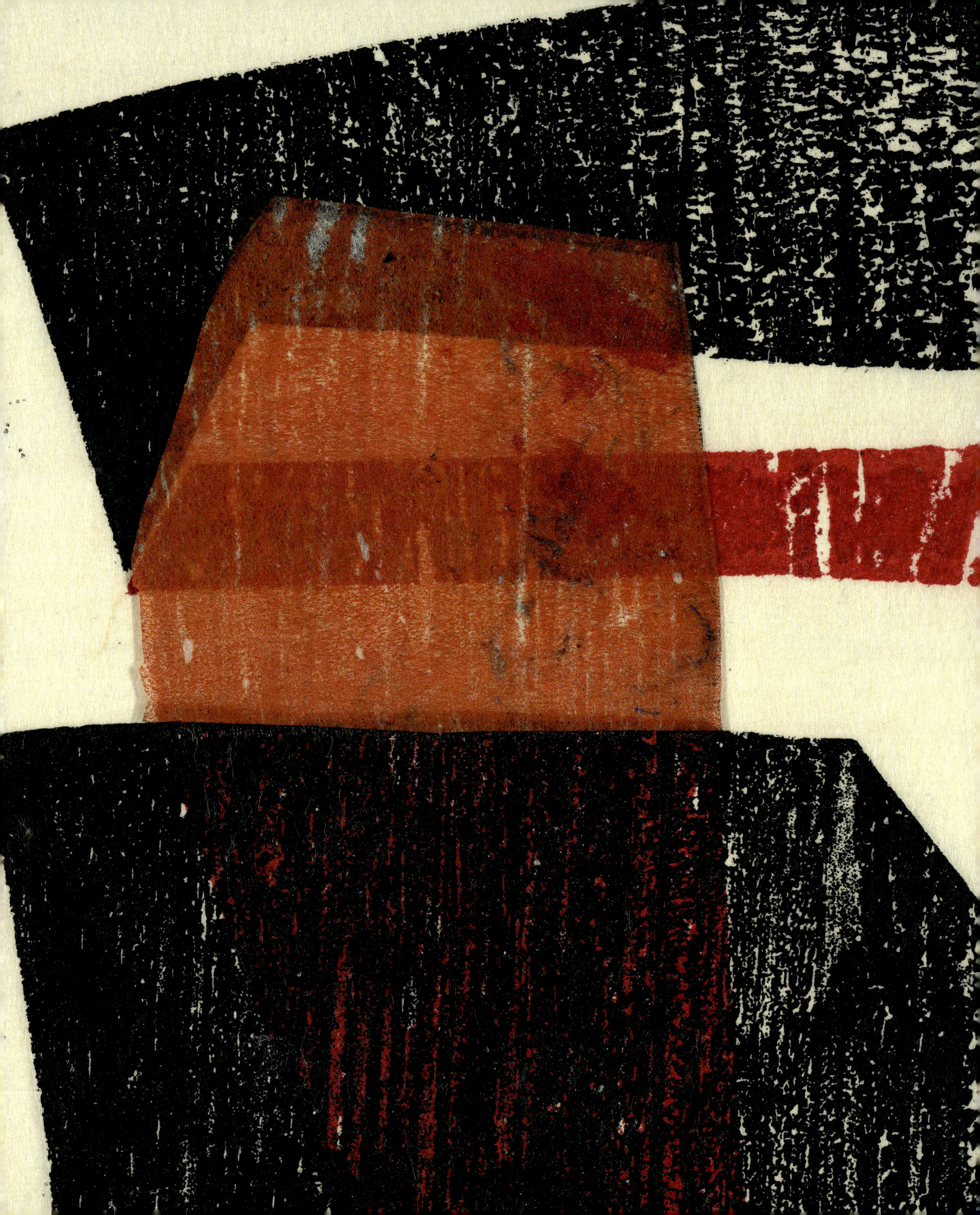

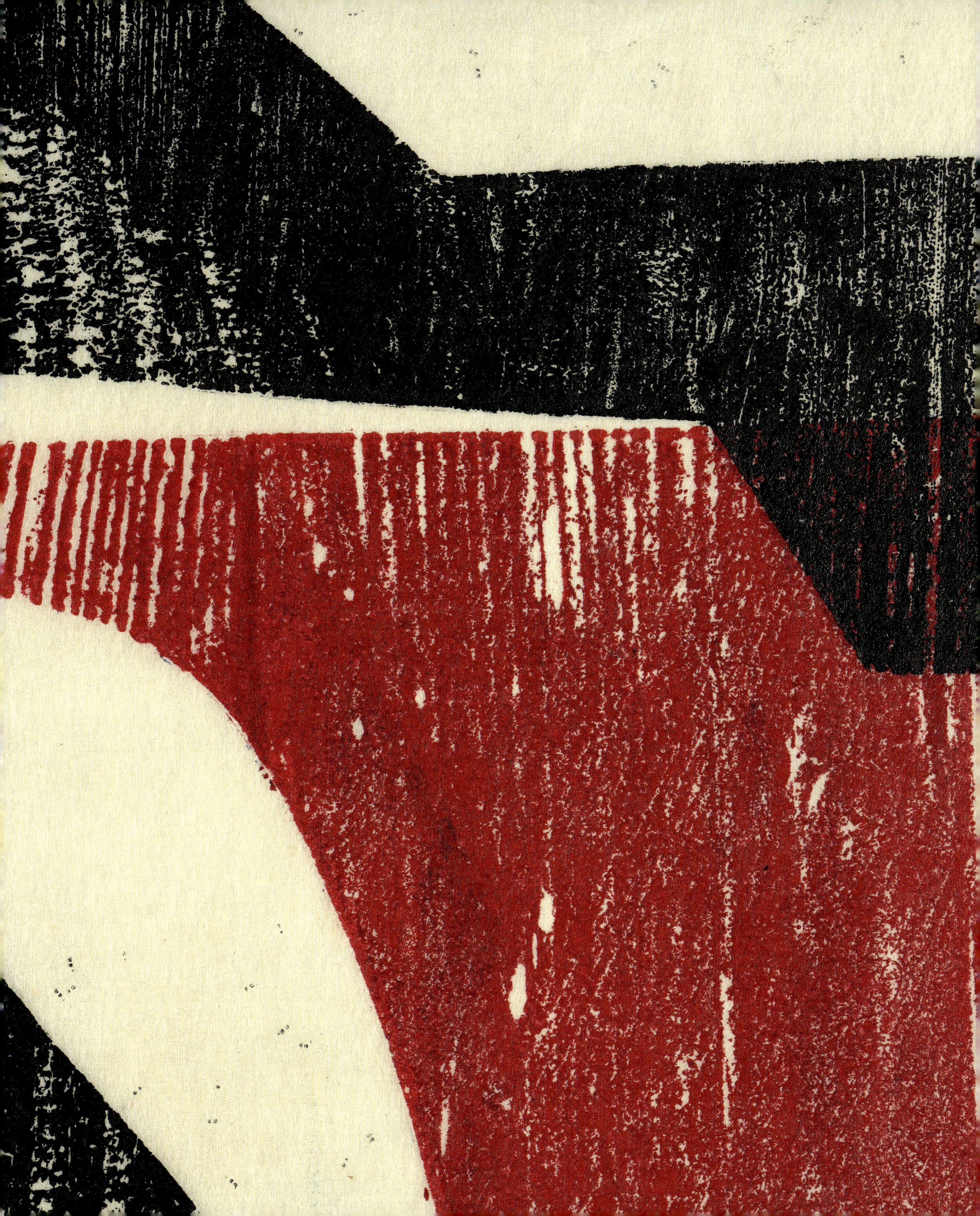

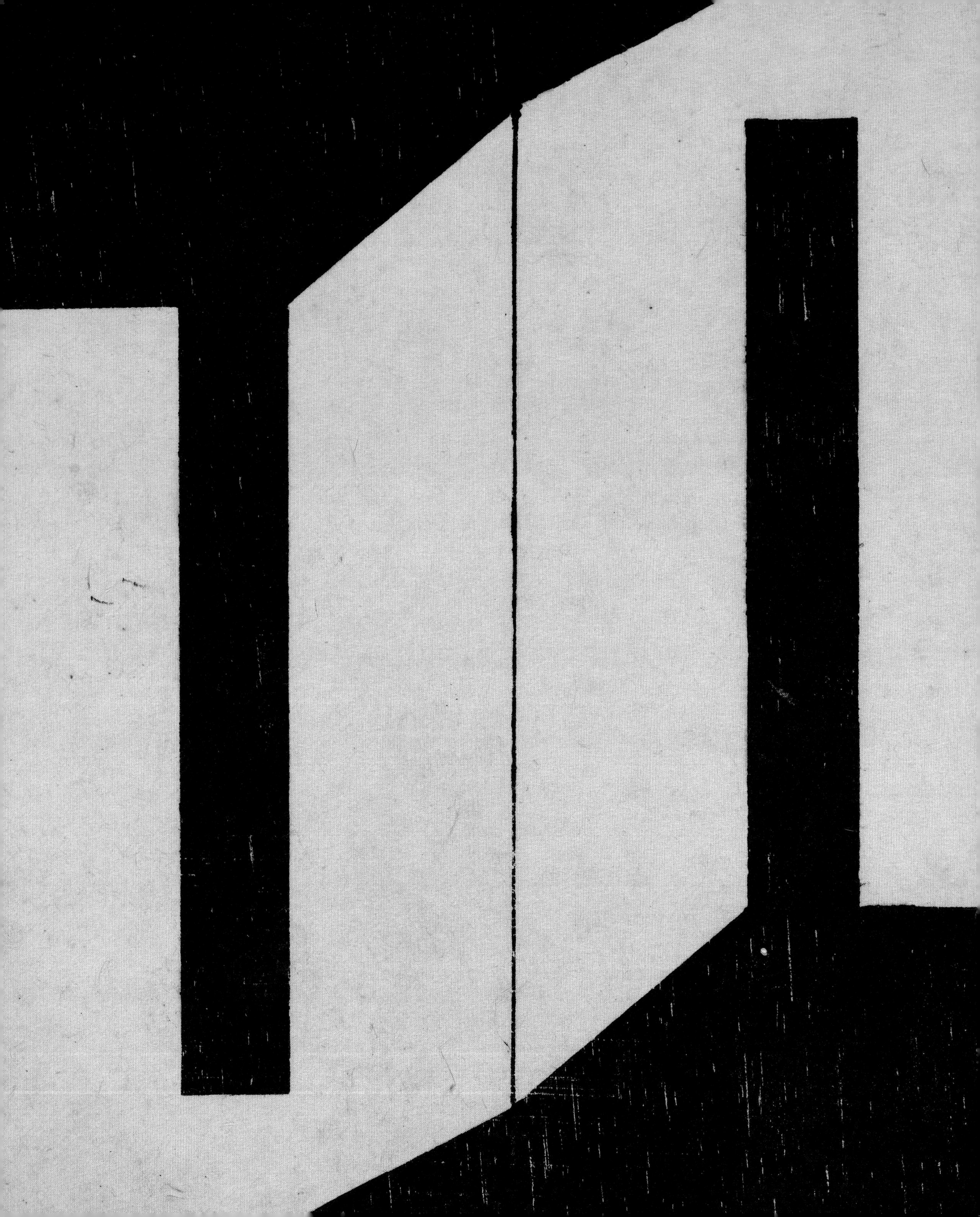

PLAY AND PRECISION: MAKING THE TECELARES

Mark Pascale

Lygia Pape began her focused investigation of printmaking in the early 1950s;
PL. 97 she effectively concluded it with her 1960 publication *Poemas–Xilogravuras* (Poems–woodcuts).[1] The prints—primarily woodcuts—she made during this relatively brief period are known collectively as *Tecelares*, a term Pape coined decades after their creation, once she fully understood their significance to her later work. In inventing the word—it has no dictionary definition in Portuguese—the artist intended the meaning of *weaving* (*Tecelar* derives from the verb *tecer* [to weave]). As art historian Adele Nelson has explained, "the new title linked her practice to a tactile craft and underscored the handmade, haptic qualities of the geometric abstract works. It posited the notion of a textile's interwoven warp and weft as an artist-authorized manner by which to understand the complex spatial activity in the works. *Tecelares* also invited a consideration of the woodcuts in relation to the artist's engagement with indigenous Brazilian culture."[2] (Pape's most literal "weavings,"
PL. 99 her late-career *Ttéia* sculptures, show how these themes recurred in her oeuvre.[3]) This catalogue is the first to focus exclusively on the Tecelares. It brings together the largest collection of these prints ever shown, some not seen since the artist exhibited them in the 1950s and 1960s. Pape's printmaking practice was highly conceptual, and her methods were unusual in the history of the medium. While she created small, limited editions of her first relief prints (several
PLS. 1–2, 7, 11, 15–16, 19 prints in this exhibition are marked with edition numbers), her deep dive into the woodblock process was distinctive in that she typically printed only one or perhaps two impressions of her compositions.

The past forty or so years have witnessed the normalization of unique prints and variants, a trend that began, broadly speaking, with *The Painterly Print: Monotypes from the Seventeenth to the Twentieth Century*, an exhibition organized by the Metropolitan Museum of Art, New York, in 1980.[4] In Western art historical tradition, prints made as one-off visual statements are called *monotypes*. The practice traces back to seventeenth-century Italian artist Giovanni Benedetto Castiglione, who smeared paint or ink onto a smooth (unetched) copper plate and, using a match or the blunt end of a paintbrush, created white lines on the dark field (SEE FIG. 1). Because the image was unfixed, the artist could make only one impression of great fidelity. Secondary impressions from such plates are called *cognates* or *ghosts* for their comparatively hazy quality. Artists such as Edgar Degas often used these ghost impressions as the basis for pastel drawings (SEE FIG. 2A–B). This kind of studio drawing is possible only if an artist has the appropriate equipment—namely, a mechanical press, which can apply sufficient pressure to the matrix (the surface that holds the image to be printed) to fully imprint the ghost impression.

Pape did not make monotypes per se. She created matrices with wood blocks (or sometimes found wood) by cutting, gouging into, and shaping unarticulated elements with saws, then arranging, inking, and impressing them, usually on very thin Japanese papers. In some cases she deliberately made multiple impressions of the same block that were not cognates, creating what are called *monoprints*: distinct prints from a fixed matrix, not duplicates but rather variations of the image. Variants could be made by means as simple as rotating the composition 180 degrees or changing the color or position of individual blocks in a multiblock composition. Pape's method of printing also made each image unique: the artist often used hand pressure instead of a mechanical press, yielding the optical qualities for which her prints are celebrated. By hand printing, she was able to vary the pressure over the block or blocks, so that some areas appear soft while others are crisply rendered. Combined with the very thin papers she used, this technique produced diverse and specific tones beyond the uniform, solid black typically achieved with a press.

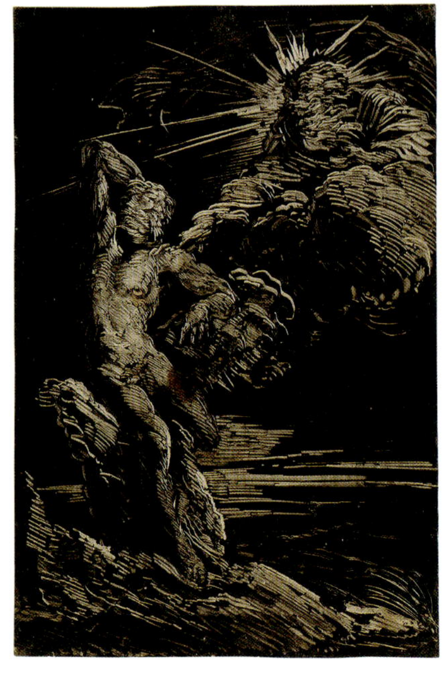

Although Pape began creating prints before she had formal training, she studied in 1954 with Fayga Ostrower (SEE FIG. 3) and visited the studio of Oswaldo Goeldi. Both artists were widely respected and specialized in printmaking, chiefly woodblock printing. Pape studied briefly with Ostrower at the Museu de Arte Moderna do Rio de Janeiro; the elder artist likely transmitted some of her Marxist ideas as well as her theories of perception, which manifested in Pape's use of printmaking as a means to "objectify ideas by graphic means."[5] Pape and her husband, Günther, collected Goeldi's prints, which are characterized by deeply expressionistic subject matter and intense contrasts of light and dark, qualities also typical of Ostrower's early work. Goeldi's hands-on methods had a particular influence on Pape's own developing woodblock process.[6] By 1955 she had established her own studio, concurrent with her family's move to the Jardim Botanico neighborhood of Rio de Janeiro. There she immersed herself in woodblock printing, as well as drawing and painting.

PLS. 1–2 The earliest prints in this exhibition, made in 1952, constitute a striking beginning to Pape's visual syntax. The two linoleum block prints are representational, depicting traditional still-life and landscape subjects, but they already demonstrate Pape's interest in framing devices, figure–ground shifts, and nondescriptive mark making. Linoleum's homogenous surface

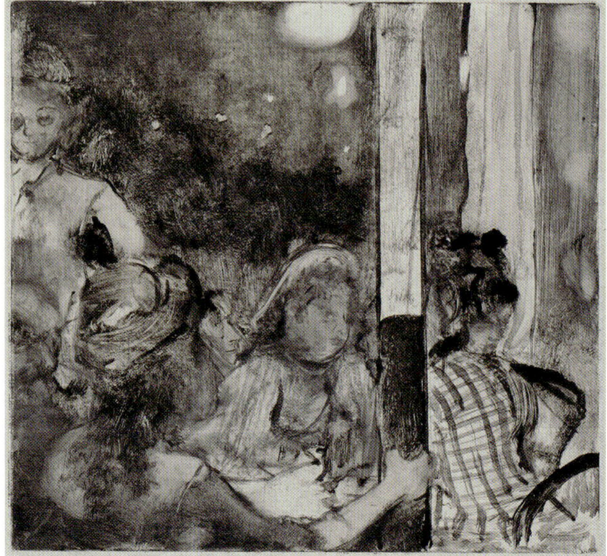

A

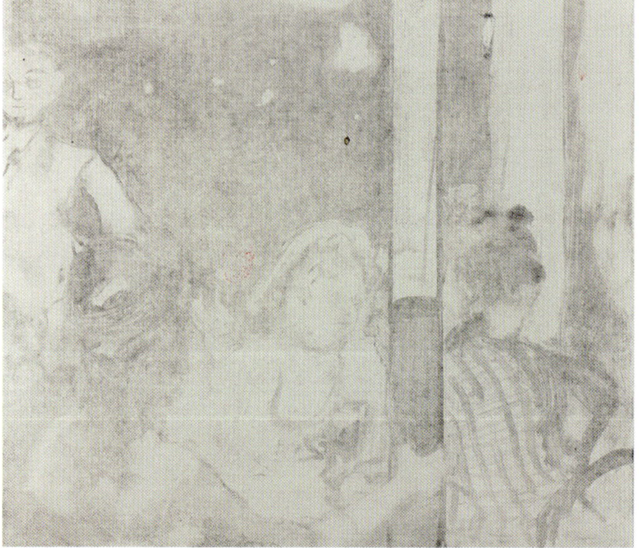

B

results in prints with a flat quality. Pape quickly realized—either through experimentation or from her exemplars Goeldi and Ostrower—that wood offered better opportunities for light and surface manipulation, and she focused on woodblock printing thereafter. A Tecelar in black and mustard yellow showcases Pape's increasing sophistication in selecting blocks with variations in softness and grain, which played a key role in her radical representations of space. There are many ways to read this print. The yellow ground is more veil-like than solid, and Pape prevented a decisive interpretation of its position by inserting black shapes that hover both in front of and behind it, blocking the viewer's ability to apprehend a consistent sense of perspective.[7] Moreover, areas of the reserved white of the paper—apertures created by the absence of printed ink—vacillate between appearing as positive and negative shapes; one small parallelogram just left of center seems to cast a shadow due to the nearly solid-black form next to it, printed from a particularly close-grained block. Here, the interplay of textures resulting from at least four different types of wood foreshadows Pape's later practice of cutting her blocks with offset parallel lines that stand out against dark fields of tight grain, as in a highly developed work from 1957. As with all of her prints from the 1950s, she made this early work using thin Japanese paper. The material's soft texture and translucency underscore the overall ethereal appearance of her images. She explored similar compositions in her painting practice at this time; a group of paintings from 1953 show the same ambiguously overlapping shapes in limited color palettes (SEE P. 30, FIG. 4).

PL. 3

PL. 39

After Pape eliminated color from her printing experiments, she seemed to discover more possibilities for unexpected frameworks and spatial investigations. Two such prints in this group are anti-formal to a profound degree, composed of distributions of printed scraps of wood that appear first as silhouettes of sculptural blocks. The stacking of the blocks and the asymmetrical distribution of light, texture, and tone push each work beyond representing any recognizable thing. Each element shows evidence of previous use—nail and tool impressions along with marks and wear that exaggerate the wood grain, features possibly exacerbated by Pape sanding or scratching the pieces with a cabinet-scraping tool. The artist's estate archive, the Projeto Lygia Pape, retains tools she used to make her woodcuts; they include the expected gouges and chisels but also flathead screwdrivers and a hand drill likely used to make the holes seen in later Tecelares. Pape had already become so experimental at this early point in her printmaking that in 1952 she also made at least one print using the remains from other block cuttings, which she stamped multiple times in a rotating movement. As with the aforementioned anti-formal prints, this one challenges any attempt to read it as a stationary, singular object; its planes and lines seem to dance in space.

PLS. 8–9

PL. 10

< FIG. 1 Giovanni Benedetto Castiglione (Italian, 1609–1664). *The Creation of Adam*, c. 1642. Monotype on laid paper; 30.3 × 20.3 cm (11 15/16 × 8 in.). The Art Institute of Chicago, gift of an anonymous donor; purchased with funds provided by Dr. William D. and Sara R. Shorey and Mr. and Mrs. George B. Young, 1985.1113.

FIG. 2A–B Edgar Degas (French, 1834–1917). Original impression (A) and cognate (B) of *Women in front of a Café, Evening*, c. 1876. Monotypes on wove paper; images: 27 × 29.8 cm (10 5/8 × 11 3/4 in.); (A) sheet: 46.5 × 54.9 cm (18 5/16 × 21 5/8 in.); (B) sheet: 27.3 × 31.2 cm (10 3/4 × 12 1/4 in.); secondary support: 31.6 × 45.6 cm (12 1/2 × 18 in.). The Art Institute of Chicago, through prior bequest of Mr. and Mrs. Martin A. Ryerson Collection, 1990.77.1–2.

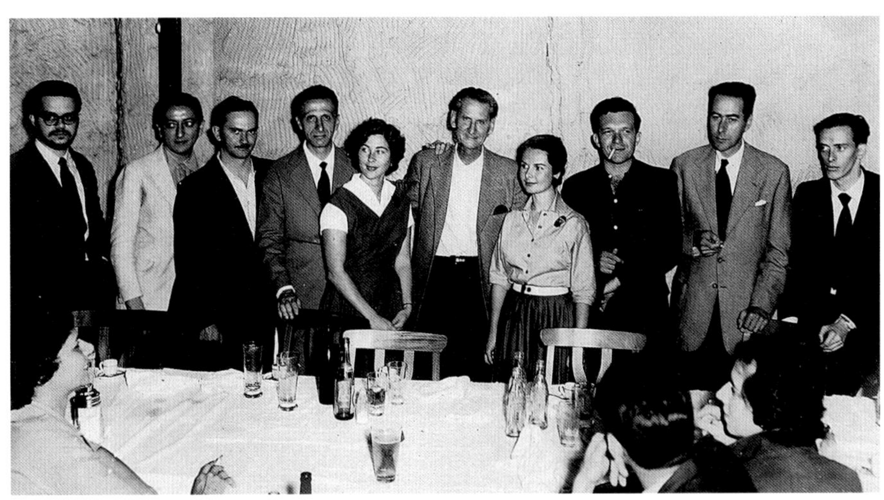

V FIG. 3 Group of Brazilian artists, c. 1960. Left to right: Cláudio Corrêa e Castro, Anísio Medeiros, Poty, Livio Abramo, Fayga Ostrower, Oswaldo Goeldi, Lygia Pape, Aurino Valenca Lins Darel, Iberê Camargo, and Marcelo Grassmann.

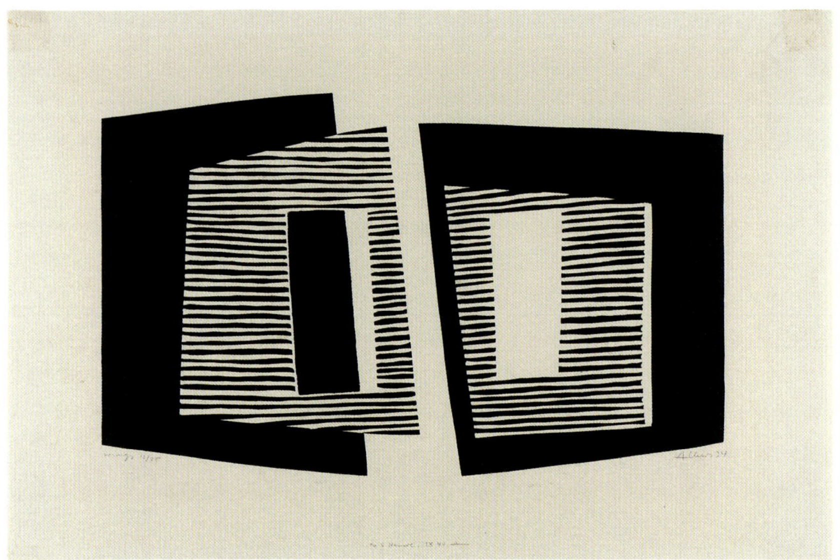

These explorations were essential to Pape's developing ideas. They also separated her from the European De Stijl, Constructivist, and Bauhaus groups, with their strict adherence to systematic abstraction. As critic Paulo Herkenhoff has explained, printmaking for Pape was a matter of "dynamically organizing the visual field rather than producing images."[8] Her model in this approach was German-born artist Josef Albers, who exhibited work in São Paulo as early as 1939 (SEE FIG. 4). He also participated in the fourth Bienal in São Paulo in 1957 and corresponded with Lygia and Günther Pape.[9] "With her precise knowledge of the history of modern engraving," noted Herkenhoff, Pape "pointed to Josef Albers as a paradigm of experimental analysis in art"; his "optical-effect regime"—rather than "predictable mathematical form"—was "the crucial reference... that broke her ties to printmaking tradition."[10] Pape's prints were thus foundational to her future experiments in other media, although the artist herself did not recognize their significance until much later.

The following year Pape undertook a series of Tecelares with elements—again, printed from wood scraps and mostly unarticulated boards—arranged in superimposed layers. Some of these she printed with black ink only; for others, she used a block in one transparent color (known as a *tint block*) to extend the tonal range of the black ink. Among the purely black
PL. 22 prints, one exquisite example stands out. Here, Pape played with a variety of shapes, including parallelograms, rectangles, and triangles. Importantly, she printed with a deft touch, paying close attention to the transparency of the different layers so that each grain, incised mark, and shape remains visible through the overlapping forms. The effect is balletic, with movement restricted to a frontal and lateral orientation reminiscent of dancers on a stage. Indeed, the work seems to foreshadow Pape's 1958 *Ballet Neoconcreto*, during which actors hidden in white cylinders and red cuboids move the shapes slowly across a stage (SEE FIG. 5).[11]

By the mid-1950s Pape regularly exhibited her woodcuts in group presentations. While she never limited herself to printmaking, her work in this medium was well respected, and she was often referred to in the press as *a gravadora* (the printmaker).[12] This acclaim seems to have fueled

< FIG. 4 Josef Albers (American, born Germany, 1888–1976). *Wings*, 1934. Woodcut on laid paper; image: 18.5 × 31.4 cm (7 5⁄16 × 12 3⁄8 in.); sheet: 26.7 × 41.6 cm (10 1⁄2 × 16 3⁄8 in.). The Art Institute of Chicago, gift of Mrs. Ernest A. Hamill, III, 1946.294. This print was shown in São Paulo at Galeria Ita's May Salon, June–August 1939.

V FIG. 5 Still from a video documenting a performance of *Ballet Neoconcreto* (cat. 98) at the Museu de Arte Contemporânea de Serralves, Porto, Portugal, in 2000.

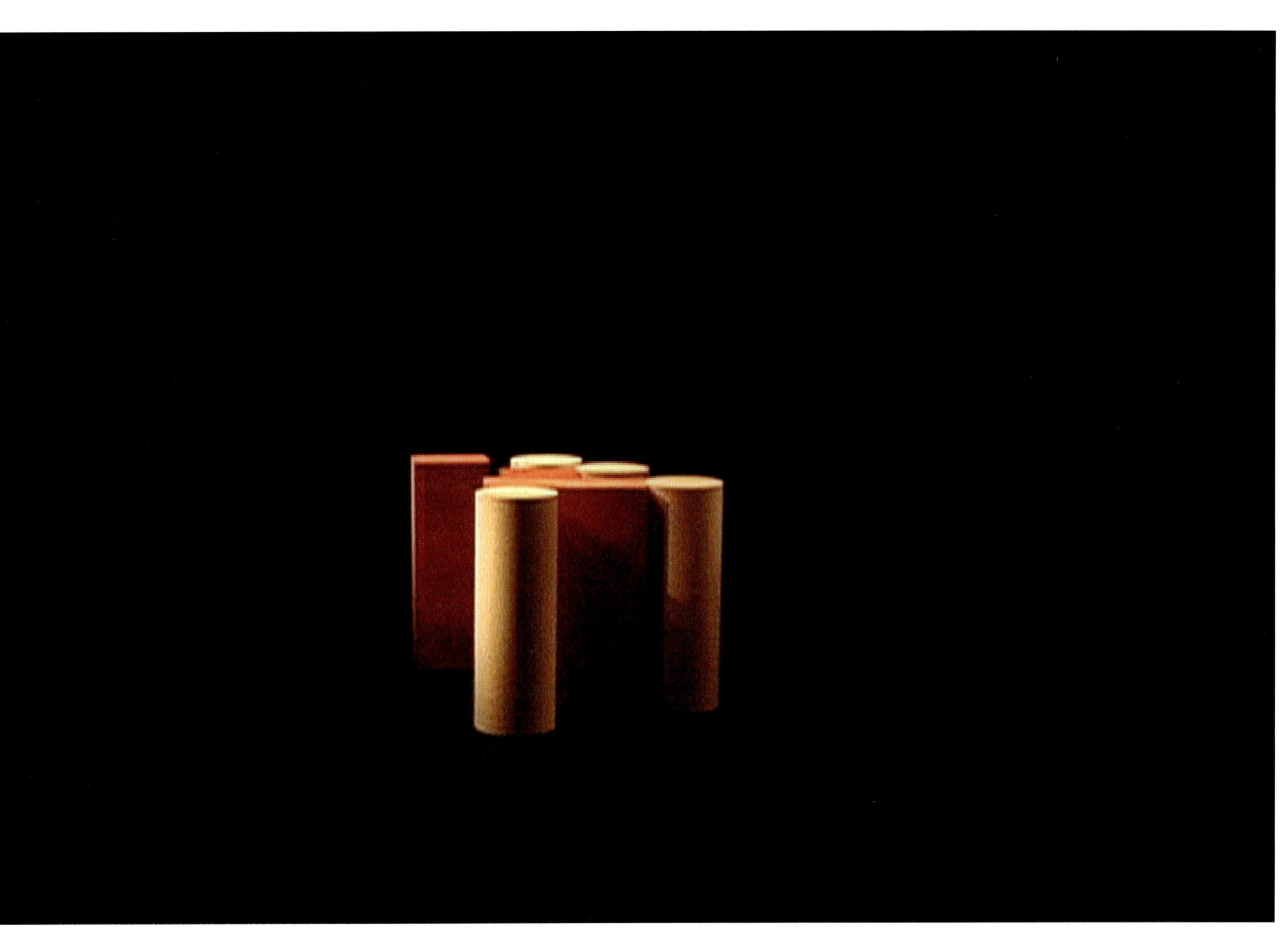

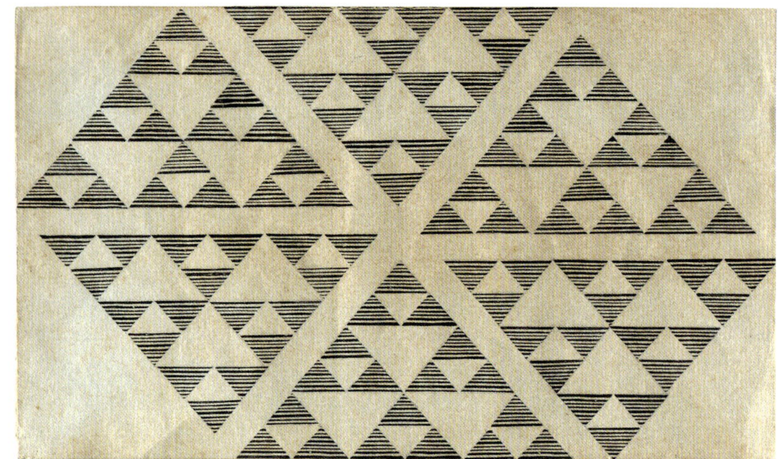
A

B

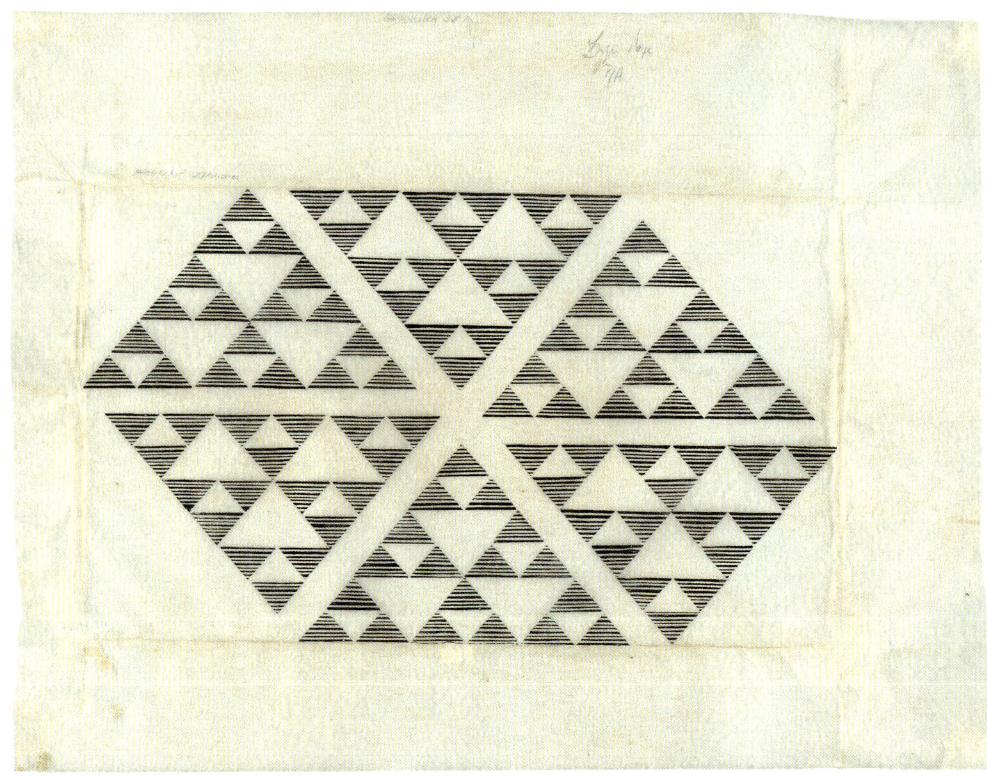
C

FIG. 6A–C Conservation images of cat. 25. The top two images show the recto (A) and verso (B) of the object as found at the Projeto Lygia Pape, wrapped around a cardboard sheet. The bottom image (C) shows the full sheet unfolded in preparation for the Art Institute of Chicago's presentation.

FIG. 7 Josef Albers (American, born Germany, 1888–1976). *Multiplex C*, 1948. Woodblock print; sheet: 40.6 × 29.2 cm (16 × 11½ in.); image: 30.3 × 20.3 cm (12 × 8 in.). Collection of Irving Stenn, Jr., Chicago.

FIG. 8 Pape, in a photograph taken by her husband, Günther, laying out Tecelares in her studio, 1958.

PLS. 25–29 her experimentation. In 1955 she created a series of Tecelares exploring the motif of triangles within triangles. It was the first time she had used repeated printings of the same blocks to construct a larger shape or composition. Some of these works retain the faint lines of graphite the artist used to guide her positioning of the blocks. She often printed these triangular compositions on very large sheets of paper, although it is unclear whether this was to make registration easier or because she intended to exhibit them in a new way. One
PL. 25 such composition was discovered in the Projeto still in its presentation form, wrapped around a piece of cardboard sized to meet the edges of the printed blocks (SEE FIG. 6A–C). Several Tecelares in the exhibition show evidence of having been similarly wrapped around board.[13] Pape may have conceived this unconventional display method in an attempt to subvert the traditional understanding of prints as two-dimensional images and instead emphasize their object-ness.

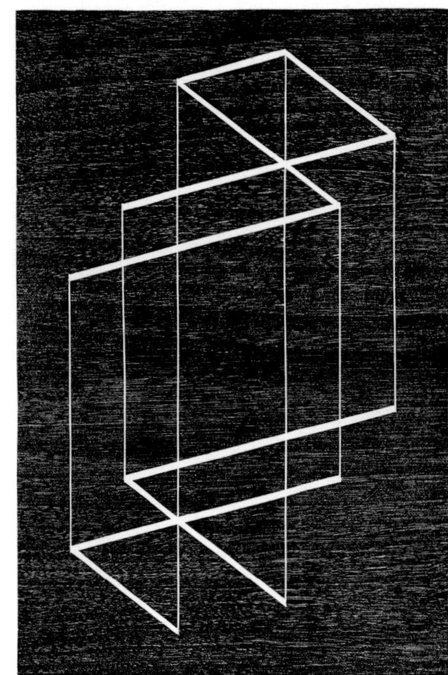

In spite of the wide variety of techniques and presentation forms Pape explored during this period, she ultimately designated all of her prints from the time as Tecelares. At first, she applied the term only to prints she made from roughly 1956 on. Dating is a complex matter with Pape, who sometimes printed blocks much earlier than the date she signed the resulting works. She may have first limited the date range for the Tecelares because of the variety and refinement of prints from later in the period; among those
PLS. 33, 35 from 1956–57 alone are her monumental dark-manner Tecelares printed from
PLS. 37–39 hard, fine-grained mahogany as well as works that more literally allude to weaving. In this latter group, Pape astutely combined myriad linear elements, from fine, handmade incisions that play off the grain of coarse wood to the lines resulting from the intersecting edges of blocks. Curiously, these prints bear an uncanny resemblance to some of Albers's woodcuts, especially those that set linear, reversible geometric forms against wood-grain backgrounds (SEE FIG. 7).[14]

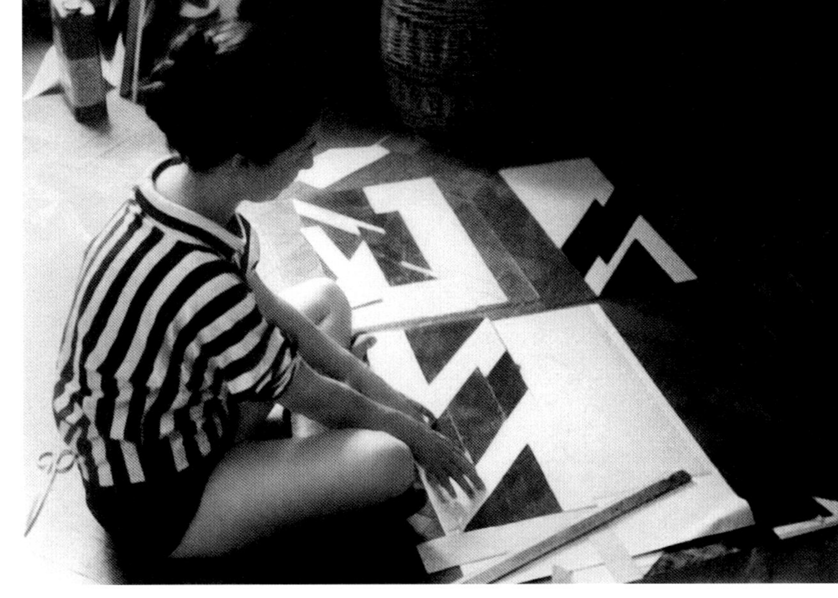

If Albers had an enduring influence on Pape, it shows most clearly in the Tecelares from
PLS. 58–59, 64, 67–72 1958. Here, like Albers, she forcefully combined planes of cut blocks to yield unexpected patterns of dark and light; line, mass, and volume; and symmetrical reversals. A photograph of Pape sitting on the floor of her studio with a ruler and scissors and laying out Tecelares from this group (FIG. 8) attests to a spirit of playful experimentation but also to the precision with which she composed and assembled her prints. In their vocabulary and finesse, these works resound with a timelessness that makes them look freshly conceived more than sixty years later. While the prints from 1958 are among her most regulated, in 1959 Pape con-
PLS. 80–85 ceived some of the most freewheeling of all the Tecelares. This group of six, selected for the exhibition from a larger body of similar works, are composed of cut circles, half-circles, parallelograms, rectangles, and squares. Some of these shapes Pape created by drilling a matrix of holes; when layered over

each other in multiple printings, they produce fields of vibrating movement. Inelegant in most every way, they constitute Pape's fearless excursions into freely distributed elements. At times the overlapping shapes suggest the clash of atomic particles, rudimentary city plans, or slides of microscopic specimens, while the patterns of drilled holes approximate punch cards or computer chips.

Striking in all of these works is their implication of limitless meaning. They invite the viewer to study them and come to their own interpretations. This openness was a central tenet of Pape's artistic philosophy: rather than trying to define an intention or control the viewer's response, Pape wished to lead by implication of the visual evidence. It was no accident that she so often left something seemingly incomplete in the prints—ephemeral passages of inadequate hand pressure and awkward forms that look more like the hollowed-out leftovers of a block than any deliberate shape. Just as life is unpredictable, so art can be daring, playful, sensual, and exhilarating. Pape's Tecelares are among the most enticingly tactile and visually striking expressions of material culture produced in the twentieth century. How remarkable that a print can resonate so long and accomplish so much.

Notes

1 Pape's engagement with printmaking in the 1950s has been studied and written about more regularly in recent years. See Adele Nelson, "Sensitive and Nondiscursive Things: Lygia Pape and the Reconception of Printmaking," *Art Journal* 71, no. 3 (Fall 2012): 26–45; and María Luisa Blanco, Manuel J. Borja-Villel, and Teresa Velázquez, eds., *Lygia Pape: Magnetized Space*, exh. cat. (Madrid: Museo Nacional Centro de Arte Reina Sofía, 2011). Both studies were foundational to this catalogue and the exhibition it accompanies.

2 Nelson, "Sensitive and Nondiscursive Things," 42.

3 As with *Tecelar*, Pape invented the name *Ttéia*, which combines the Portuguese words *teia* (web) and *teteia*, a colloquial term for a graceful person or thing.

4 See Colta Ives, Eugenia Parry Janis, David W. Kiehl, Michael Mazur, Sue Welsh Reed, and Barbara Stern Shapiro, *The Painterly Print: Monotypes from the Seventeenth to the Twentieth Century*, exh. cat. (New York: Metropolitan Museum of Art, 1980).

5 Paulo Herkenhoff, "Lygia Pape: The Art of Passage," in *Lygia Pape: Magnetized Space*, 28.

6 For more on this subject, see Iria Candela, "The Risk of Invention," in *Lygia Pape: A Multitude of Forms*, ed. Iria Candela, exh. cat. (New York: Metropolitan Museum of Art, 2017), 2–15.

7 Because Pape used hand pressure and impressed wet ink into wet ink, the layers of her printing are particularly difficult to discern, even under technical observation. The results, however, are extremely rich and specific to her vision.

8 Herkenhoff, "Lygia Pape: The Art of Passage," 30.

9 See Sérgio B. Martins, "An Anticlass in Avant-Gardism," in *Lygia Pape: A Multitude of Forms*, 182n10. Pape did not participate in the Bienal but likely attended.

10 Herkenhoff, "Lygia Pape: The Art of Passage," 30–31.

11 Reviews from the period suggest that the ballet was originally titled *Ballet Concreto*. Pape may have retitled it after the Neo-Concrete group published its manifesto in 1959.

12 For details see Vivian A. Crockett, "Chronology," in *Lygia Pape: A Multitude of Forms*, 168–69.

13 Several Tecelares in the exhibition had traces of graphite layout lines and damage caused by acid migration from the cardboard mounts around which Pape wrapped the prints for exhibition. The Projeto preferred that this damage be minimized and the works be given a more traditional presentation, matted and framed under glazing.

14 See Martins, "An Anticlass in Avant-Gardism," 27.

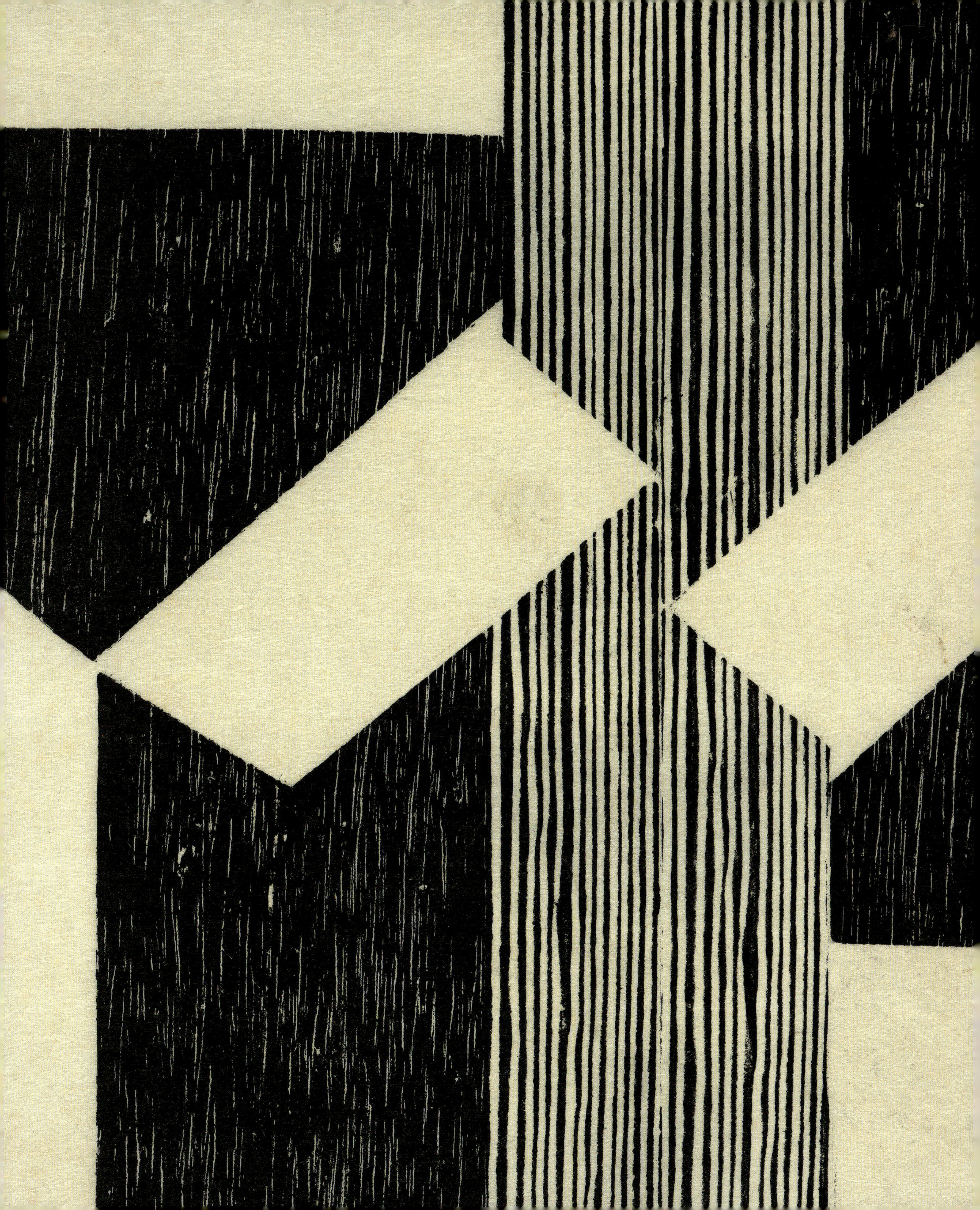

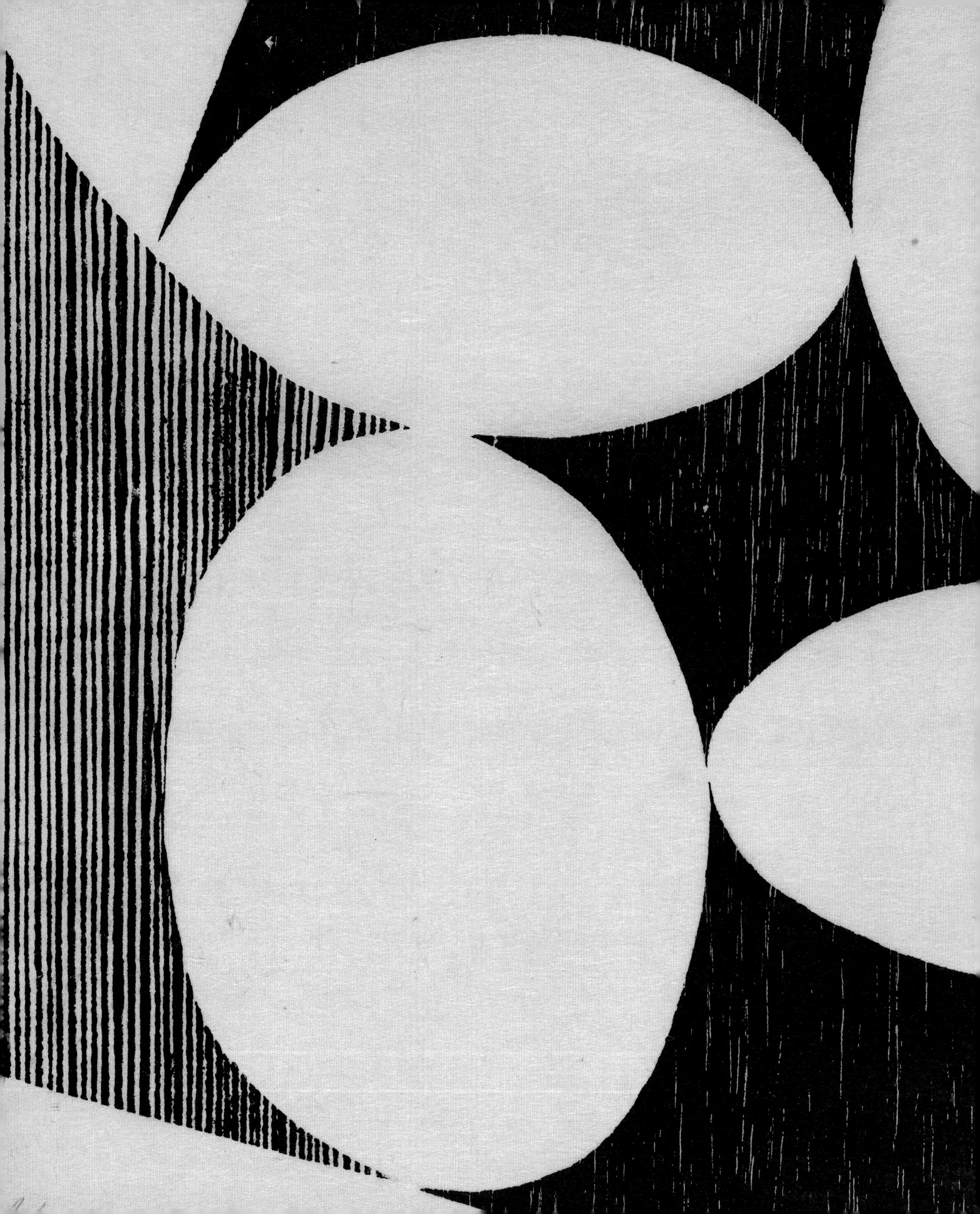

Adele Nelson

GENDER AND GENRE: LYGIA PAPE'S SELF-FASHIONING IN PRINT

Following World War II, media and art institutions in many industrialized and industrializing nations treated women artists not only as creators but also as the ideal consumers of modern art and design—as the faces of an expanding commercial culture. This was the case in rapidly developing 1950s Brazil. Women there won the right to vote, albeit with many restrictions, when artist Lygia Pape was a young child.[1] Some of the limits on women's voting rights—explicitly tied to education, labor, and marital status and implicitly to class and race—were slowly removed starting in the late 1940s and into the early 1960s, as Pape established her career. Historians of twentieth-century Latin America have detailed how the woman worker functioned as a cultural paradox: visible and lauded yet treated as a threat to gender norms and targeted for reinscription into patriarchial values.[2]

From her privileged position as a white, middle-class woman working in the visual arts, a field associated with wealth, Pape traversed societal divisions between working and non-working women and between consumers and producers of art. In many ways, she perfectly performed the role of spokeswoman for modern Brazil, even exploiting this position to the benefit of her career. But through her printmaking she also expanded and subverted expectations for women artists. In the woodcut prints she produced in the 1950s and early 1960s, as well as in her accompanying writing and self-presentation, Pape plumbed the material and conceptual capacities of printmaking to create visual spaces of intersection and contrast in which sight and touch, word and image, and, I suggest, woman and worker
PL. 97 form unexpected, novel relationships. In her 1960 poem book, *Poemas–Xilogravuras* (Poems–woodcuts), Pape literally bound the practices of printmaking and poetry together. Just as the titular dash both joins and separates the two media, the work itself resists their linking even as it juxtaposes them.[3] This idea of the *break*—of relationship through rupture, connection across distance—continued to inform the artist's work long after she stopped making prints.[4] But the active joining together of elements also builds on the assembly process intrinsic to her approach to printmaking, in which she cut, carved, abutted, adhered, and printed distinct wood grains and shapes.

I have previously studied Pape's innovative redefinition of printmaking, arguing that, through repeated reinterpretations over the course of her fifty-plus-year career, she positioned her woodcuts as a conceptual foundation for her artistic practice as a whole.[5] Her most significant reimagining of the prints occurred in the late 1970s and early 1980s, when she retitled the works, originally presented as *Xilogravuras*, as *Tecelares*, which translates roughly to *Weavings*. In what follows I trace the connections between the less-studied start and end of her woodcut period—namely, the prints she created from about 1952–55, which were not refashioned as Tecelares by the artist during her lifetime, and *Poemas–Xilogravuras*, arguably her last major print work. I analyze these works and their display, including press coverage of the exhibitions in which they appeared, to show that Pape's rhetorical and photographic self-fashioning during these moments of publicity reveal how she negotiated the gendered ways in which the public imagined the producers and consumers of abstract art.

> FIG. 1 Photograph of striking textile workers published in *Voz Opéraria*, September 12, 1953, 6.

WOMEN PROTAGONISTS AND NEW ART INSTITUTIONS

Abstract art in postwar Brazil developed in a milieu defined, on the one hand, by a host of new modern-art entities like the São Paulo Bienal and, on the other, by the contested relationships between artists and these emerging institutions.[6] Artists founded Concrete-oriented collectives—Grupo Ruptura in São Paulo and Grupo Frente in Rio de Janeiro—that sought an abstraction free from any ties to representation. In 1959 former members of Grupo Frente—Lygia Clark, Hélio Oiticica, and Pape included—initiated the Neo-Concrete movement, arguing for a new art that remained grounded in geometry but focused on transforming the viewer from a passive spectator into an active participant. As the group's manifesto put it, their artworks addressed the viewer as an an "eye-body" rather than an "eye-machine"—as a mobile, feeling, social being rather than a static and purely rational observer.[7] Pape alone embraced printmaking as a medium well suited to activating this kind of experiential, phenomenological relationship. Although her production was manifestly multimedia, during the 1950s it was primarily via her identity as a printmaker that Pape not only pursued her artistic aims but also challenged expectations for women artists.

The Rio press, from daily newspapers to art magazines, showered attention on Grupo Frente, hailing them as a youthful avant-garde. They also described the artists in capitalistic terms as "producers," treating them as central characters in a developmentalist narrative of national economic progress. Critics trumpeted the artists' youth, their explorations of new materials, and their relations with industry as "renovating" the national artistic scene and, by extension, Brazil's international reputation as a dynamic modern society.[8] The group held exhibitions in Rio, then the nation's capital, and the surrounding area from June 1954 to June 1956. Those were politically turbulent years in Brazil. In 1954 the country's authoritarian, nationalist, and populist president, Getúlio Vargas, took his life when it was revealed that those close to him had attempted to assassinate journalist Carlos Lacerda. The subsequent election and inauguration of Juscelino Kubischek was challenged by multiple coup attempts. In a key text defining Grupo Frente's aim, Mário Pedrosa, an eminent art critic and political activist, envisioned the movement's archetypal artist as an ethical, nonideological citizen, engaged and informed but standing apart from the craven corruption, manipulation, and partisanship he saw as dominating Brazilian politics.[9] This belief in a model citizen was articulated and visualized by the artists and their interlocutors most effectively around the female members of the group.

Brazilians reimagined citizenship following World War II, as the country transformed from a dictatorship (instituted by Vargas from 1937 to 1945) back to a democracy. The postwar period saw rapid industrialization accompanied by an expanding urban middle class and consumer culture. The press lauded women's status as increasingly enfranchised and visible citizens, although class and racial barriers, along with patriarchal values, persisted. In 1945 voting became obligatory for working women, leaving women who did not work outside the home with the right but not the requirement to vote.[10] Coincident with these electoral reforms and amid accelerated industrialization, women played a prominent role in the fight for workers' rights; for instance, predominantly female textile workers led labor actions that culminated in the twenty-four-day "strike of the 300,000" in 1953 (SEE FIG. 1).[11] Not until 1962 could married women legally work without the permission of their husbands, and only in 1965 did voting become compulsory for all literate women regardless of their marital or employment status. This system of yoking enfranchisement to social identity is the background against which representations of women artists must be understood.

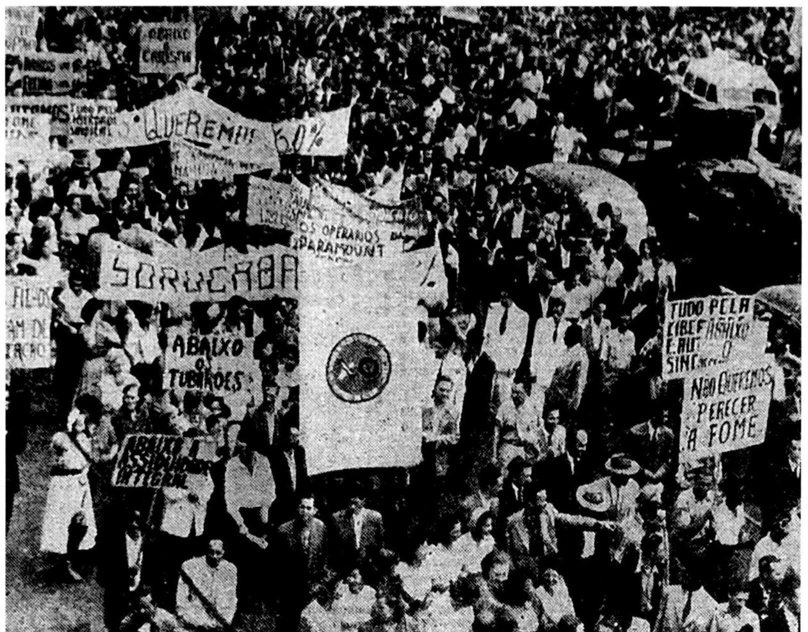

Media portrayals of women as citizens included new visibility for, and growing acceptance of, professional women, artists included. The three female artists in Grupo Frente—Clark, Elisa Martins da Silveira, and Pape—figured prominently in the emerging popular image of the woman worker. Stories about the collective moved out of the cultural pages as its members engaged with politics. In 1953 Pape and other artists publicly supported a free-press initiative.[12] On election day in 1955, Clark, along with other prominent women in Rio, went on record in favor of the presidential candidate supported by *Tribuna da Imprensa*, a center-right daily newspaper.[13] Founder Lacerda made a concerted effort to mobilize middle-class urban women in support of establishment, non-populist, and anti-Vargas candidates.[14] Press coverage of creative and academic professional women reflected their wider emancipation but also instrumentalized it to provide vivid depictions—and idealizations—of the engaged urban woman "with long pants," as one article put it.[15] In other words, the representation of Grupo Frente's women artists went hand-in-glove with electoral politics, which were broadly prodemocratic and, in some instances, specifically anti-Vargas. But, as we will see, this treatment was equally if not more concerned with expanding postwar media and consumer culture.

Writing about visual art appeared in newspaper sections aimed at women in addition to the cultural pages; women artists—particularly affluent and middle-class white women like Pape—benefitted from visibility in both. But they also navigated a double bind of representation: cast as the passive viewers and consumers of the new art, it was less clear how women could be positioned as active, autonomous creators. In its two-year run from 1954 to 1956, art magazine *Forma* repeatedly featured Pape, publishing praise for the artist from both the printmaking and Concrete art circles associated with the magazine.[16] The predominance of women in the magazine's leadership made it an outlier in the midcentury publishing world: Luiza Elza Massena was its director, and the editorial board was split nearly evenly between men and women.[17] *Forma* was not presented or received as a women's magazine, a burgeoning genre at the time, but the line delineating the art press from media aimed at women consumers was far from definite. As Alzira Alves de Abreu has shown, the Sunday supplement of the *Jornal do Brasil*, which from its inception in 1956 served as a key intellectual forum for abstract artists in Rio, initially targeted female readers.[18] *Forma* was also immersed in women-run organizations, including an informal group—led in part by Pape—that facilitated sales of artist-designed Christmas cards and Carnival masks at the magazine's headquarters. Art club Tajiri, founded in 1954 by artists and critics and hosted by wealthy women at homes in and around Rio, also overlapped with *Forma*'s writers and likely with their subscribers.[19] Paying members convened monthly, and their dues entitled them to participate in raffles of artworks. Although the club's leadership was co-ed, it functioned as a women-run organization, with printmaker Vera Bocayuva Mindlin most frequently mentioned as leader and Pape connecting the magazine's staff and contributors with the club.[20] The Museu de Arte Moderna do Rio de Janeiro (MAM Rio) was a larger link between these groups, as was the daily newspaper *Correio da Manhã*, owned by Paulo Bittencourt, husband of MAM Rio's director, Niomar Moniz Sodré.

The new museums and art institutions were also inextricably entangled with the expanding consumer culture—the confluence of art, diplomacy, shopping, and tourism that historian Tony Bennett termed the "exhibitionary complex."[21] A 1955 photograph of a storefront display comprised of mannequins posed next to works of art on easels attests to Brazilians' widespread appreciation for abstract art in this period (FIG. 2).[22] The display advertised a traveling exhibition from the United States, previously shown at the third Bienal, along with clothing and accessories sold at the store. Organized by the Instituto Brasil–Estados Unidos, the exhibition was held at high-end department store Mesbla, located in an Art Deco building in downtown Rio. What at first seems like a straightforward scene is in fact mired in the discourses of class, consumption, gender, and race that controlled the reception of abstract art in Brazil: white, female mannequins donning pearls and gloves pose as both art admirers and as objects of admiration themselves. A male viewer in a suit and tie, cropped and in shadow at the right edge of the image, takes in the scene. Is he contemplating the artwork? Is he appraising the clothing, jewelry, and perfume for sale? Or is he perhaps consuming the visual spectacle of the elegant stand-ins for women? As a woman artist, Pape risked being similarly objectified. She mitigated this risk by taking steps to control her image—most notably by crafting her identity as a printmaker.

ARTIST–PRINTMAKER

Consistently identified in the press as *a gravadora* (the printmaker), Pape developed a reputation as the sole printmaker among the artists in Rio and São Paulo who adopted the nonobjective practices that came to define

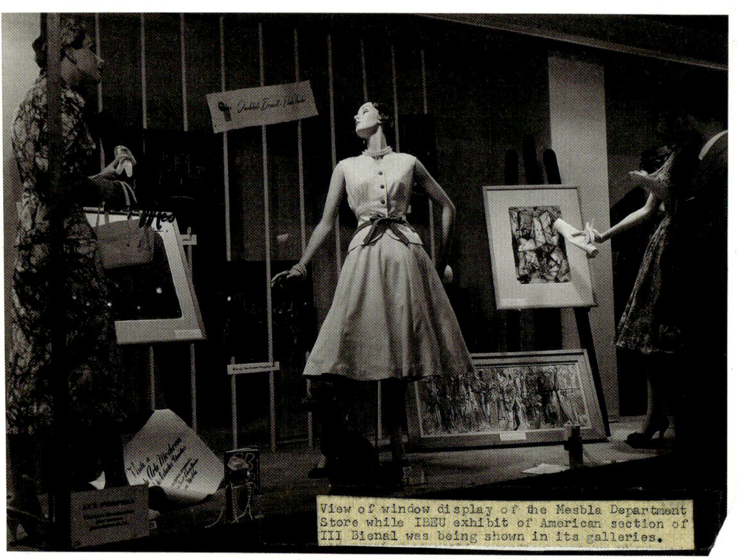

∨ FIG. 2 Display at Mesbla department store promoting an exhibition of art from the United States, Rio de Janeiro, 1955.

> FIG. 3 Fayga Ostrower (Brazilian, born Poland, 1920–2001). *5907*, 1959. Color aquatint with drypoint on paper; 32.3 × 49.5 cm (29 ⅝ × 39 ⅜ in.). The Art Institute of Chicago, gift of Mr. and Mrs. John Frankel, 1960.549.

Concrete art. The name was initially coined and promoted by European artists Theo van Doesburg and Max Bill to describe art devoid of any reference to the natural world, composed of geometric forms, and focused on mathematical relationships and rhythms. Following World War II, print workshops and graphics biennials proliferated in Latin America, where printmaking was often hailed as a technique suited to developing economies.[23] Prints were relatively affordable to produce and disseminate (compared, for example, to paintings, which typically required expensive imported oil paints), and they had established practical and political applications. The medium also had a lauded history in the region—for instance, the Taller de Gráfica Popular in Mexico and the work of Oswaldo Goeldi in Brazil. Amid this renewed interest in the artform, Brazilian artists like Maria Bonomi and Fayga Ostrower produced multihued, technically expert prints (SEE FIG. 3) and received international praise, with Ostrower winning the top printmaking prize at the Venice Biennale in 1958.[24] Although Pape participated in exhibitions of Brazilian prints in the 1950s, she criticized the alternately prevailing rarified and utilitarian definitions of the medium among her contemporaries, many of whom worked in gestural abstraction. Pape's process also resisted convention. She did not systematically sign and date her prints at the moment of creation. Over the course of the 1950s, she stopped consistently indicating edition size and proof number and began exhibiting impressions of the same image with different mountings and orientations. These choices, paradoxically, resulted in multiple originals. In part because of the distance she asserted from mainstream practices, Pape sidestepped critics' sexist dismissal of many female printmakers.[25] Her insistence on the medium's parity with painting, sculpture, and ultimately poetry gained increasing traction among other Concrete artists as well as art critics in the late 1950s and early 1960s.

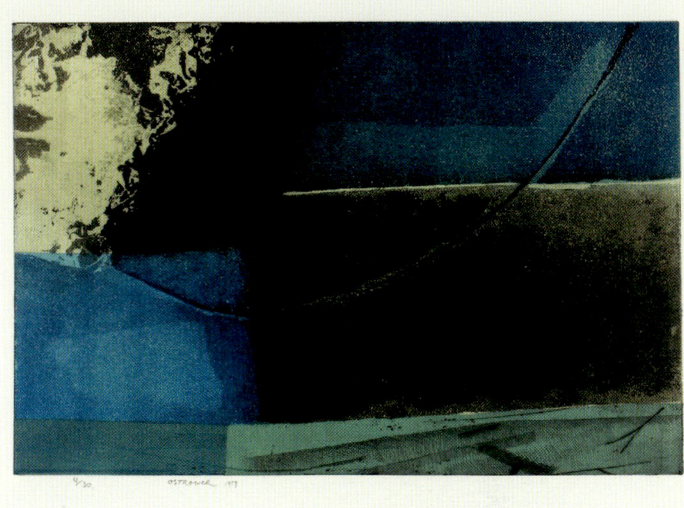

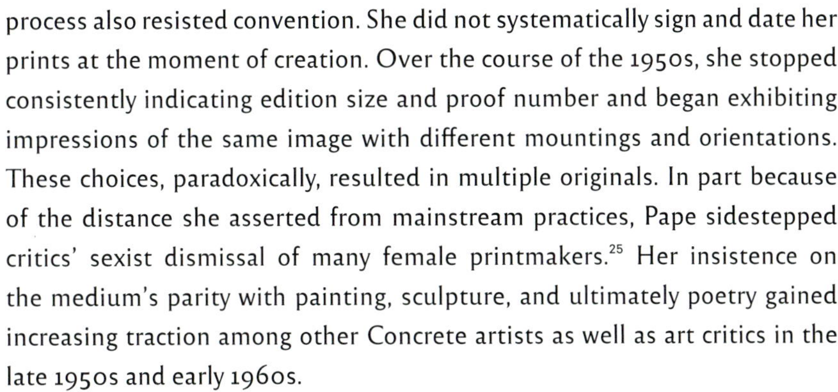

In a few short months, from December 1954 to March 1955, Pape shot to prominence in the Rio press as the sole printmaker dedicated to Concrete art; occasional mentions of her presence at openings expanded suddenly to features on the front page of the arts section. This new visibility coincided with media interest in Grupo Frente; notably, however, it occurred during a period when the collective did not have an exhibition on view, and Pape was often singled out rather than discussed as a member of the group. Moreover, this newfound attention was directed for the most part at her prints. Pape later explained that her painting and print practice developed simultaneously in the 1950s.[26] But that retrospective assertion is complicated by the few mentions of her paintings at the time as well as the variability inherent to the dates now assigned to her early production. She exhibited abstracted figurative works in both media at salon exhibitions at the start
PLS. 1–2 of the decade, including prints originally titled *Still Life* and *Trees* at the second and third national salons of modern art. Several of her paintings were displayed in the important *Exposição nacional de arte abstrata* (National Exhibition of Abstract Art) in 1953, possibly abstract works assembling an

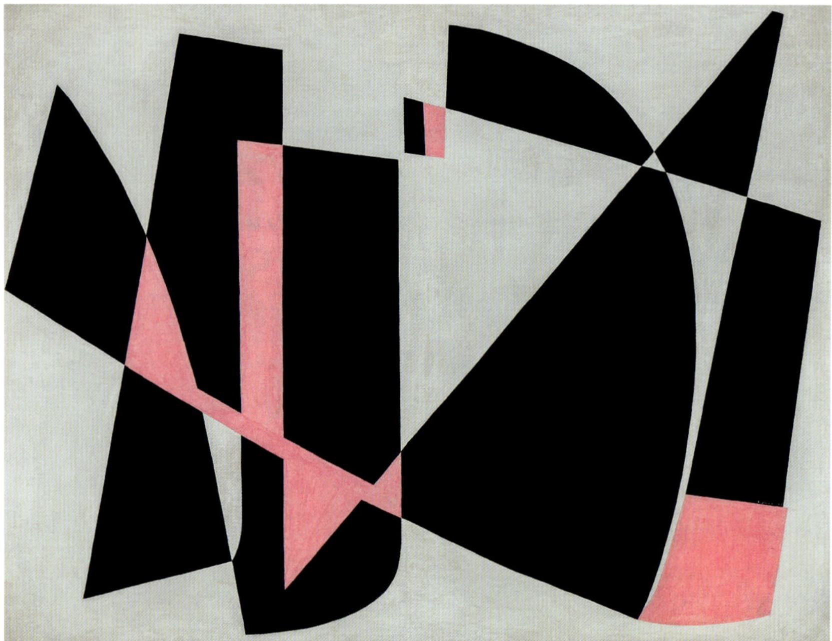

< FIG. 4 Lygia Pape (Brazilian, 1927–2004). *Pintura* (Painting), 1953. Oil on canvas; 75 × 100 cm (29 ⅝ × 39 ⅜ in.). Projeto Lygia Pape.

> FIG. 5 Images from a feature on jewelry designs (including Pape's, center) showcased at the Museu de Arte Moderna do Rio de Janeiro, *Correio da Manhã*, December 4, 1954, 10.

↓ FIG. 6 Pape with her print portfolio at the Museu de Arte Moderna do Rio de Janeiro, 1955.

interwoven cluster of flatly painted rectilinear and curved forms in the center of uniform white grounds (SEE FIG. 4); the overlapping forms echo in some of PLS. 3–7, 11–13 her early woodcuts.[27] These painted and printed works appear to have developed in tandem, oriented by Pedrosa's theory of perception and enlivened by the frequent get-togethers between Pedrosa and the artists who went on to comprise Grupo Frente.[28] That being said, the paintings and prints employ different materials, palettes, and scales and thus create distinct effects, with the paintings suggesting weightlessness, the woodcuts interlocking rotation. Pape's known painting practice of the 1950s also extended to sharply rendered, geometric paintings and low reliefs—works that do not form such a legible dialogue with her prints. Documentation establishes that Pape at least considered submitting to and perhaps exhibited paintings at the third and fourth Grupo Frente exhibitions in 1956.[29]

With these exceptions, Pape, to the best of my knowledge, showed woodcuts at exhibitions of the 1950s, along with jewelry on a few occasions. It is possible that the artist elected to foreground her prints given the uneven reception of her paintings. The second Bienal (1953–54) rejected the paintings she submitted.[30] She was not the only one snubbed: unrealized plans for an artist-organized *salon des refusés* were announced, and Clark and sculptor Zélia Salgado proposed an exhibition of women artists to draw attention to the Bienal's overzealous selection process and its disproportionate exclusion of women.[31] It is also possible that Pape's painting practice gradually became a more private facet of her production. What seems certain is that her dedication to printmaking was informed not only by her training and by the vibrant discourse around the medium in postwar Brazil and Latin America more broadly but also by the opportunity to pioneer a Brazilian Concretist approach to the medium. Reviews of the first Grupo Frente exhibition in 1954 identified Pape as "maybe the only Concrete printmaker in Brazil."[32]

It was nevertheless her jewelry designs that first received sustained solo press attention.[33] In December 1954 Pape's jewelry was included in a celebration of the third iteration of an annual exhibition of art by children in Ivan Serpa's classes at MAM Rio. The show and its surrounding events were timed to coincide with the Christmas season and included a large, experimental tree sculpture created by an artist or designer. The accompanying displays featured jewelry by Pape and two other artists, including her teacher, Ostrower; furniture by Abraham Palatnik; and a sale of recent art books from Europe and the United States. All of these received substantial media coverage, and the press lauded the events not only for their artistic merit but also as shopping opportunities.

By foregrounding Grupo Frente's leader, Serpa, and two of its artists, Palatnik and Pape, this holiday celebration aligned with the support and visibility MAM Rio gave to the collective in the mid-1950s. The press praised Pape's enamel and copper brooches, earrings, and necklaces, though in explicitly gendered and patriarchal terms. Articles described modern artistic jewelry as a welcome expansion of feminine taste, with husbands as the purchasers. In addition to the snapshots of enthusiastic shoppers peering into vitrines of jewelry, *Correio da Manhã* showcased the designs on the silhouetted heads and necks of culturally prominent women, including artist Noemia Mourão, identified not by her name but as the wife of painter Emiliano Di Cavalcanti (FIG. 5).[34] Pape subsequently showed jewelry and prints in the second Grupo Frente exhibition in 1955. That exhibition positioned the applied arts as a vital pathway for innovative artists to shape industry and consumer tastes, but Pape's work resisted such ready instrumentalizing. Her jewelry designs were decidedly idiosyncratic, handcrafted objects accented with experimental, brushy passages of enamel. They mark the artist's attempt to blur the distinctions between fine and applied arts and promote a realm of design typically regarded as minor and feminine relative to the period's more lauded design fields, such as architecture.

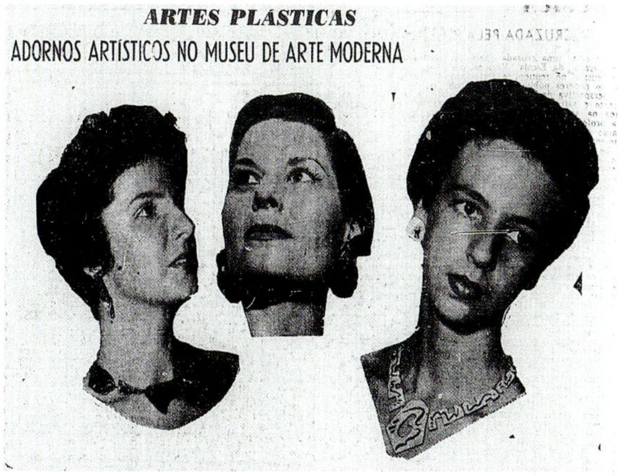

ARTES PLASTICAS
ADORNOS ARTÍSTICOS NO MUSEU DE ARTE MODERNA

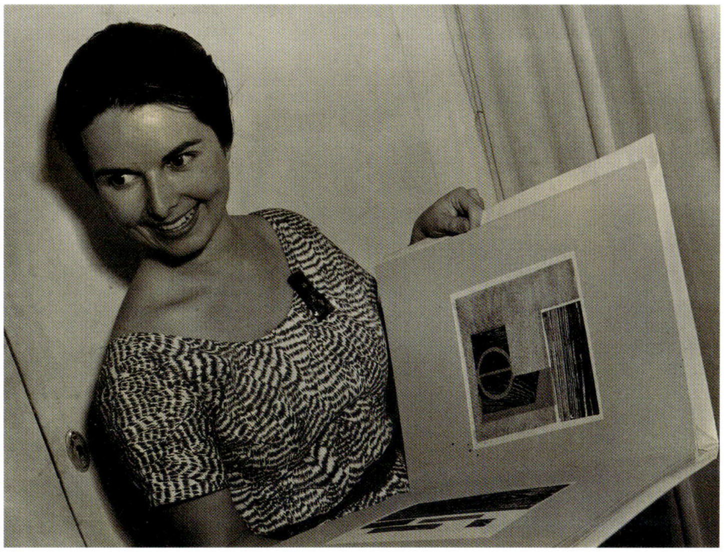

In January and February 1955 Pape again made the news, this time for the release of a print portfolio of ten small-format, colored woodcuts in an edition of twenty.
PLS. 15–16 (Two of these prints appear in this catalogue.) Daily newspapers ran multiple stories about the portfolio, noting that it was on sale at MAM Rio and at one point using identical language, surely copied from the same museum press release, to rave about the prints' quality and bargain price.[35] A photograph of Pape (FIG. 6) accompanied a short, upbeat interview celebrating the young artist's promising future.[36] She is pictured wearing a brooch, likely of her own design, and smiling broadly, holding the portfolio open to two of her prints.

The photograph of Pape with her portfolio illustrates a tension that recurred in the cultural press then as it does now, in which women artists are regularly showcased alongside new art and design pieces (including their own), donning stylish outfits coordinated with the works on hand. The picture presents Pape as both the maker of the prints and the customer for her own jewelry. Here, as in a number of other photographs of the artist in the 1950s, she wears a dress with a vibrant pattern, perhaps deliberately selected as an eye-catching backdrop to make her jewelry visible in grainy newspaper reproductions. But the overall effect is of a beautiful, coordinated tableau—down to the coiffed hair and cheery expression—that casts the artist as spokesmodel. Such images of Pape with her own works coexisted in the subsequent months and years with photographs of her at openings or cultural events in front of artworks that were not her own. Pape, along with other women artists, thus served as an elegant embodiment of Rio's vibrant cultural scene.

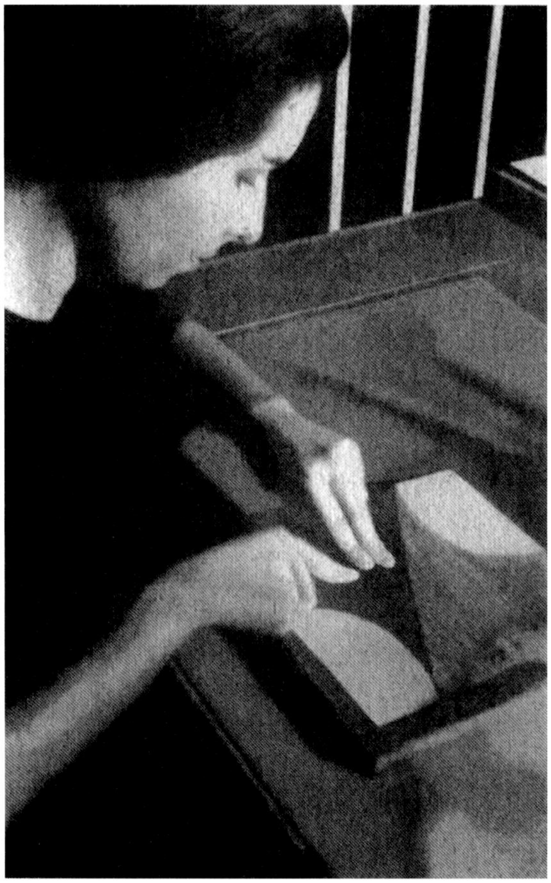

Pape took steps to control her public image. Her husband, Günther, photographed her making works repeatedly over the 1950s. At least one of his photographs served as a headshot in an exhibition catalogue, but most of them were not published until late in the artist's life or posthumously.[37] Still, they provide important documentation of Pape's working processes. In these studio pictures, Pape sometimes wears fashionable outfits that coordinate with the art; as such, even these representations toe the line of woman as consumer while they attempt to make space for woman as producer. But they notably foreground her labor, not her face, centering her fingers pressed against her work (SEE FIG. 7) or her body hunched over a collage on the floor of her studio (SEE P. 21, FIG. 8).

It was via printmaking itself that Pape most fully constructed and asserted her status as a creator. In early 1955 she released her print portfolio and simultaneously submitted works to the third Bienal, where her prints were featured prominently alongside sculptures by nationally renowned artist Maria Martins (SEE FIG. 8). The Bienal's organizers placed prints in a central gallery, demonstrating the high esteem Brazilian printmaking enjoyed at the time. The ten portfolio woodcuts and four additional prints Pape exhibited honed the collage-like lexicon of her early woodcuts.[38] The small-format works overtly juxtapose different wood types and different tonalities of gray and black with areas of vivid, saturated color. Geometric shapes made up of impressions of wood grains of disparate scales and orientations adjoin and crisscross in the playful, teetering compositions. Some works, like her earlier prints, use the warm white of the paper as a ground for interaction between forms. In one, Pape vertically stacked irregu-
PL. 15 lar gray and black rectangles printed from different wood grains; on the edge of one rectangle, she placed, as if on a shelf, a deep-red circle. She showcased the rough-hewn quality of the shapes, calling to mind the leftovers

of a woodshop and downplaying the technical precision necessary to realize such a multiblock print. In other works she filled the picture plane to create
PL. 16 a background of black and gray wood grain. One such print sees translucent blue and red circles float atop the interlocking, rectilinear surfaces of two wood grains, punctuating their different scales and tonalities. The proportions of Pape's geometric building blocks and the scales of some wood grains at times appear enormous relative to the sheets, contributing to the animation and physicality of the forms. The two-dimensional prints feel like found objects cut, arranged, and pasted together.

In a 1955 article about her prints in *Forma*, Pape explained that her work "takes advantage of the material of printmaking itself."[39] Rather than using the wood block as a uniform support to be carved, inked, and printed, Pape assembled impressions of surfaces of a variety of woods, which are legible in her works as distinct, physical objects. The adventurous mix of elements in the prints extends to the materials, which combine common and fine domestic and imported woods. Pape spoke poetically of the qualities of her different woods—the "beautiful drawings" of common pine, the "sinuous and accentuated veins" of Scots pine, and the "porous and fine texture" of peroba.[40]

For the second Grupo Frente exhibition in 1955, the most ambitious and visible of the group's initatives, Pape elected to display a group of prints that varied widely in color, shape, sensibility, and format. They were united by an emphasis on materiality—that is, by a palpable sense of their physical con-

< FIG. 7 This photograph by her husband, Günther, shows Pape in her studio working on the block for cat. 91.

V FIG. 8 Installation view of the third São Paulo Bienal in 1955 showing four of Pape's prints (left of center) displayed amid sculptures by Maria Martins.

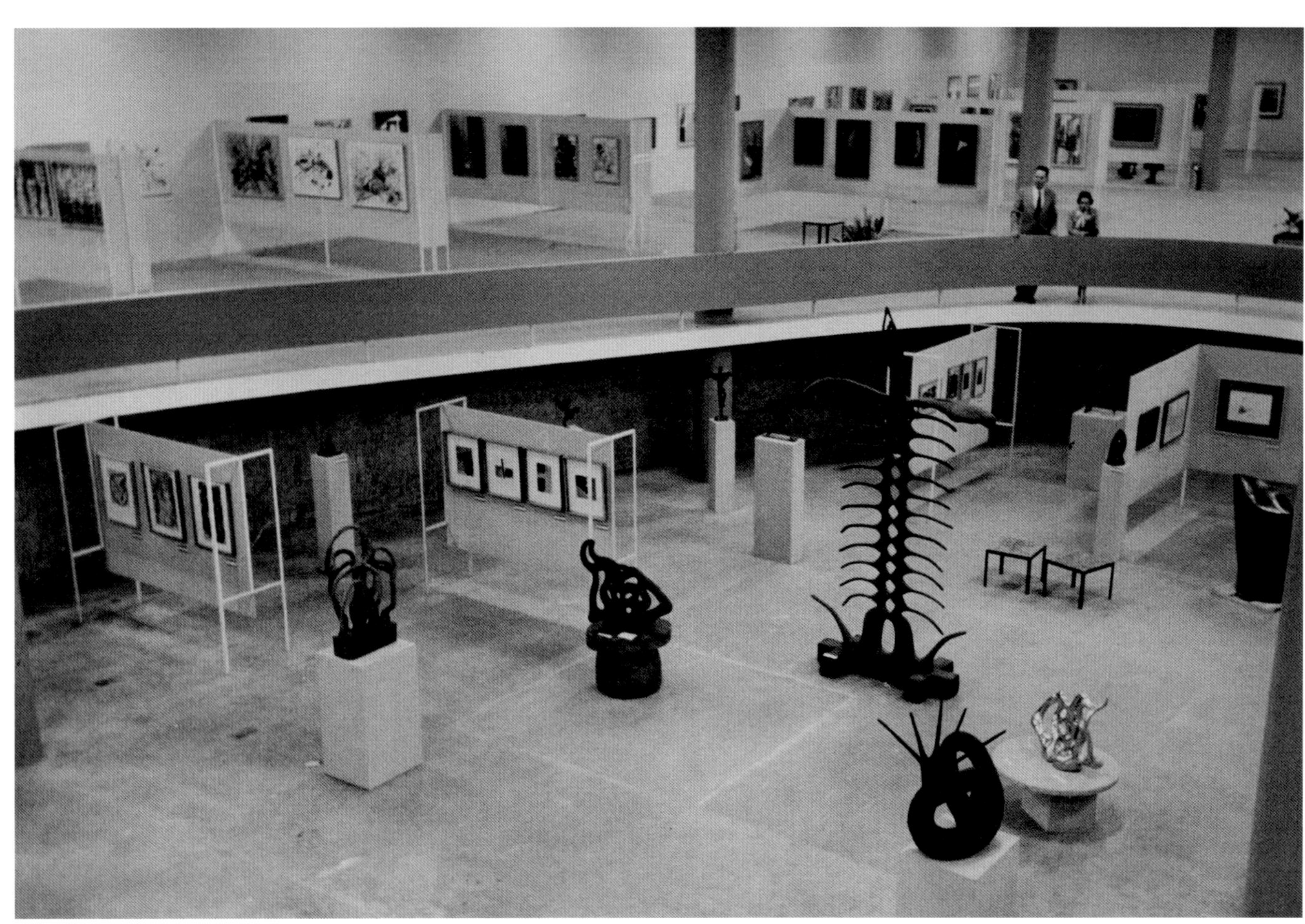

struction and of the labor that bound together the different elements. Pape's seven small- and medium-format prints were the first works visitors encountered upon entering the exhibition. Some of these prints retain the precise edges, overt juxtaposition of different wood grains, and palette of blacks with pops of color from the portfolio.[41] But others deviate in a host of ways, their backgrounds composed of a single surface of
PL. 19 largely uniform wood grain. In one print, muted-pink and warm-gray forms coexist with black
PL. 21 shapes. In another, pointy, oblique trapezoids and triangles repeat and seem to morph into a central band across the horizontal composition. In contrast to her earlier collage-like prints, this work and others seem to capture kinetic relationships among the elements, with some marks reading as scratches and some shapes reading as shadows or echoes of others.

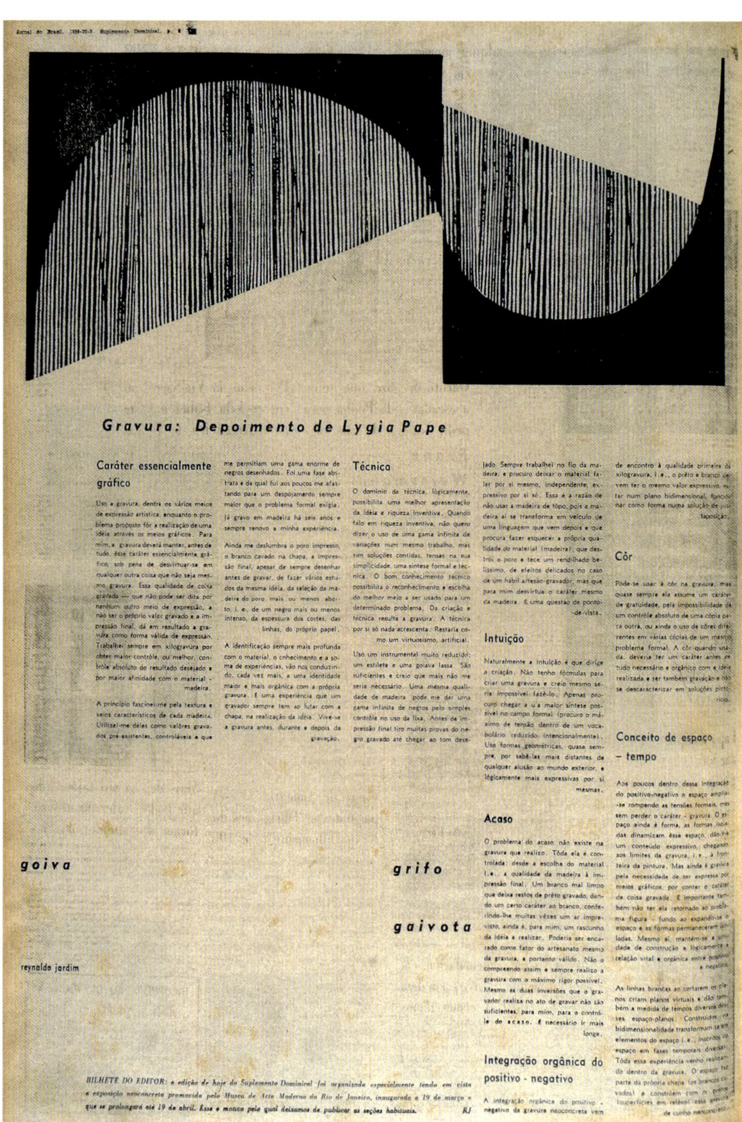

Gravura: Depoimento de Lygia Pape

Caráter essencialmente gráfico

Uso a gravura, dentre os vários meios de expressão artística, enquanto o problema proposto fôr a realização de uma idéia através os meios gráficos. Para mim, a gravura deverá manter, antes de tudo, êsse caráter essencialmente gráfico, sob pena de desvirtuar-se em qualquer outra coisa que não seja mesmo gravura. Essa qualidade de coisa gravada — que não pode ser dita por nenhum outro meio de expressão, a não ser o próprio valor gravado e a impressão final, dá em resultado a gravura como forma válida de expressão. Trabalhei sempre em xilogravura por obter maior contrôle, ou melhor, contrôle absoluto do resultado desejado e por maior afinidade com o material - madeira.

A princípio fascinei-me pela textura e veios característicos de cada madeira. Utilizei-me dêles como valôres gravados pré-existentes, controláveis e que me permitiam uma gama enorme de negros desenhados. Foi uma fase abstrata e da qual fui aos poucos me afastando para um despojamento sempre maior que o problema formal exigia. Já gravo em madeira há seis anos e sempre renovo a minha experiência.

Ainda me deslumbra o poro impresso, o branco cavado na chapa, a impressão final, apesar de sempre desenhar antes de gravar, de fazer vários estudos da mesma idéia, da seleção da madeira do poro mais ou menos aberto, i. e., de um negro mais ou menos intenso, da espessura dos cortes, das linhas, do próprio papel.

A identificação sempre mais profunda com o material, o cnhecimento e a soma de experiências, vão nos conduzindo, cada vez mais, a uma identidade maior e mais orgânica com a própria gravura. É uma experiência que um gravador sempre tem ao lutar com a chapa, na realização da idéia. Vive-se a gravura antes, durante e depois da gravação.

Técnica

O domínio da técnica, lògicamente, possibilita uma melhor apresentação da idéia e riqueza inventiva. Quando falo em riqueza inventiva, não quero dizer o uso de uma gama infinita de variações num mesmo trabalho, mas sim soluções contidas, tensas na sua simplicidade, uma síntese formal e técnica. O bom conhecimento técnico possibilita o reconhecimento e escolha do melhor meio a ser usado para um determinado problema. Da criação e técnica resulta a gravura. A técnica por si só nada acrescenta. Restaria como um virtuosismo, artificial.

Uso um instrumental muito reduzido: um estilete e uma goiava lassa. São suficientes e creio que mais não me seria necessário. Uma mesma qualidade de madeira pode me dar uma gama infinita de negros pelo simples contrôle no uso da lixa. Antes de impressão final tiro muitas provas do negro gravado até chegar ao tom desejado. Sempre trabalhei no fio da madeira, e procuro deixar o material falar por si mesmo, independente, expressivo por si só. Essa é a razão de não usar a madeira de tôpo, pois a madeira aí se transforma em veículo de uma linguagem que vem depois e que procura fazer esquecer a própria qualidade do material (madeira), que destrói o poro e tece um rendilhado belíssimo, de efeitos delicados no caso de um hábil artesão-gravador, mas que para mim desvirtua o caráter mesmo da madeira. É uma questão de ponto-de-vista.

Intuição

Naturalmente a intuição é que dirige a criação. Não tenho fórmulas para criar uma gravura e creio mesmo seria impossível fazê-lo. Apenas procuro chegar a u'a maior síntese possível no campo formal (procuro o máximo de tensão dentro de um vocabulário reduzido intencionalmente). Uso formas geométricas, quase sempre, por sabê-las mais distantes de qualquer alusão ao mundo exterior, e lògicamente mais expressivas por si mesmas.

Acaso

O problema do acaso não existe na gravura que realizo. Tôda ela é controlada: desde a escolha do material i.e., a qualidade da madeira à impressão final. Um branco mal limpo que deixa restos de prêto gravado, dando um certo caráter ao branco, conferindo-lhe muitas vêzes um ar imprevisto, ainda é, para mim, um rascunho da idéia a realizar. Poderia ser encarado como fator do artesanato mesmo da gravura, e portanto válido. Não o compreendo assim e sempre realizo a gravura com o máximo rigor possível. Mesmo as duas inversões que o gravador realiza no ato de gravar não são suficientes, para mim, para o contrôle do acaso. É necessário ir mais longe.

Integração orgânica do positivo - negativo

A integração orgânica do positivo - negativo da gravura neoconcreta vem

Côr

Conceito de espaço – tempo

goiva

grifo

gaivota

reynaldo jardim

BILHETE DO EDITOR: a edição de hoje do Suplemento Dominical foi organizada especialmente tendo em vista a exposição neoconcreta promovida pelo Museu de Arte Moderna do Rio de Janeiro, inaugurada a 19 de março e que se prolongará até 19 de abril. Êsse é motivo pelo qual deixamos de publicar as seções habituais. RJ

The attention Pape received as the only Concrete printmaker increased in the late 1950s, as did the precision of her marks and geometry once she eliminated color inks and began experimenting with larger formats. She received one of the inaugural Leirner contemporary art prizes in 1956.[42] Her prints were featured in the *Exposição nacional de arte concreta* (National Exhibition of Concrete Art) in Rio and São Paulo in 1956–57 and in the first Neo-Concrete exhibition in Rio in 1959. Her work also became a mainstay of exhibitions of Brazilian art (organized by MAM Rio in conjunction with the federal government) that traveled to Europe and South America. She participated in a series of published debates on printmaking in 1957–58 and published theoretical texts about her production.[43] In these, she positioned herself as an avant-garde artist and her prints as originals rather than as products of a reproducible, technical process. Pape argued that the formal qualities inherent to printmaking—and to woodblock prints above all—made it the best medium for achieving the dynamic spatial relations Concrete artists pursued. She continued to be photographed as an idealized consumer of her own art; however, in the Sunday supplement to the *Jornal do Brasil*, it was no longer photographs of the artist but instead illustrations of her woodcuts—cropped to the edges, silhouetted, and set into the graphic design of the sparse page layouts—that accompanied discussion of her work (SEE FIG. 9). Moreover, stark installation views, unpopulated by visitors, became a mainstay in arts journalism. This new visual representation of Pape's work was reinforced by her own writing, especially her 1960 *Poemas-Xilogravuras*, in which she sought to definitively articulate her artistic identity as a creator and author rather than a spokeswoman or consumer.

< FIG. 9 An illustration of cat. 93 accompanies an article by Pape in an issue of the *Jornal do Brasil* dedicated to the launch of the Neo-Concrete movement, March 22, 1959, 8.

PL. 97 In 1960 Pape produced her final major print work, *Poemas–Xilogravuras*. Besides marking the culmination of a decade of in-depth experimentation with the woodcut medium, the project reveals how the artist productively maintained and conceptualized fissures in her multimedia practice and in her identity. The dash in the work's title participates in a larger practice among her Brazilian, Concrete-oriented contemporaries. Several artists used the punctuation mark in composite titles, such as *Forma–Objeto* (Form–object), to express their engagement with theories of form and abstract art histories.[44] In Pape's case the dash signals the material and conceptual labor entailed in binding together the practices of printmaking and poetry. This mix of media, one visual and the other textual, was also explicitly gendered, because postwar art critics cast printmaking as feminine and therefore minor compared to poetry's masculine power and relevance. Their juxtaposition thus represented a complex salvo against misogyny: the work does not equate the artforms but instead maintains their difference even as it brings them together, an act I suggest reflects the tension inherent to Pape's identity as a woman worker and artist in the face of patriarchical norms and circumscribed legal rights.

Pape built on her status as the only Concrete printmaker to join the otherwise male ranks of Concrete poets. Published in May 1960, *Poemas–Xilogravuras* was the fifth and final volume in the *Coleção Espaço* (Space collection), a series of poetry books produced by the *Jornal do Brasil*.[45] She displayed the poem book alongside her first participatory work, *Livro da criação* (Book of creation; FIG. 10), at the second Neo-Concrete exhibition in Rio in late 1960. Both works were subsequently displayed at the third and final Neo-Concrete exhibition in São Paulo in 1961.

The poem book is unbound and housed in a folded folio printed with the black outline of a square. The inaugural page—which the reader accesses by folding back two flaps of the folio along a centered vertical cut—reads "*em quebra / revela*" (on breaking / reveals). Pape thereby endowed the gesture of pulling back the cover with transformative potential, narrating the act of opening the book as a breach that reveals. She also suggested a meaning for the work's title: the poems and prints are not equivalent; instead, in the chasm between them and in their adhering together, something is unveiled. In a text published during the second Neo-Concrete exhibition, Pape described the book as composed of two distinct parts: poems and prints. She wrote, "The two, side by side, lose their expressive independence in favor of another catalyst, which encompasses both parts, merging them together into new content."[46] Pape thus eschewed the longstanding proposition that visual art conjures an ineffable experience for its viewers in favor of underlining the experience of the "spectator–reader," who negotiates and merges unlike things.[47] She noted that the spectator–reader is obligated to take time to attempt to reconcile the poems and prints and that this "duration" itself fosters a "new expressivity."[48] In the poem and print combinations, the temporality Pape suggests is cyclical and spatial; it endures, replicates, rotates, and wanders.

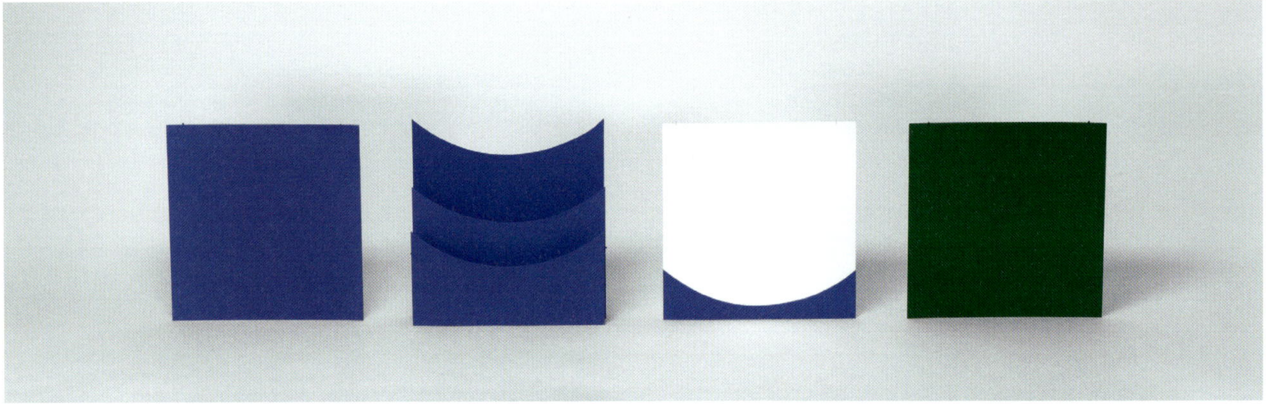

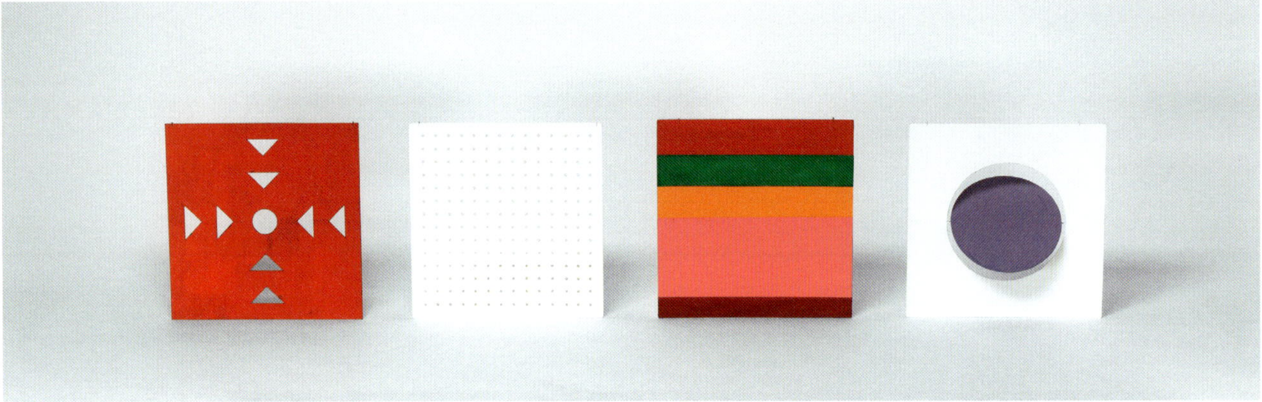

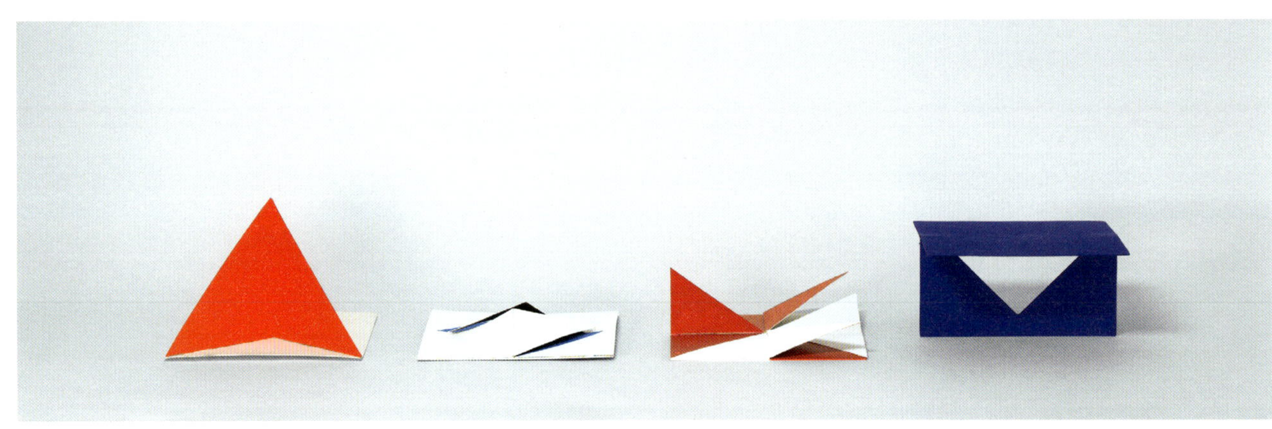

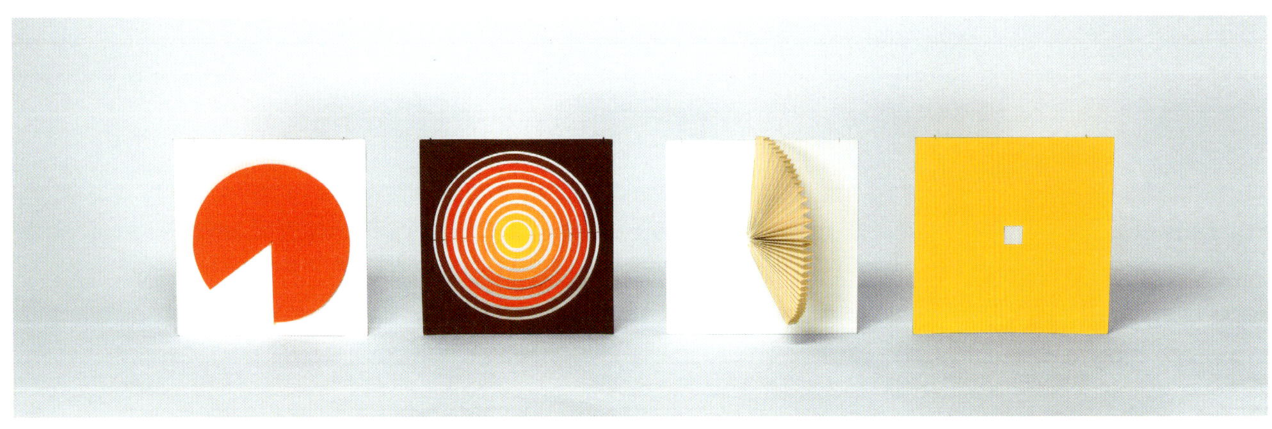

< FIG. 10 *Livro da criação* (Book of creation), 1959–60. Artist's book with sixteen unbound pages, some with gouache on board, paper, and string; each: 30.5 × 30.5 cm (12 × 12 in.). The Museum of Modern Art, New York, gift of Patricia Phelps de Cisneros, 1349.2001.a–r.

Following the first page, the sheets of *Poemas-Xilogravuras* are folded in half, and the reader must open each to view the conjunction of poem and print. The reading experience thus entails encountering a sequence of blank, white squares that one physically opens and then closes again. In this way, the square on the folio cover foretells the rhythm of reading the book. The sheets of the work have been displayed in different configurations, seemingly by Pape's design.[49] The order of the book featured in this exhibition and catalogue is different from the version I studied in 2017, which read as follows:

em quebra / revela (on breaking / reveals)
em brado / campo / em claro (in shout / field / in light)
cal / moi (lime / grind)
no veio / no verde / nomeia (in the grain / on the green / names)
fio / foz (thread / river mouth)
cheio / vagar (full / to wander)
de vento / de tempo (of wind / of time)
em eco / gizes (in echo / chalks)
em meio / girava (in the middle / it rotated)
em avêsso / aço (in reverse / steel)
aço / gorja / azul (steel / keel / blue)
os trigais / os mesmos (the wheat fields / the same ones)
em verde / perdure (in green / endures)
em brado / campo / em claro (in shout / field / in light)[50]

The poems typeset on the left side are juxtaposed, on the right side, with woodcut and photoengraved prints on Japanese paper adhered to cardstock. Pape repurposed the compositions of existing woodcuts, carving new square blocks in some instances or working with a print shop in Rio to create photoengraved versions of earlier blocks.[51] Among the works she repurposed
PLS. 87–88 was one of her best-known compositions from the late 1950s, with three square voids stacked down the central vertical axis, which was exhibited in the first Neo-Concrete exhibition and the fifth Bienal in 1959. The majority of the book's prints drew from previous works composed of high-contrast wood grain, with the grain further heightened by the photoengraving technique. It appears that Pape also created several new prints specifically for the poem book, including those that accompany the second and last poems.

The second and last poems are identical: "em brado / campo / em claro." Their accompanying prints share the same composition—triangles jutting in from the four corners—but in the earlier iteration the triangular planes are filled in with flatly printed, solid black ink, while in the latter they are delineated with thick black lines. Matched to geometric, streamlined prints that do not seem to have anything to do with the words, these opening and closing poems evoke an animate presence in nature or a multisensory experience of nature: the sound of a shout, the physical location of a field, and the feel of light. The final words, "em claro," can also be translated as *awake* to describe the state of consciousness of whatever being has uttered or heard the shout. The repetition of the poems and the shift from black to white in the prints also suggests a teleological movement from darkness to lightness, from ignorance to enlightenment. Notably, these sheets were absent when the work was displayed in 1961, another layer of variability Pape maintained in the work: not only does the book lack a set order, it can also be displayed in part and still be considered "complete."

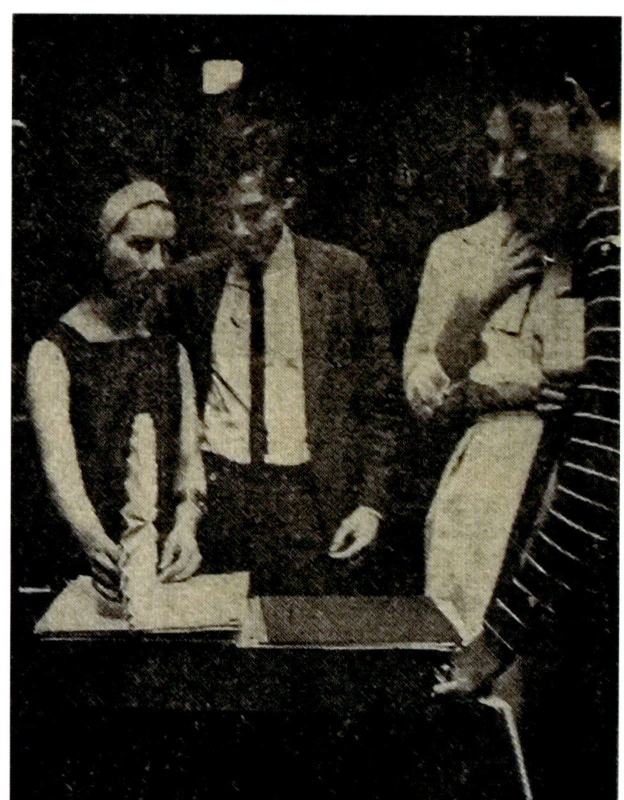

Compositionally, the forms in many of the prints replicate and invert across a central axis—whether horizontal, vertical, or diagonal—to create doubled, dynamic spaces. The shapes of forms and the textures of Pape's carving in the wood matrices of certain prints echo the imagery of the poems. A print of an undulating *S* curve composed of rough-hewn, oblique lines and intervening triangles accompanies the poem "fio / foz." Dense diagonals and stacked chevrons appear next to the poem, "os trigais / os mesmos." Similarly, the placement of the words often corresponds to the structure of the prints; for example, the staggered lines of "de vento / de tempo" seem to follow the angle of the slash that bisects the companion print.

Color plays a captivating role in the poem book, underlining the breach signaled on the opening page. Pape used colored ink in just one instance: alongside the poem "aço / gorja / azul," she printed the woodcut in a vibrant ultramarine, a visual shock among the otherwise uniformly white and black pages. In contrast, two poems mention green ("no veio / no verde / nomeia" and "em verde / perdure"), but the color does not appear in the accompanying prints, which are composed of solid and striped blacks with unprinted areas of warm-white Japanese paper. Pape asks the spectator-reader to mentally conjure the color but does not prescribe where they should—or whether they should—apply these visualizations to the prints. Are the blacks meant to evoke the fecundity of sowing grain? Do the whites represent endurance?

Poemas-Xilogravuras is not pictured in any known installation views of the second Neo-Concrete exhibition in Rio, but written accounts state that the work was displayed as individual panels on the wall under glass.[52] Pape exhibited *Livro da criação* in a vertical stack on a waist-high table positioned along the wall, which allowed participants to open and turn the pages (SEE FIG. 11). Philosopher and critic José Guilherme Merquior explained that *Livro da criação* was shown with just "a few words of guidance," an explanatory caption to accommodate viewers unmoored by the non-textual book.[53] In São Paulo Pape displayed the individual panels of *Livro da criação* on a long, low pedestal in various positions—some flat, some upright. *Poemas-Xilogravuras* was installed on the wall above, under glass (SEE FIG. 12).[54] As in Rio, visitors could manipulate the panels of *Livro da criação*, although only with some effort, given the low height of the pedestal. The allusion to the book form is less obvious than in the Rio presentation, where photographs of the exhibition in the Sunday supplement of the *Jornal do Brasil* convey a freewheeling interactivity: artists demonstrating the participatory nature of their works and children and adults exploring the space and the art. In the installation photography by Neo-Concrete artist Willys de Castro, the São Paulo exhibition is devoid of people, highlighting instead Oscar Niemeyer's streamlined design for the large gallery. In these photographs, *Livro da criação* reads primarily as sculpture, its pages registering as three-dimensional forms to be inspected as aesthetic objects rather than interacted with.

By placing the two projects in such close proximity in São Paulo, Pape emphasized an original and radical component of *Livro da criação*: the withholding of language that makes perceptible the representational and expressive labor she enlisted visuality to undertake. But the two works also functioned as auxiliaries for each other in the exhibition. In *Poemas-Xilogravura*, we read of fields, wind, wheat, and a river mouth as well as of green and blue, words that form a wellspring of allusions to an animate, cyclical nature. Similarly, the kaleidoscopic monochromes of *Livro da criação* amplify the sites and spaces described in the poems and prints.

At the time, Pape and critics discussed the two works, both unbound books of similar lengths, as interconnected projects.[55] The artist's 1960 text "*Poemas-Invenção*" (Poems-invention) suggested a progressive shift between the two works: *Poemas-Xilogravuras* remains in "virtual space," while "the next book, *Livro da criação*, materializes real space."[56] The contrast between virtuality and reality was one Pape deployed going forward to explain her leap from prints to participatory works. Yet despite her description of the differences between the two works, her original installation establishes a deep sense of their continuity. Furthermore, in her writing about the two

< FIG. 11 Photograph of Lygia Pape demonstrating *Livro da criação* at the second Neo-Concrete Exhibition at the Ministério da Educação, *Jornal do Brasil*, November 23, 1960, 8.

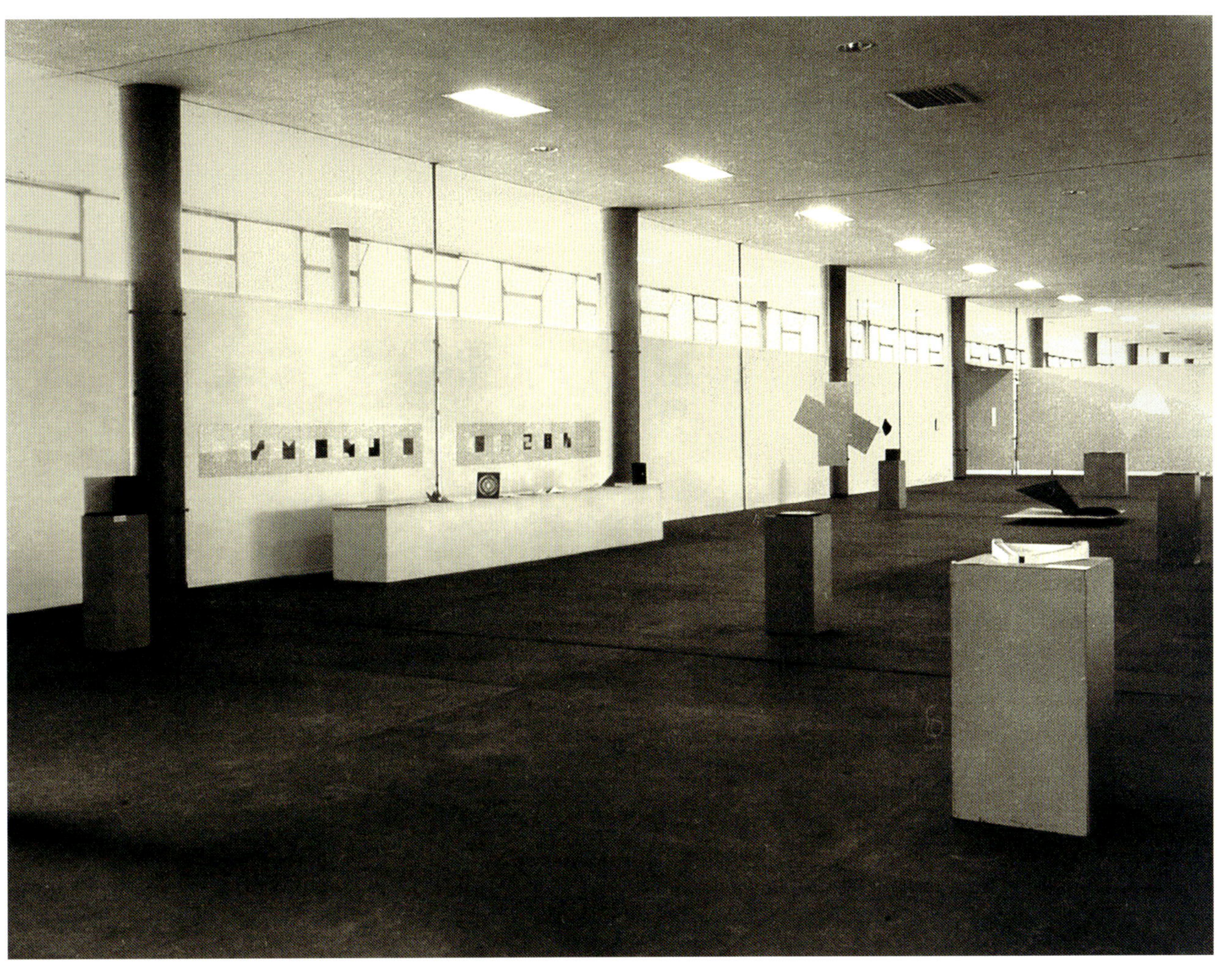

V FIG. 12 Photograph of the *Exposição Neoconcreta* at the Museu de Arte Moderna de São Paulo by Brazilian artist Willys de Castro, 1961. Pape's works line the back wall, with cat. 97 framed above a platform displaying pages from *Livro da criação*.

works, she positioned *Poemas–Xilogravuras* as inaugurating an examination of the break between language and image, another key subject of Pape's practice going forward.

The prominence of *Poemas–Xilogravuras* in the Neo-Concrete exhibitions of 1960 and 1961 soon receded in accounts by Pape and others, and the work has been little studied by historians. Scholars have instead privileged *Livro da criação*, which has seemed a better fit for the participatory component of Neo-Concretism that has always received more attention. But other factors may have played into the work's diminished prominence—not only hierarchies of media and the persistent secondary status of printmaking but also Pape's more fraught understanding of spectatorship in *Poemas–Xilogravuras*, which offers tension rather than reconciliation. The reader–viewer is continually made aware of the difference between visual and textual representation: the prints emphatically do not illustrate the poems. This kind of experience was out of sync with Neo-Concrete artists' increasingly liberatory gloss, in subsequent years, on the kind of participation offered by their works.[57]

Considering *Poemas–Xilogravuras* alongside Pape's prints of the 1950s provides new insight into how the materials and meanings of printmaking informed her conception of "the break." She described how prints "form an invisible weft" that is "very expressive through its proper techniques: whites, lines formed by the mismatch of fiber, scratched blacks, etc."[58] The pioneering manner in which Pape sutured different materials, forms, and disciplines makes legible a neglected but crucial facet of the transformation of viewership abstract artists enacted in Brazil after World War II. Friction rather than resolution prevail. Difference is held together provisionally. That this was also the social and legal condition even for a privileged woman like Pape in Brazilian society at the time is essential to grasping the stakes of her media juxtapositions. By establishing herself as the singular Concrete printmaker *and* woman Concrete poet, Pape both considered and countered her portrayal as an attractive sideshow in the art world. The break she first explored in printmaking was also a means of expressing and subverting the limits placed on women artists, the means by which she fashioned herself not as a consumer but as a creator.

This essay is indebted to the critical insights of an anonymous reader and Kit Shields, and benefitted from dialogue about Lygia Pape's work with Aglaíze Damasceno and Luiz Camillo Osorio over several years. The study of artworks in conservation labs, storage, and study rooms and the expertise of conservators, curators, and registrars have been fundamental to my understanding of Pape's prints. I thank Mark Pascale and María Cristina Rivera Ramos for sharing their knowledge of works in the present exhibition, and Erika Mosier at the Museum of Modern Art, New York. The Pape family afforded me precious access to works in their collection over an extended period. During a 2017 exhibition at the Metropolitan Museum of Art, New York, Allison Barone, Iria Candela, Jeff Elliott, Marina Ruiz Molina, and Michele Wijegoonaratna allowed me to examine *Poemas-Xilogravuras* on a non-public day with the kind permission of the artist's family and the assistance of António Leal. I thank Tie Jojima, Thiago Ferreira, and Maria Luisa Tavora for research assistance. All translations from Portuguese are my own unless otherwise noted.

1 In 1932 Brazil became the second Latin American nation (after Ecuador) to extend suffrage to women, although voting was not compulsory for women as it was for men and myriad barriers existed.

2 See Ann Farnsworth-Alvear, *Dulcinea in the Factory: Myths, Morals, Men, and Women in Colombia's Industrial Experiment, 1905–1960* (Durham, NC: Duke University Press, 2000); and John D. French and Daniel James, eds., *The Gendered Worlds of Latin American Women Workers: From Household to Factory to the Union Hall and Ballot Box* (Durham, NC: Duke University Press, 1997).

3 An expanse of blank paper divides the title on the final page of the book, but Pape rendered the separation between *Poemas* and *Xilogravuras* with a dash in her contemporaneous (and later) writing. See Lygia Pape, "Poemas-Invenção, livro: Poemas-Xilogravuras," *Jornal do Brasil*, November 26, 1960, 6.

4 I draw here on Pape's use of the word *quebra* (break or breach) in *Poemas-Xilogravuras*, as well as critic Mário Pedrosa, who refers to the theme of *brecha* (breach) in her work. Mário Pedrosa, "To Lygia Pape," in Luis Otávia Pimental, Lygia Pape, and Mário Pedrosa, *Lygia Pape* (Rio de Janeiro: Funarte, 1983), 1.

5 See Adele Nelson, "Sensitive and Nondiscursive Things: Lygia Pape and the Reconception of Printmaking," *Art Journal* 71, no. 3 (Fall 2012): 26–45. Foundational studies and sources on Pape's print-making by Brazilian scholars include Lygia Pape, *Lygia Pape: Entrevista a Lúcia Carneiro e Ileana Pradilla* (Rio de Janeiro: Lacerda Editores, Centro de Arte Hélio Oiticica, 1998); Ronald Duarte, Glória Ferreira, and Paulo Venancio Filho, "Dossiê Lygia Pape: Entrevista de Lygia Pape," *Arte e ensaios* 5, no. 5 (1998): 7–16; Denise Mattar, *Lygia Pape: Intrinsecamente anarquista* (Rio de Janeiro: Relume Dumará, 2003); Maria Luisa Luz Távora, "Lygia Pape: Gravuras ou antigravuras? Deslocamentos possíveis da tradição," *Arte e ensaios* 11, no. 11 (2004): 58–65; Luis Camillo Osorio, "Lygia Pape: Experimentation and Resistance," *Third Text* 20, no. 5 (September 2006): 571–83; and Paulo Herkenhoff, "Lygia Pape: The Art of Passage," in *Lygia Pape: Magnetized Space*, ed. María Luisa Blanco, Manuel J. Borja-Villel, and Teresa Velázquez, exh. cat. (Madrid: Museo Nacional Centro de Arte Reina Sofía, 2011), 19–59.

6 For extended discussion of these developments, and of Grupo Frente, see Adele Nelson, *Forming Abstraction: Art and Institutions in Postwar Brazil* (Berkeley: University of California Press, 2022).

7 Ferreira Gullar, "Neo-Concrete Manifesto (1959)," in *Inverted Utopias: Avant-Garde Art in Latin America*, ed. Mari Carmen Ramírez and Héctor Olea, trans. Laura Pérez, exh. cat. (New Haven, CT: Yale University Press, 2004), 497.

8 See, for example, Jayme Maurício, "No Museu de Arte Moderna: gente moça renovando a paisagem artística," *Correio da Manhã*, July 15, 1955, 12, 14.

9 See Mário Pedrosa, "Grupo Frente (1955)," in *Mário Pedrosa: Primary Documents*, ed. Glória Ferreira and Paulo Herkenhoff (New York: Museum of Modern Art, 2015), 269–72.

10 See John D. French and Mary Lynn Pedersen Cluff, "Women and Working-Class Mobilization in Postwar São Paulo, 1945–1948," in *Gendered Worlds*, 182–83, 197. A literacy prerequisite, which persisted until 1985 and excluded uneducated women, exemplifies the implicit class- and race-based discrimination codified in Brazilian law. At midcentury half the population (across genders) could not read. In practice, the disenfranchisement targeted rural populations, since urban workers could often vote, regardless of literacy status, having been enrolled by their employers; see Brodwyn Fischer, *A Poverty of Rights: Citizenship and Inequality in Twentieth-Century Rio de Janeiro* (Palo Alto, CA: Stanford University Press, 2008); and James Holston, *Insurgent Citizenship: Disjunctions of Democracy and Modernity in Brazil* (Princeton, NJ: Princeton University Press, 2008).

11 See Joel Wolfe, *Working Women, Working Men: São Paulo and the Rise of Brazil's Industrial Working Class, 1900–1955* (Durham, NC: Duke University Press, 1993), 178–83. Barbara Weinstein suggests that women's labor leadership was more limited than Wolfe proposes; Barbara Weinstein, "Unskilled Worker, Skilled Housewife: Constructing the Working-Class Woman in São Paulo, Brazil," in *Gendered Worlds*, 99n66.

12 "Apoio à campanha da Tribuna da Imprensa," *Tribuna da Imprensa*, July 6, 1953, 2.

13 "Mulheres de várias atividades antecipam a sua escolha," *Tribuna da Imprensa*, October 3, 1955, 9.

14 See Bryan McCann, "Carlos Lacerda: The Rise and Fall of a Middle-Class Populist in 1950s Brazil," *Hispanic American Historical Review* 83, no. 4 (November 2003): 666.

15 "Mulheres de calças cumpridas prendem artistas ao bairro," *Tribuna da Imprensa*, July 8, 1955, 6.

16 See, for example, A. L. [Anna Letycia] Quadros, "Grupo Frente," *Forma*, no. 2 (August 1954): n.p.; "Cartões de Natal," *Forma*, no. 4 (December 1954): n.p.; and "Lygia Pape," *Forma*, no. 5 (April 1955): n.p.

17 There were other women editors and writers in the Brazilian art press. Lina Bo Bardi directed *Habitat: Revista das Artes no Brasil* in São Paulo, although it was published and backed by publicist Rodolfo Klein. Maria Eugênia Franco was the rare arts and culture critic who regularly contributed to newspapers outside the sections targeted at women; see Talita Trizoli, "Maria Eugênia Franco e os ensaios sobre a II Bienal de São Paulo" (virtual lecture, Congresso Associação de Brasilianistas na Europa, Prague, September 20, 2021).

18 See Alzira Alves de Abreu, "Revistando os anos 1950 através da imprensa," in *O moderno em questão: a década de 1950 no Brasil*, ed. Rugai Bastos, Glaucia Villa Bôas, and André Botelho (Rio de Janeiro: Topbooks, 2008), 216.

19 See "A loteria do Clubinho Tajiri," *Correio da manhã*, October 31, 1954, 12.

20 Pape, along with Mário Pedrosa, joined the leadership of the club in 1955. See "Tout court," *Correio da manhã*, March 2, 1955, 10.

21 Tony Bennett, "The Exhibitionary Complex," *New Formations* 4 (Spring 1988): 73–102.

22 International Council and International Program Records, I.B.124, MoMA Archives, New York.

23 See, for example, Silvia Dolinko, *Arte plural: el grabado entre la tradición y la experimentación, 1955–1973* (Buenos Aires: Edhasa, 2012); and Maeve Coudrelle, "The Imprint of Hemispheric Exchange: The Bienal Americana de Grabado, 1963–1970," *OBOE Journal: On Biennials and Other Exhibitions* (forthcoming 2022).

24 On the postwar history of printmaking in Brazil, see Maria Luisa Luz Távora, "A gravura brasileira—anos 50/60," *Gávea* 5 (April 1988): 42–56. On the stakes of Pape's adoption of woodcuts in this milieu, see Sérgio B. Martins, "An Anticlass in Avant-Gardism," in *Lygia Pape: A Multitude of Forms*, ed. Iria Candela (New York: Metropolitan Museum of Art, 2017), 27–29.

25 On sexism in art criticism of postwar printmaking, see Ana Avelar, "Pintoras e gravadoras expressivas: um capítulo à parte, informalismo e expressismo-abstrato no Brasil," *Modos: Revista de História da Arte* 5, no. 1 (January–April 2021): 160–77.

26 Lygia Pape, quoted in Mattar, *Lygia Pape: intrinsecamente anarquista*, 63–64.

27 For illustrations of Pape's early paintings and reliefs, see Candela, *Lygia Pape: A Multitude of Forms*, pls. 1–26.

28 On Pedrosa and Gestalt theory, see Mário Pedrosa, "Da natureza afetiva da forma na obra de arte," in *Arte, forma e personalidade, 3 estudos* (São Paulo: Kairós, 1979), 12–86; and Kaira M. Cabañas, *Learning from Madness: Brazilian Modernism and Global Contemporary Art* (Chicago: University of Chicago Press, 2018), 83–107.

29 In an unpublished text at the Projeto Lygia Pape, Ivan Serpa relays his impressions of Pape's new paintings and reliefs during a 1955 studio visit. He also mentions her plan to exhibit the works at a Grupo Frente exhibition. To the best of my knowledge, there was no discussion of Pape's paintings and reliefs in the press during the mid-1950s. See Ivan Serpa, "Text for the New Exhibition of Works by Grupo Frente: Lygia Pape and Her Production (Reliefs and Paintings)," in *Lygia Pape: Magnetized Space*, 63.

30 According to records at the Arquivo Histórico Wanda Svevo (hereafter AHWS) at the Fundação Bienal de São Paulo, Pape submitted five gouache-on-canvas paintings in April 1953. In June 1953 she received permission to substitute five oil-on-canvas paintings because of condition issues with the gouache works. The selection jury met in September and October 1953, and her entry cards were stamped *recusada* (rejected). Neither her prints nor her paintings appear in either the catalogue or in any known photography of the event. Lygia Pape, entry forms, April 29, 1953, box 02/17, folder 7, and box 02/20, folder 1; Lygia Pape to the Museu de Arte Moderna de São Paulo, June 11, 1953, box 02/16, folder 6; Arturo Profili to Lygia Pape, June 26, 1953, box 02/16, folder 6; and Lygia Pape to Arturo Profili, July 1, 1953, box 02/16, folder 6, all 02 Bienal de São Paulo, MAM, AHWS.

31 "Exposição paralela à Bienal," *Tribuna da Imprensa*, September 30, 1953, 8.

32 Quadros, "Grupo Frente."

33 Pape's jewelry is a subject for further research. Black-and-white photographs of her wearing her own designs were a mainstay of the 1950s Brazilian art press.

34 See "Adornos artísticos no Museu de Arte Moderna," *Correio da Manhã*, December 4, 1954, 10; "A Embaixatriz e os adornos modernos," *Correio da Manhã*, December 16, 1954, 14; and "Arte de moda em três vitrinas," *Correio da Manhã*, December 22, 1954, 9.

35 "Gravuras de Lígia Pape," *Tribuna da Imprensa*, January 25, 1955, 3; and "Gravuras de Ligia Pape," *Correio da manhã*, January 26, 1955, 10.

36 "Album de gravura," *Correio da Manhã*, February 5, 1955, 12.

37 *Grupo Frente*, exh. cat. (Rio de Janeiro: Instituto Brasil–Estados Unidos, 1954), n.p.

38 Based on photographs of the third Bienal, it is likely that at least one work in the portfolio was exhibited. In addition to fig. 8, AHWS holds two other installation views showing Pape's prints. See 03-00001-03835 and 03-00001-03833, AHWS.

39 "Lygia Pape," *Forma*, no. 5 (April 1955): n.p.

40 Ibid. As she would later recount to Távora, Pape sourced what she called "common pine" for her prints from boxes for salt cod at a warehouse near her studio; Távora, "Lygia Pape: gravuras ou antigravuras?," 61.

41 See illustrations and discussion in Nelson, *Forming Abstraction*, 230, 234–35.

42 Isaí Leirner established an annual prize for contemporary art to acquire works for the Museu de Arte Moderna de São Paulo. See Regina Teixeira de Barros, "A Galeria das Artes de Folhas e Prêmio Leirner de Arte Contemporânea: arte e meio artístico em São Paulo, 1958–1962" (PhD diss., Universidade de São Paulo, 2020).

43 Pape's key early texts include Lygia Pape, "Debate sobre a gravura, afirma Lygia Pape: 'os jovens devem abrir o seu próprio caminho,'" *Jornal do Brasil*, December 15, 1957, 2; "Novos depoimentos sobre a gravura: Goeldi, 'desde 1900 não fazemos senão marcar passo,' Lygia Pape, 'minha fantasia é controladíssima como a de Lívio,' Edith Behring, 'Villon practica a heresia de misturar técnicas,'" *Jornal do Brasil*, February 2, 1958, 2; and "Gravura: Depoimento de Lygia Pape," *Jornal do Brasil*, March 22, 1959, 8 (pictured in fig. 9). For analysis, see Nelson, "Sensitive and Nondiscursive Things," 33–37.

44 See Nelson, *Forming Abstraction*, 70–81.

45 The series, begun in 1958, also included books of poetry by Ferreira Gullar, Theo Spanudis, Reynaldo Jardim, and Carlos Fernando do Fontes de Almeida. There were unrealized plans for other books. From the first announcement of the book series, Pape's planned volume was mentioned, though occasionally it was described as a book of her prints with no mention of her poems.

46 Pape, "Poemas–Invenção," 6. Pape repurposed much of this text in a subsequent interview by Vera Martins, "Neoconcretos falam de sua exposição: Lígia Pape," *Jornal do Brasil*, April 26, 1961, 2. Slight variations in this second interview inform my translation.

47 Martins, "Neoconcretos falam," 2.

48 Ibid.

49 The work was illustrated in a different order during Pape's lifetime and in a scholarly study by Maria Clara Amado Martins, "Os 'livros' de Lygia Pape" (master's thesis, Universidade Federal do Rio de Janeiro, 1996), 37–46.

50 Pape's poems resist definitive translation. Many words and phrases have multiple meanings. I am grateful to Tie Jojima for her excellent insights on the translation, which also draws, with modifications, on that of several poems in Blanco, Borja-Villel, and Velásquez, *Lygia Pape: Magnetized Space*, 177. See also "Sete poemas de Lygia Pape," *Jornal do Brasil*, June 20, 1959, 2.

51 The photo-relief-etched blocks are stamped on the verso: "S. Batista Fotogravura."

52 See Ferreira Gullar, "Palavra, humor, invenção," *Jornal do Brasil*, December 10, 1960, 3.

53 José Guilherme Merquior, "A criação do Livro da Criação," *Jornal do Brasil*, December 3, 1960, 3.

54 Critic and poet Roberto Pontual noted at the time that the São Paulo exhibition essentially re-presented the Rio exhibition. Roberto Pontual, "Neoconcretos em São Paulo: não objetos verbais: diversidade de experiências," *Jornal do Brasil*, April 22–23, 1961, 2.

55 See Lygia Pape, "Poemas–Invenção," 6; and Roberto Pontual, "O não-objeto verbal como síntese," *Jornal do Brasil*, December 18, 1960, 4–5.

56 Pape, "Poemas–Invenção," 6.

57 On the differences between Pape's approach to spectatorship and those of other Neo-Concretists, see Alexander Alberro, "'Like the Skin of a Whale': The Pluri-Sensorial Art of Lygia Pape," in *Lygia Pape* (New York: Hauser & Wirth, 2018), 9–24; and Monica Amor, "Black Is White and White Is Black: Lessons on Form and Ways of Seeing in Lygia Pape's Tecelares," in *Lygia Pape*, ed. Francesco Stocchi (London: Koenig Books, 2019), 62–75.

58 Pape, "Poemas–Invenção," 6.

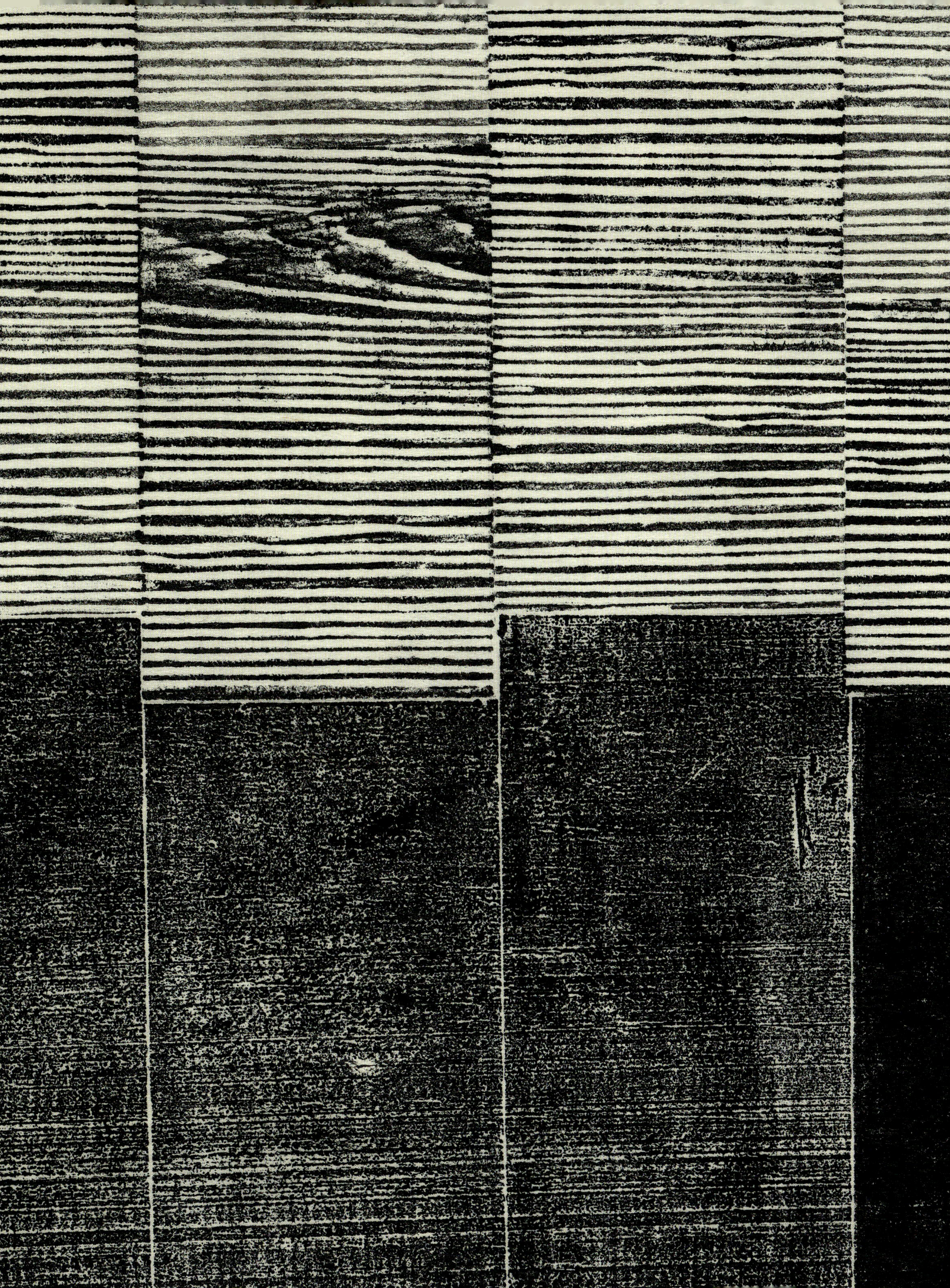

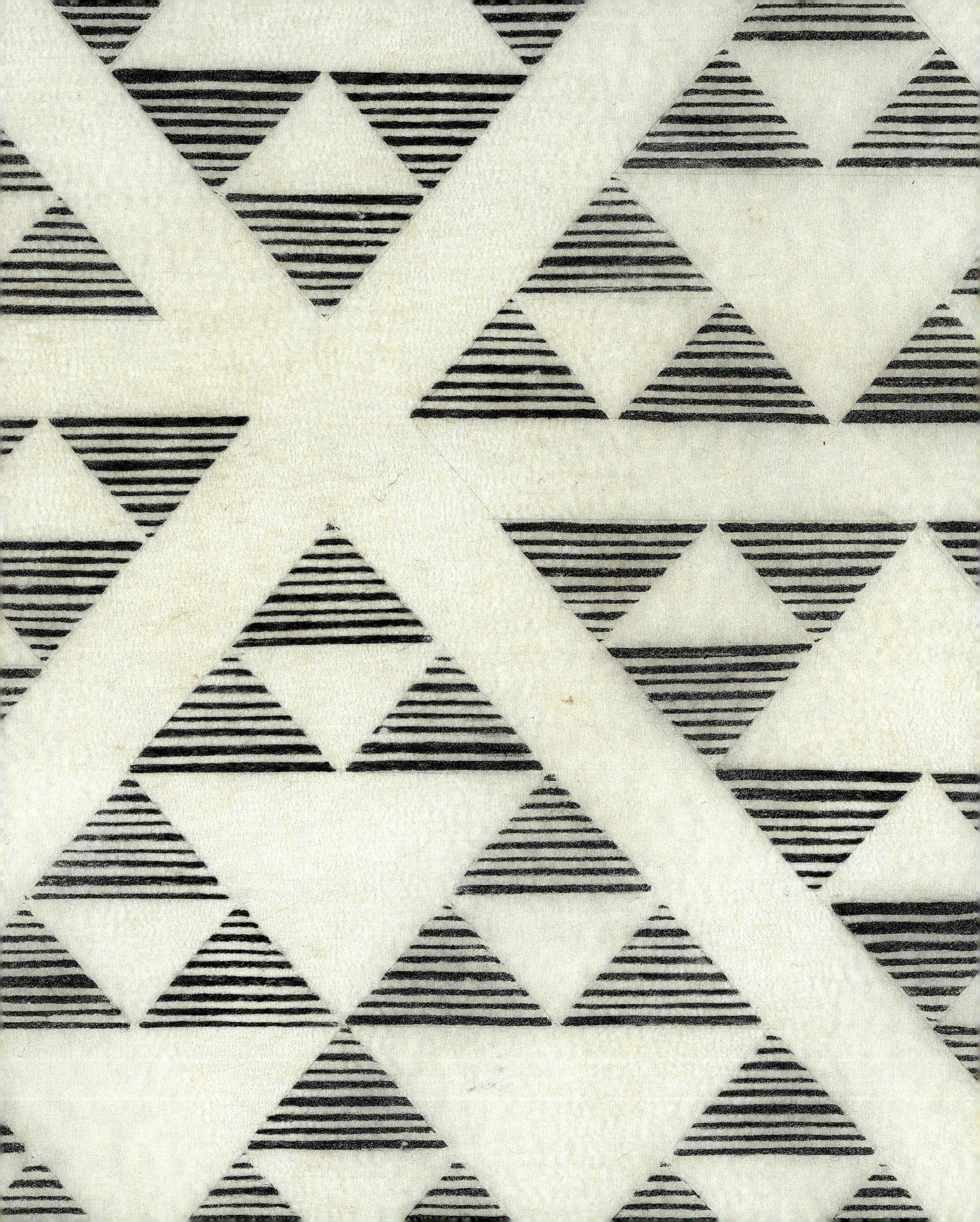

María Cristina Rivera Ramos

CONTROLLED ANARCHY: LYGIA PAPE AND HER MATERIALS

"The problem of chance does not exist in the sort of printmaking I do. All of it is controlled: from the choice of material . . . to the final print."[1] Artist Lygia Pape wrote these words, part of a statement for the *Jornal do Brasil*, in 1959, the year before she effectively stopped making prints. Throughout most of the 1950s, Pape deliberately chose printmaking as the vehicle for her Concrete and early Neo-Concrete explorations. Scholars have argued that her predilection for woodcut reflects her desire to subvert long-established hierarchies in the visual arts, which tend to privilege painting.[2] But Pape also subverted expectations for printmaking: she employed a reproductive technique associated in Latin America with traditional craft and the dissemination of sociopolitical discourse to create largely unique works focused on formal inquiry. Close examination of the *Tecelares* (Weavings) reveals how Pape pursued these aims, not only through her choice of medium but also through her choice of materials.

Even in these earliest years of her artistic production, Pape's aesthetic, formal, material, and technical decisions were revolutionary. Her choices suggest an ethos of experimentation but also a deep awareness and command of the various elements of her craft. The artist tended to select gossamer-thin Japanese papers, which must have been exceedingly challenging to use in combination with the sharp relief of her hardwood and metal matrices. But the translucency of those papers gave her the freedom to, for example, privilege the verso of a print over its recto. Throughout her printed oeuvre, Pape repeated, reworked, and reformatted her compositions to discover new resonances within her groupings of hand-carved, geometric forms. Not content with the sterility of the early Concrete aesthetic, Pape invented her own language of making by incorporating the vocabulary of craft. By investigating Pape's materials and process, we can start to decipher that language and interpret the quiet power of her prints.

PAPER, POROSITY, AND ABSORBANCE

Pape predominantly used Japanese papers as the support for her prints.[3] The material suited her interest in depicting dynamic space through light. In his discussion of her series *Poemas-Luz* (Poems-light), critic Sérgio B. Martins noted that "black and white become materially equated with translucency and opaqueness" in Pape's prints.[4] Japanese paper—which differs from Western papers in fiber selection and preparation, sheet formation, drying, and finish—was essential to achieving this quality. Japanese papers are made from long fibers that are softened and separated rather than cut, resulting in thin sheets with considerable wet strength. They are dried slowly and are not treated with sizing, which leaves them more flexible and very absorbent.[5] All of these factors result in a more open structure comprised of a dimensionally stable

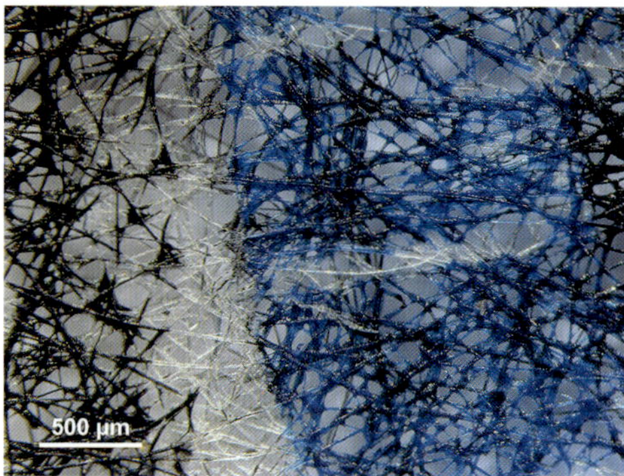

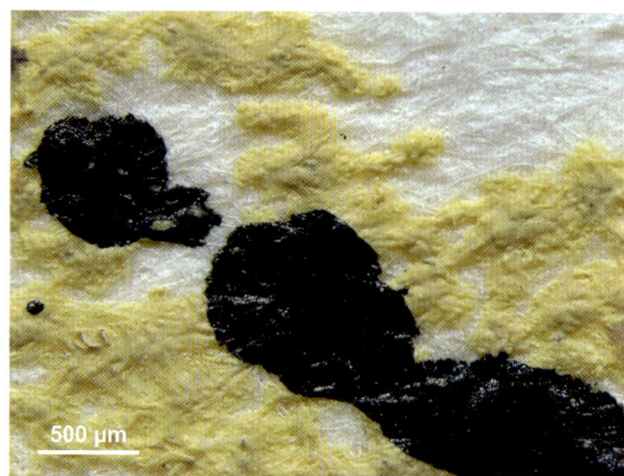

<< FIG. 1 Photomicrograph detail of cat. 16 showing the open fiber network structure characteristic of the tissue-like Japanese kozo paper used by the artist.

< FIG. 2 Photomicrograph detail of Georg Baselitz (German, b. 1938). *Untitled*, 1966. Woodcut on laid paper; image: 27.9 × 27.9 cm (11 × 11 in.); sheet: 40.6 × 33.7 cm (16 × 13 ¼ in.). The Art Institute of Chicago, Margaret Fisher Endowment Fund, 2022.62. The denser microstructure is typical of Western papers and leads the ink to lay on the surface of the paper matrix rather than penetrating it as with the more open-structured Japanese papers Pape used.

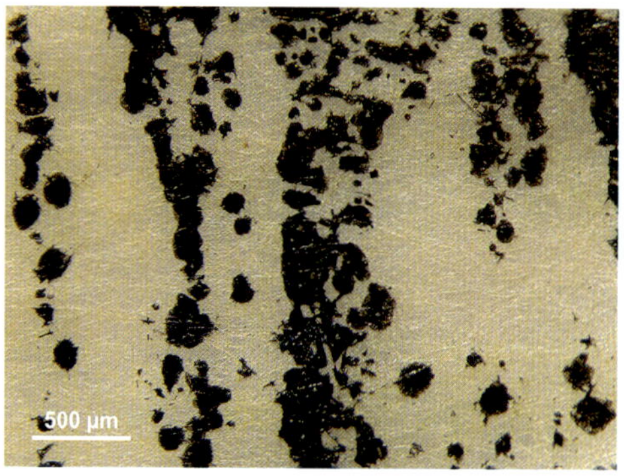

∟ FIG. 3 Photomicrograph detail of cat. 21 revealing the presence of neri in the interstices of the paper's fibrous network. This material prevents the ink from fully penetrating the extremely thin, partially translucent gampi paper.

V FIG. 4 Photomicrograph detail of cat. 19 showing varying degrees of ink seepage into the soft kozo paper. The thinner blue ink penetrates the support and coats its fibers, while the black and lilac inks remain concentrated on the surface.

fibrous network (SEE FIG. 1) completely different from that of both hand- and machine-made Western papers typically used for printmaking (SEE FIG. 2).[6]

These qualities appealed to Pape from the beginning of her graphic output. Two early prints, both from 1953, show how the artist achieved different effects through paper selection as well as ink color and application.
PL. 21 For the first print, Pape selected a gampi sheet (composed of the inner bark of the gampi plant) well suited to diffusing light. During sheet manufacture, gampi fibers are traditionally coated in neri, a viscous agent that fills the interstices of the paper and allows ink to glide over the paper's surface and deposit in an even layer (SEE FIG. 3). Pape devised an image that incorporates an array of wood grains and treatments, knowing that the paper's smooth surface would capture fine details. The paper also enabled her to print these elements not only in pure black but also in the lighter tones she achieved by experimenting with different methods of applying ink to her matrices.[7] For
PL. 19 the second print, the artist used a more absorbent kozo (mulberry) sheet. This paper provided Pape with another opportunity to play with the boldness and subtlety of her inks, which varied this time as a function of absorbency. A detail image (FIG. 4) shows the different degrees to which three of the four inks used in the print absorbed into the sheet. The thinner blue ink coated the paper fibers and seeped further into the support. The black and lilac inks, on the other hand, appear more thickly applied and as a result remain concentrated on the surface of the sheet. By leveraging the material qualities of this specific paper and her different inks, Pape imparted dimensionality to the diaphanous sheet, creating the illusion of depth and multiple spatial planes, despite the paper's millimetric thickness and flat surface.

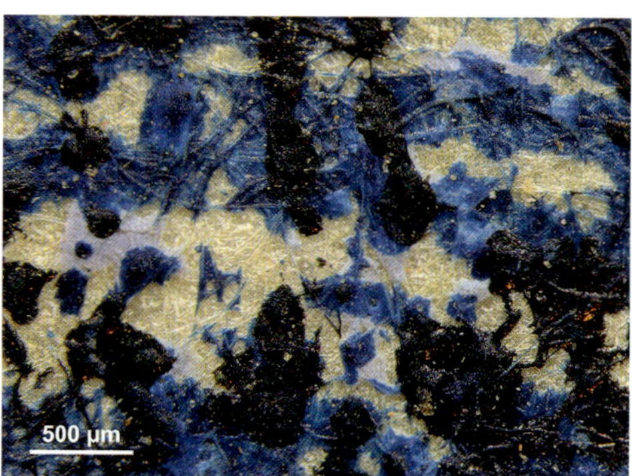

Pape family lore holds that a friend of the artist's father provided the Japanese papers she used for her woodcuts.[8] But other artists living in Brazil at the time, such as Mira Schendel, also used Japanese papers, suggesting that the material might have been readily available.[9] Pape did employ a particularly wide variety of Japanese papers in her graphic oeuvre. Close examination of more than forty of the artist's works spanning her printmaking period (1952–60) shows that her supports ranged from strong, matte, and soft kozo papers to very thin, uniform, and transparent gampi sheets.

The latter are easily recognizable because of their silky luster, characteristic rattle, and vulnerability to creasing.[10] She also used extremely thin, tissue-like kozo sheets, where the open structure of the fiber matrix is clearly visible under magnification.

VERSO AS FINAL IMAGE

In the course of examining the interaction between ink and paper in the works included in the exhibition, it became clear that Pape occasionally selected a print's verso as the final image. She nevertheless consistently signed her woodcuts on the recto—that is, the side on which the ink was printed. The only exceptions in this group were those works that she intended to wrap around boards as a method of compositional framing and display. However,
PL. 17 in a print from 1953, the artist's signature and the year appear below the image on what conventionally would have been the verso of the print. In looking for additional examples of this radical choice in Pape's early practice, I discovered that the print accompanying the poem "*em avêsso / aço*"
PL. 97 (in reverse / steel) in her 1960 poem book, *Poemas-Xilogravuras* (Poems-woodcuts), had been adhered to its secondary support face down, conclusive evidence that the artist preferred the verso image. Pape's treatment of these two prints demonstrates not only her innovative approach but also her sensitivity to the nuances she could achieve by exploiting the properties of her materials.

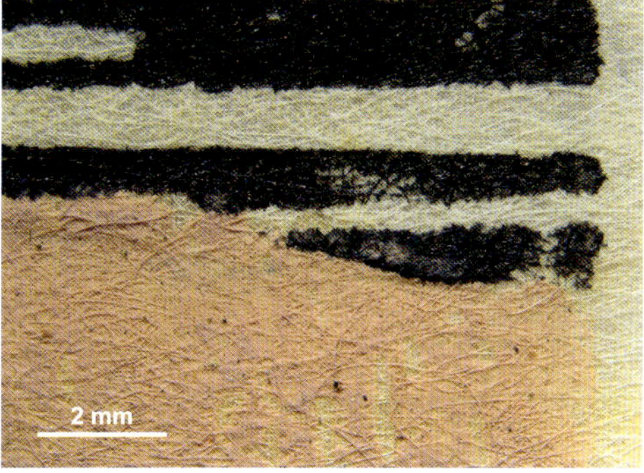

A B

V FIG. 5A–B Photomicrograph details of cat. 17. Pape used the verso of this print as the final work. The Japanese paper she selected has a porous, open structure when compared to Western papers used for printmaking. As a result, the printing ink is subtly visible on the verso of the sheet (A). The side of the sheet that was in direct contact with the matrix exhibits a more saturated appearance (B), as these fibers are more fully coated and developed areas of ink buildup.

Prints on thin Japanese papers are typically legible from both the recto and verso, with the latter showing the ink that has seeped through the paper during printing. The reverse image is typically hazier becauase of the partial saturation and interference of bare fibers, and the inverted order of the ink layers causes the inks that were printed first to feature more prominently (SEE FIG. 5A–B). Pape's artistic philosophy prompted her to experiment with the verso. She was interested, in her own words, in "the principle of ambiguity, no privilege[d] position for a base or bottom (a work could be inverted without being stripped of all its characteristics)."[11] Perhaps it seemed obvious to her that the recto should be whichever side of the print best captured the play between plane and space, regardless of whether it had been in contact with the matrix (the surface holding the image). Such radical decisions may have come naturally to an artist who referred to herself as "intrinsically an anarchist" with a "terrible inclination to not respect rigid structures."[12]

But Pape's choice also aligns with a long tradition among connoisseurs of Japanese woodblock prints, who glean insights about a work's history from studying the verso (SEE FIG. 6A–B). Scholars and collectors rely on ink saturation and the subtle topography on the back of a print to assess its quality and relative age (earlier or later printing).[13] Pape may have been aware of

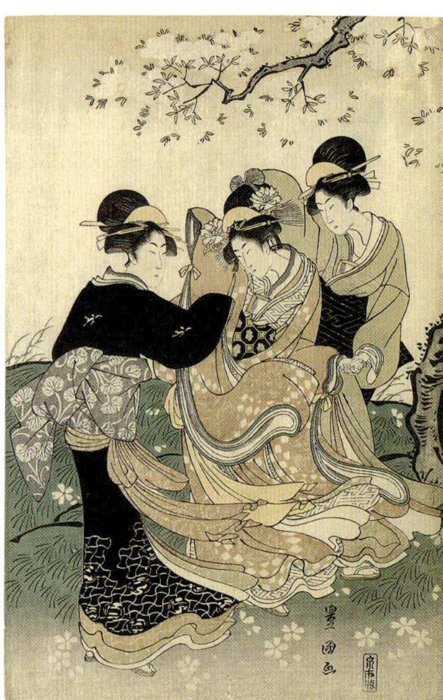

A

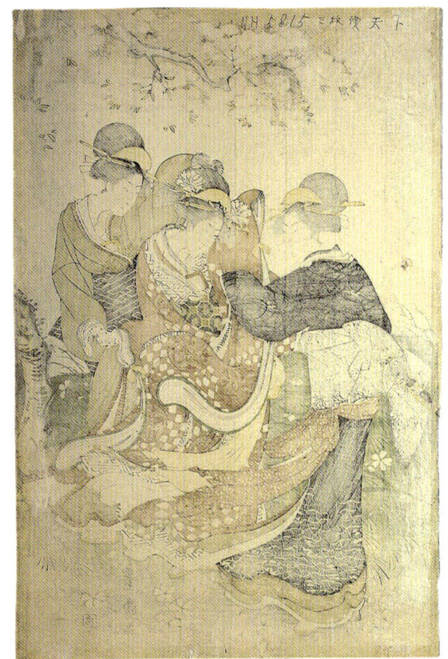

B

< FIG. 6A–B Recto and verso of left print from Utagawa Toyokuni I (Japanese, 1769–1825). *A Windy Day under the Cherry Trees*, c. 1797. Triptych of color woodblock prints on paper; 37.9 × 25.5 cm (14 15/16 × 10 1/16 in.). The Art Institute of Chicago, Clarence Buckingham Collection, 1925.2313. The verso (B) shows a more subtle image than the recto (A). Scholars and collectors of traditional Japanese prints often examine the verso to glean information about the work.

∨ FIG. 7A–B Photomicrographic details of cats. 44 (A) and 25 (B) with graphite ruling lines and marks Pape made in the process of creating her precise, mirrored compositions. Pape most likely used such markings as guides for stamping multiple smaller blocks (as opposed to one block containing the entire image).

this practice, since she was interested not only in Japanese paper but also in Japanese art more broadly. She alluded to the influence of traditional Japanese aesthetics on her own work, specifically her poster for director Nelson Pereira dos Santos's 1961 film, *Mandacaru vermelho* (Red mandacaru).[14] And she described herself as "fascinated" by Japanese haiku, noting that it appealed to the Concrete poets as well. She admired haiku's precision and "economy," descriptors that certainly apply to her own poetry.[15] Perhaps Pape found this same "poetic" quality in the versos of those two prints—a subtlety and simplicity revealed only from the back.

REPETITION

Around 1955 Pape transitioned from loose, playful explorations of shape and wood grain to careful constructions of mirrored images, which she created by repeating smaller units or groups of shapes. In an attempt to understand if she made these prints using a single matrix or by reprinting smaller blocks in a precise formation, the works were examined under magnification and manipulated in Photoshop to allow for accurate transpositions.[16] Two prints from this group, one from 1955 and one from 1957, reveal that Pape used graphite lines and registration marks (SEE FIG. 7A–B) to help her organize her small blocks into larger, almost seamless patterns. It is notable that she made these marks on the recto of the sheet, which is consistent with printing multiple smaller blocks. The typical process for printing a single block requires making such marks on the verso of the sheet. When printing with one block, the artist lays the paper over the block and uses an implement to apply pressure; in such cases, the verso is visible when printing, as the recto is facedown on the matrix. Smaller blocks are printed more like stamps, with the recto of the sheet facing the artist, meaning that registration marks can be made on that side. The technique necessitates a higher degree of precision, but it enables greater compositional flexibility.[17]

PLS. 25, 44

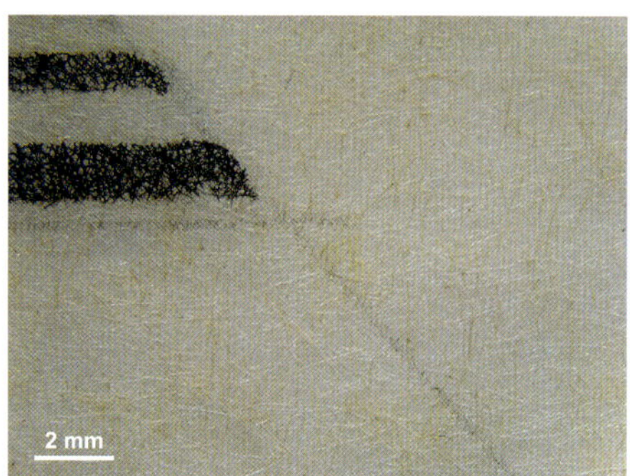

A

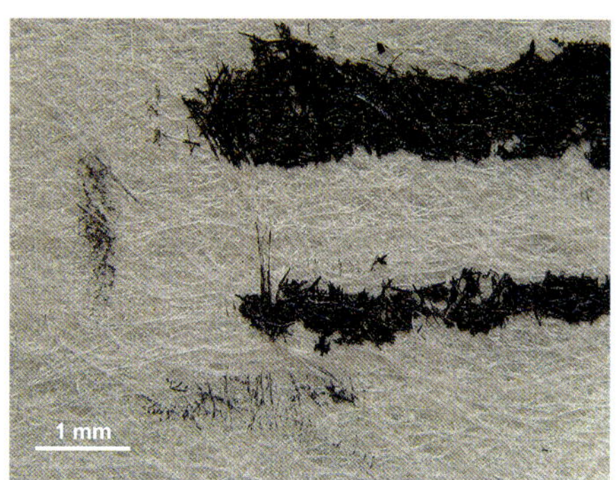

B

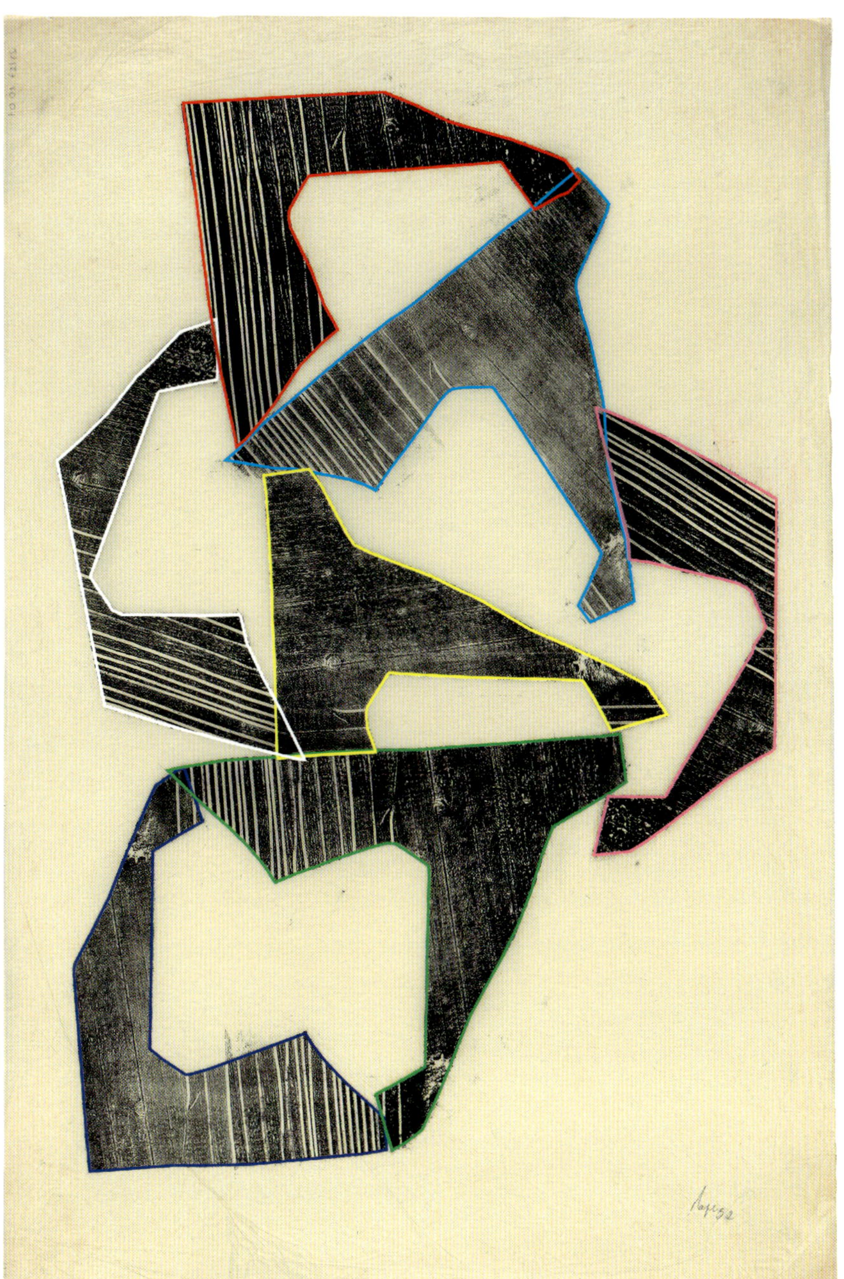

< FIG. 8 Annotated image of cat. 10 showing the eight impressions of the same block that make up this composition. Pape used masking to alter the shape as she printed it.

PL. 10 One of Pape's earliest prints, made in 1952, clearly informed later Tecelares printed from smaller blocks in multiple orientations. It lacks the rigorous balance and symmetry of that body of work—she arranged the components more chaotically and printed them less uniformly—and the shapes of individual elements vary. Close examination, however, shows that this work was in fact an early exploration of the idea of printing a single, smaller unit multiple times to form a composition (SEE FIG. 8). A distinctive knot in the grain of one of the individual elements (SEE FIG. 9A) can be found in all of the other shapes. Where the knot was not clearly reproduced, other prominent features of the grain align perfectly from shape to shape. That these identical grain structures reappear in compositional elements of varied shapes and sizes means that Pape must have employed masking to delineate different printable areas on a single block. Offset media in areas around some of the shapes (SEE FIG. 9B) likely result from ink oozing out from behind the material

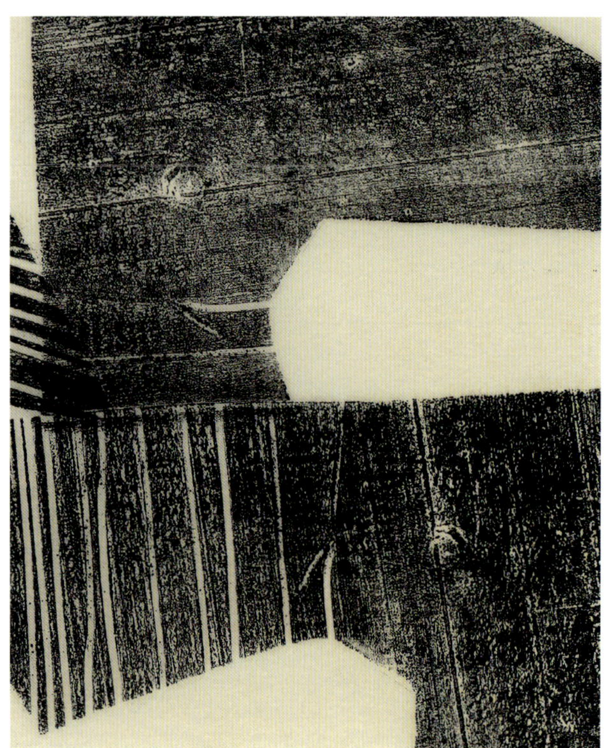

A

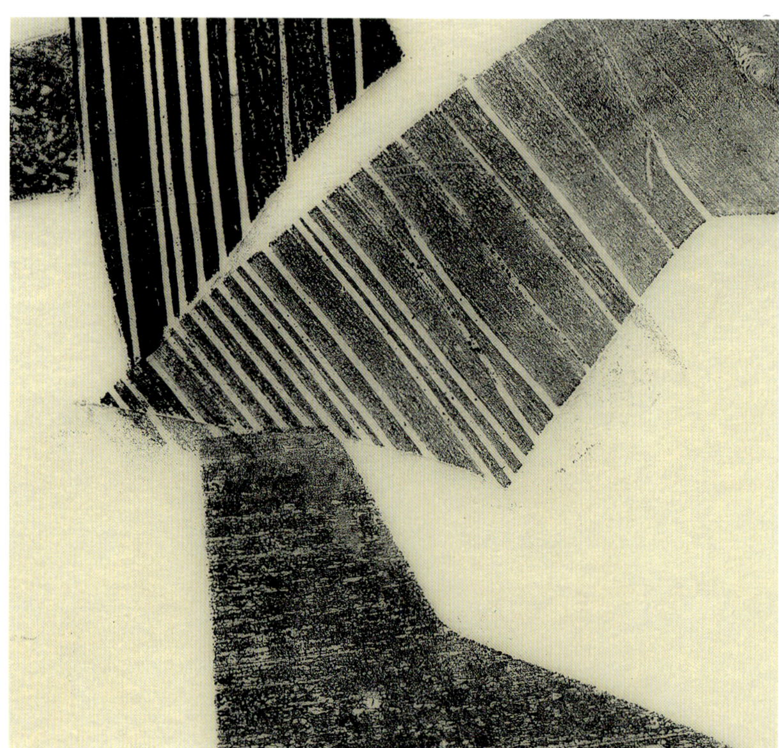

B

used to create the mask. These unplanned marks were part of the process of developing a composition, Pape explained: "A less-than-clean white that leaves the remains of black on the [printed] surface, lending a certain character to the white part, often gives it an unexpected air and is a sketch of the idea to be materialized, for me." She claimed, however, not to accept such chance occurences in the fully realized print, for which only the "utmost possible rigor" would suffice.[18] That she signed this particular work in spite of its offset media may indicate that her approach was less strict than she stated, at least at this early moment in her career.

REFORMATTING

Pape regularly modified her works after printing, sometimes revisiting them years later to change the orientation of the image or the size of the support.
PL. 51 One example of this reformatting, a Tecelar from 1957, retains markings the artist made to delineate the new boundaries of the image area. She achieved
PL. 33 this same effect in another print, also from 1957, by simply folding the sheet for display, reducing the negative space to the left of the printed shape and dramatically altering the aspect ratio of the composition. Both the marked vertical fold and the offset of the image on the left side of the sheet attest to the modification. Degradation products from the oils in the printing ink, which yellow as they age, migrated to the blank portion of the sheet and produced a kind of ghost image. Notably, Pape did not alter these works permanently—for instance, by cutting away excess paper. Rather, she kept the door open for future reformatting, including a return to displaying the whole sheet.

In one of her most idiosyncratic presentations, Pape wrapped one PL. 25 of her aforementioned mirrored prints around a cardboard sheet, folding the paper at the very edge of the composition and forgoing elements of traditional presentation like matting and framing. A conservation photograph of the object (P. 20, FIG. 6B) shows the excess material Pape tucked away on the back of the board. Due to the extreme fragility of the paper where the work was folded, it had to be unwrapped from the board to be stabilized (SEE P. 20, FIG. 6C). This provided an opportunity to view the entirety of the sheet and the work's original proportions, demonstrating the difference in perception PL. 63 Pape achieved through this reformatting. Another print, from 1959, shows signs of having once been similarly displayed. Although it has since been flattened and presented matted and framed, the sheet retains creases indicating that it too was once wrapped around a board. It is not clear if Pape herself unwrapped and flattened the print, but to do so would have been consistent with her continual reassessment of past works.

Perhaps no work better epitomizes this practice of reformatting than PL. 24 a Tecelar from 1954 that includes the artist's signature in multiple orientations. First deeming the print an artist's proof or some other early step in her process, Pape annotated it as such in what she then considered the lower right corner of the sheet. Later, having apparently rethought its orientation, she signed it again in the opposite corner and dated it 1954. These signatures and flattened folds speak not only to histories of display but also to the artist's enduring relationship with these early works.

< FIG. 9A–B Details of cat. 10. One (A) shows a repeat of the same knot and checkmark shape formed by a carved line meeting a diagonal scratch in the surface of the matrix. These unique markings are present in each shape printed on the sheet, confirming that the same matrix was used to print all of the units in the work. The other detail (B) shows offset media at the edge of one of the impressions, which likely occurred where Pape used masking to alter the shape of the matrix.

REUSING AND REWORKING

Scholar John Rajchman has argued that much of Pape's oeuvre wrestles with ideas stemming from her early print production, noting that she was "ever revising, recasting, revitalizing what had come before."[19] Even during the decade or so that she made woodcuts, Pape rigorously investigated concepts by constantly reworking and refining compositions, carving multiple blocks dedicated to similar explorations, and reusing or revisiting imagery. Three prints spanning this period exhibit media additions, physical signs of Pape's revising hand enhancing or extending existing lines, adding new marks or color, and PL. 54 sometimes obscuring printed lines (SEE FIG. 10A–C). On a Tecelar from 1957, she

V FIG. 10A–C Photomicrograph details of cats. 54 (A), 78 (B), and 5 (C) showing media the artist applied to rework the images. Pape used the graphite marks seen in (A) to emphasize existing printed lines and make new ones. (B) also shows graphite lines modifying the image as well as white dry media applied to obscure ink lines that extend beyond the new boundary suggested by the additions. (C) shows the pastel Pape used to add color.

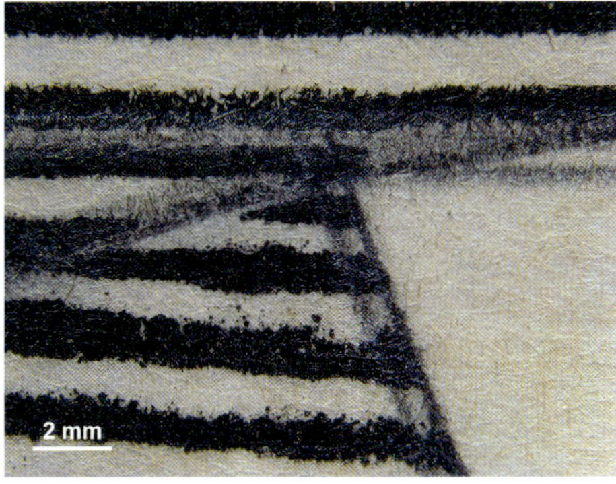

A

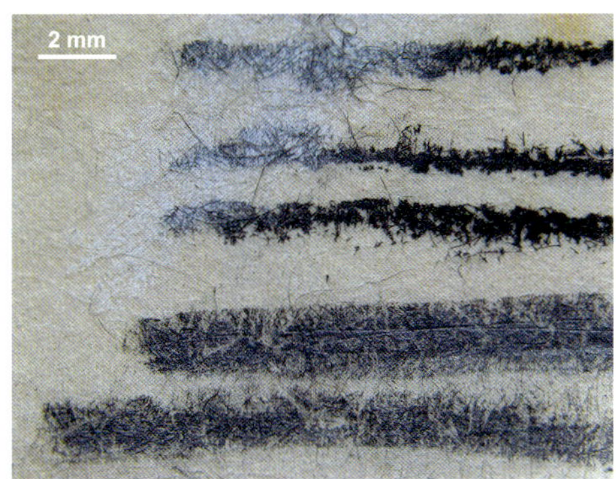

B

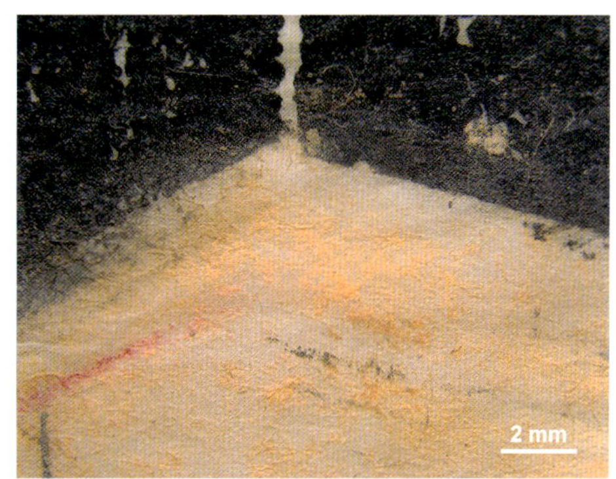

C

used a pencil to draw new lines and emphasize existing ones by increasing
PL. 78 their thickness. In another reworked print from 1958, Pape extended some
of the printed lines with graphite and applied white pastel over others as a
PL. 5 means of erasure. And in one of her earliest prints, the artist added areas of
light orange in pastel to complete the composition rather than printing an
PLS. 52–53 orange shape. Two other Tecelares from 1957 illustrate a thematic progression,
in which Pape rotated the composition ninety degrees. Notably, the difference in size of the printed images confirms that Pape revisited the design by carving a completely new block in the new configuration, as opposed to simply changing the orientation of the original matrix. These changes elucidate the artist's thought process as she worked to reestablish the boundaries between image and negative space.[20]

Poemas-Xilogravuras reuses imagery from earlier years of Pape's
graphic production to accompany the written word.[21] The print accompanying
PL. 31 the poem "*cheio / vagar*" (full / empty) derives from a work the artist made
in 1957. This time Pape did not carve a new block, choosing instead to use another impression pulled from the original matrix. As such, both prints exhibit the same holiday—an area where ink did not transfer adequately from the matrix to the support—corresponding to a chip in the upper right of the block. Another work from the poem book—the only color print in this iteration of the series—appears to be the result of much refashioning and experimentation. We are fortunate to have access to the original wood blocks, close examination of which can supplement interpretation of the prints and shed new light on Pape's process. She carved numerous blocks around variations of the composition that ultimately accompanied the poem "*aço / gorja / azul*" (steel / keel / blue). All of the blocks depict three squares vertically aligned along the center, with thin lines radiating from the corners. The lines give the impression that the shapes are suspended in place by threads. The poem book itself changed and evolved over time: not only did

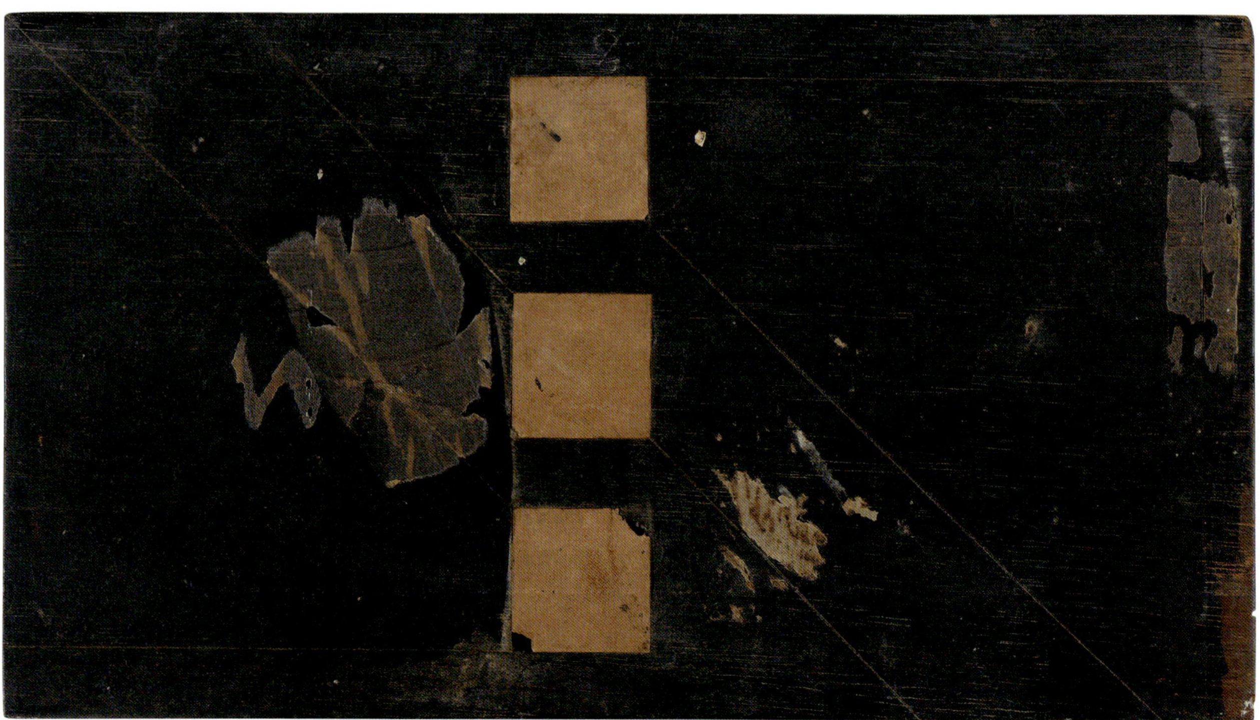

∨ FIG. 11 Verso of cat. 86, with a partially carved rendition of one of Pape's most popular compositions, versions of which appear in cats. 87–88 and 97 (accompanying the poem "aço / gorja / azul"). Pieces of paper mark the positions of the central squares; traces of another translucent paper adhered to the block are likely remnants of a wrapping that once covered it.

the order and number of pages vary, but the work sometimes included color. PL. 95 The matrix for the "aço / gorja / azul" print retains remnants of the blue ink chosen by the artist for the later impression seen in this catalogue; earlier versions were black.[22]

PL. 86 A second block in the exhibition is carved on one side with a mirror image of the composition described above, with the lines extending farther horizontally, resulting in a wider composition. The other side of this block (FIG. 11) is a partially carved, preliminary stage for an elongated rendition of the print next to "aço / gorja / azul"; the thin, shallow cuts for the radiating lines are visible, while the positions of the squares are demarcated with pieces of paper adhered to the matrix. (There are other pieces of translucent paper stuck to the block, but these appear to be remnants of a wrapping used to protect it.) It makes sense that multiple blocks exploring similar ideas survive; as the artist explained, "I always do a drawing before cutting, and make several studies for the same idea."[23] The partially realized side provides further insight into the artist's process. Both sides of the block are covered in a layer of black stain or ink. On the side Pape abandoned mid-carving, the black media extends below the pieces of paper that mark the placement of the squares in the composition, as can be seen in the spaces exposed by the two missing corners in the topmost paper square. This could suggest that Pape stained or painted the wood prior to carving it, perhaps to better envision the final work and how various approaches to the process might alter the finished product. This thoughtful experimentation shows the degree to which the artist was attuned to her materials as well as the control she exercised over her process. Her continual reuse and reworking, she explained, was not about achieving "an infinite range of variations within the same work"; instead, she sought "restrained solutions that are rigorous in their simplicity, and a formal technical synthesis. Sound technical knowledge facilitates the identification and selection of the best medium to use for a given problem. Creativity plus technique make for a print. Technique for its own sake adds nothing. It would be just artificial virtuosity."[24]

Pape maintained throughout her life that she had "no interest in creating a piece that 'works' and ten more like it to supply the market and make lots of money." As she went on to explain, "It's not that I consider the attitude unethical, but it does bore me somewhat. Sometimes I prefer to just sit and think and meditate, grievously suffering to produce a new invention, something that will really satisfy me."[25] This is one reason why, in spite of devoting so much energy to single compositional explorations (including carving multiple blocks), she rarely pulled more than a few impressions from any given matrix. Rather than creating many prints of the same image, she seems to have been satisfied with the few works she generated during her exploration of a particular concept. Pape developed her pared-down visual vocabulary through careful paper selection, knowledge of the natural imagery and patterns introduced by different wood grains, and precise geometry. She refined this vocabulary through a cadence of repetition, reformatting, reuse, and reworking, and shrewd material selection allowed her to efficiently achieve her artistic vision. These methods imbue her oeuvre with a formal strength that informed her work in other media and continues to fascinate viewers decades later.

1 Lygia Pape, “Gravura: Depoimento de Lygia Pape,” *Jornal do Brasil*, March 22, 1959, 8, translated in *Lygia Pape: Magnetized Space*, ed. María Luisa Blanco, Manuel Borja-Villel, and Teresa Velásquez, exh. cat. (Madrid: Museo Nacional Centro de Arte Reina Sofía, 2011), 86.

2 Paulo Herkenhoff, for example, argues that Pape’s woodcuts “constitute a triple detour from the art canons of Brazil.... This was Pape’s first transgression: producing geometric-abstract images through the medium—woodcut engraving—previously reserved for Expressionist art in the modernist production of Oswaldo Goeldi and Lasar Segall; for Stalinist Social Realism; and for the illustration of Brazilian *cordel* (string) literature—folk novels, poems, and songs displayed on strings by street vendors”; Paulo Herkenhoff, “Lygia Pape: The Art of Passage,” in *Lygia Pape: Magnetized Space*, 25. Similar claims can be found in Sérgio B. Martins, “An Anticlass in Avant-Gardism,” and John Rajchman, “Lygia Pape’s Vital Ideas,” both in *Lygia Pape: A Multitude of Forms*, ed. Iria Candela, exh. cat. (New York: Metropolitan Museum of Art, 2017), 27, 35. Adele Nelson has shown that Pape’s approach to printmaking was equally radical: “The artist sidelined the medium’s traditional reproductive and technical capacities and foregrounded its elemental, material components in order to create new types of conceptual space and to posit a phenomenological conception of knowledge”; Adele Nelson, “Sensitive and Nondiscursive Things: Lygia Pape and the Reconception of Printmaking,” *Art Journal* 71, no. 3 (Fall 2012): 27.

3 Typically, Japanese paper is handmade and composed of the inner bark of gampi, mitsumata, or mulberry plants. Although these papers are not watermarked, they often retain faint mould impressions from the bamboo screens on which they were made.

4 Martins, “An Anticlass in Avant-Gardism,” 28–29.

5 Paper sizing is a material additive—most commonly gelatin or glue—incorporated internally in the pulp stage or applied to the surface of the formed paper during its manufacture to increase its resistance to water penetration (from ink or watercolor). The process of applying the size layer is called sizing.

6 Western handmade and European machine-made papers are composed of shorter fibers prepared through mechanical or chemical processes, formed into sheets using a mould or machinery, dried under tension, sized, and finished.

7 “From wood of the same quality, I can get an endless range of blacks simply by controlling the use of sandpaper. Before final printing, I make many proofs from the engraved block until I get the tone I am looking for. I have always worked with the grain of the wood, and I try to let the material, independent, expressive, speak for itself.” Pape, “Gravura,” 86.

8 Paula Pape shared this background on Pape’s papers with Mark Pascale, who relayed it to me.

9 Mira Schendel’s graphic oeuvre includes a series of two thousand monotypes on Japanese paper. In her *Droguinhas* (Little Nothings), Schendel twisted, braided, and knotted Japanese paper to create tangled webs of rope-like material.

10 No fiber analysis was conducted for the works examined; papers were identified based on their physical characteristics alone.

11 Lygia Pape, “Depoimento,” 91.

12 Lygia Pape, “Birds of Marvelous Colors,” interview by Lúcia Carneiro and Ileana Pradilla, 1998, excerpt translated in *Lygia Pape: A Multitude of Forms*, 23.

13 By examining the back of Japanese prints, it is possible to tell how much the blocks (both keyblock and color blocks) have abraded. Lines or color coming through sharply and neatly on the back are associated with early editions. This is often particularly evident in the cartouche lines and color, especially with a red ink often used for cartouches. The long tradition of scholars and connoisseurs needing access to the back of prints to determine quality prompted a conservation rule of thumb to avoid lining or permanently mounting such works to secondary supports as much as possible. Janice Katz, Roger L. Weston Associate Curator of Japanese Art at the Art Institute of Chicago, generously shared her insights on this topic.

14 “Soon I began designing the titles and posters for all the Cinema Novo films. The first one I worked on was Nelson’s *Mandacaru vermelho*. It had a texture and a red ball that resembled the sun. That poster was sort of Japanese even though the setting of the film was the Northeast of Brazil. The black lettering had subtle textures, and they were printed on almost transparent paper. Nowadays I keep thinking how I wasted that wonderful paper to make film titles!” Lygia Pape, “Outside the Frame of the Screen,” interview by Angélica de Moraes, March 1998, excerpt translated in *Lygia Pape: A Multitude of Forms*, 42.

15 “Haiku is economy itself. In precisely three lines—of five, seven, and five syllables, respectively—you have to say something about the real world. It’s like imagist poetry.” Pape, “Birds of Marvelous Colors,” 21.

16 Overlays were created for five of the mirrored Tecelares (cats. 25, 42, 44, and 46–47) in an attempt to digitally assess the smallest printing units the artist used. These efforts to establish Pape’s methods did not yield conclusive results; further work is needed regarding this group of prints.

17 The rigor of printing with smaller blocks appealed to Pape: “I use separate blocks (if using blocks) because, given what I propose doing, a large plate does not offer the same possibility of achieving precision, which is a very important part of my work.” Cited in English translation in Herkenhoff, “Lygia Pape: The Art of Passage,” 31.

18 Pape, “Gravura,” 86.

19 Rajchman, “Lygia Pape’s Vital Ideas,” 34.

20 In a related print from the time (cat. 79), Pape incorporated the changes in dry media made to cat. 78, carving the lines added in graphite and shortening the lines partially blocked out with white chalk. Two other works from 1958 included in this exhibition (cats. 76–77) provide further insight into the progression of this formal inquiry.

21 The artist was adamant that the images included in the book do not function as illustrations of the poems: “The verbal aspect is installed in the printmaking with a new expressivity. The engraving is no longer an illustration of the poem, as in the old tradition. Here it is the poem or verbal aspect that will nourish the engravings, and at this point it is enriched by a new semantic charge.” Lygia Pape, “Quarenta gravuras neoconcretas,” *Jornal do Brasil*, July 17, 1975, translated in *Lygia Pape: Magnetized Space*, 90.

22 In the version of the poem book illustrated in the Reina Sofía’s catalogue, this print is black. Blanco, Borja-Villel, and Velásquez, *Lygia Pape: Magnetized Space*, 204.

23 Pape, “Gravura,” 85. There are also multiple matrices related to the print accompanying the poem “*cal / moi*” (lime / grind); the image was originally carved in wood and later etched on metal for the production of the book.

24 Ibid.

25 Pape, “Birds of Marvelous Colors,” 19.

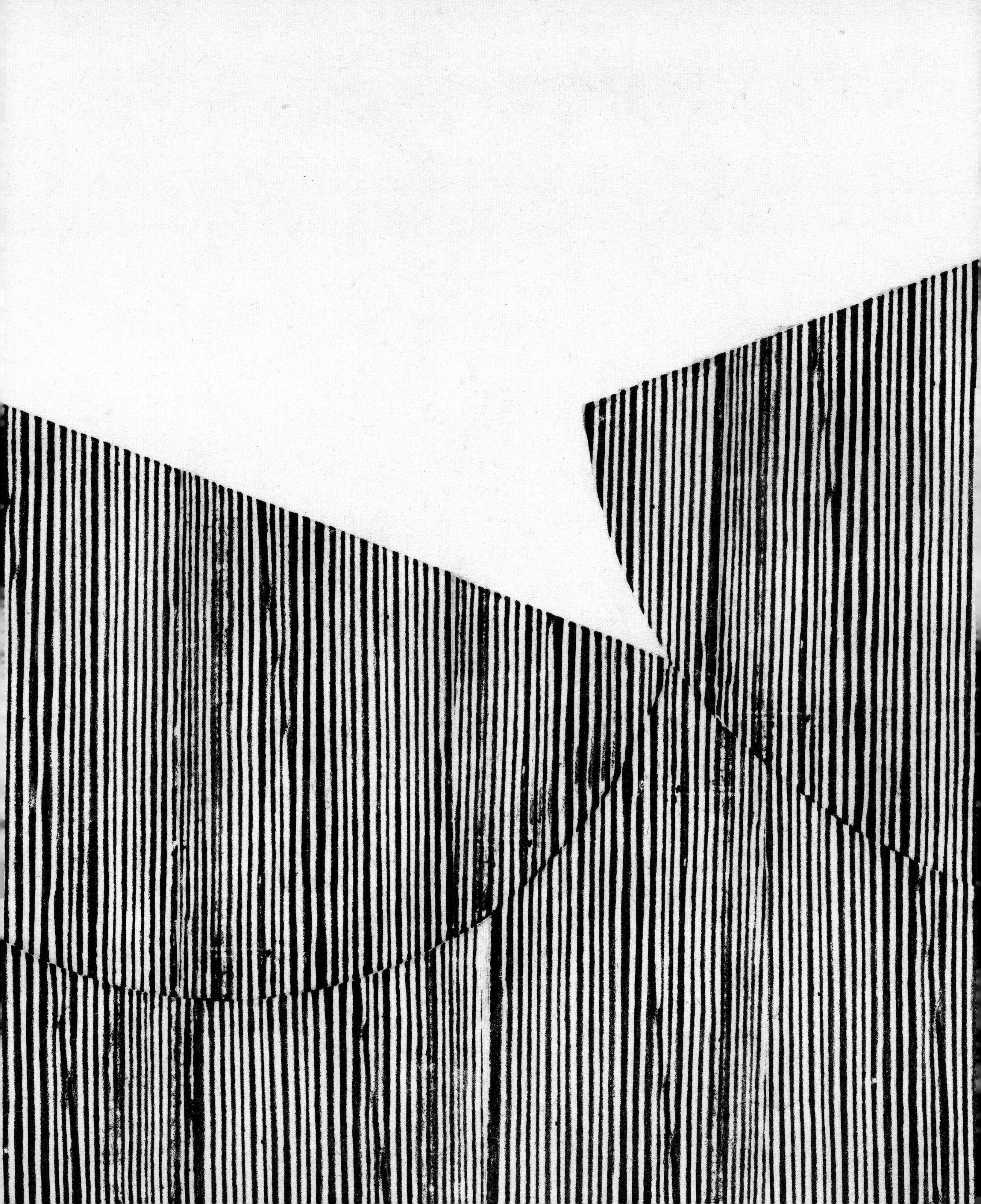

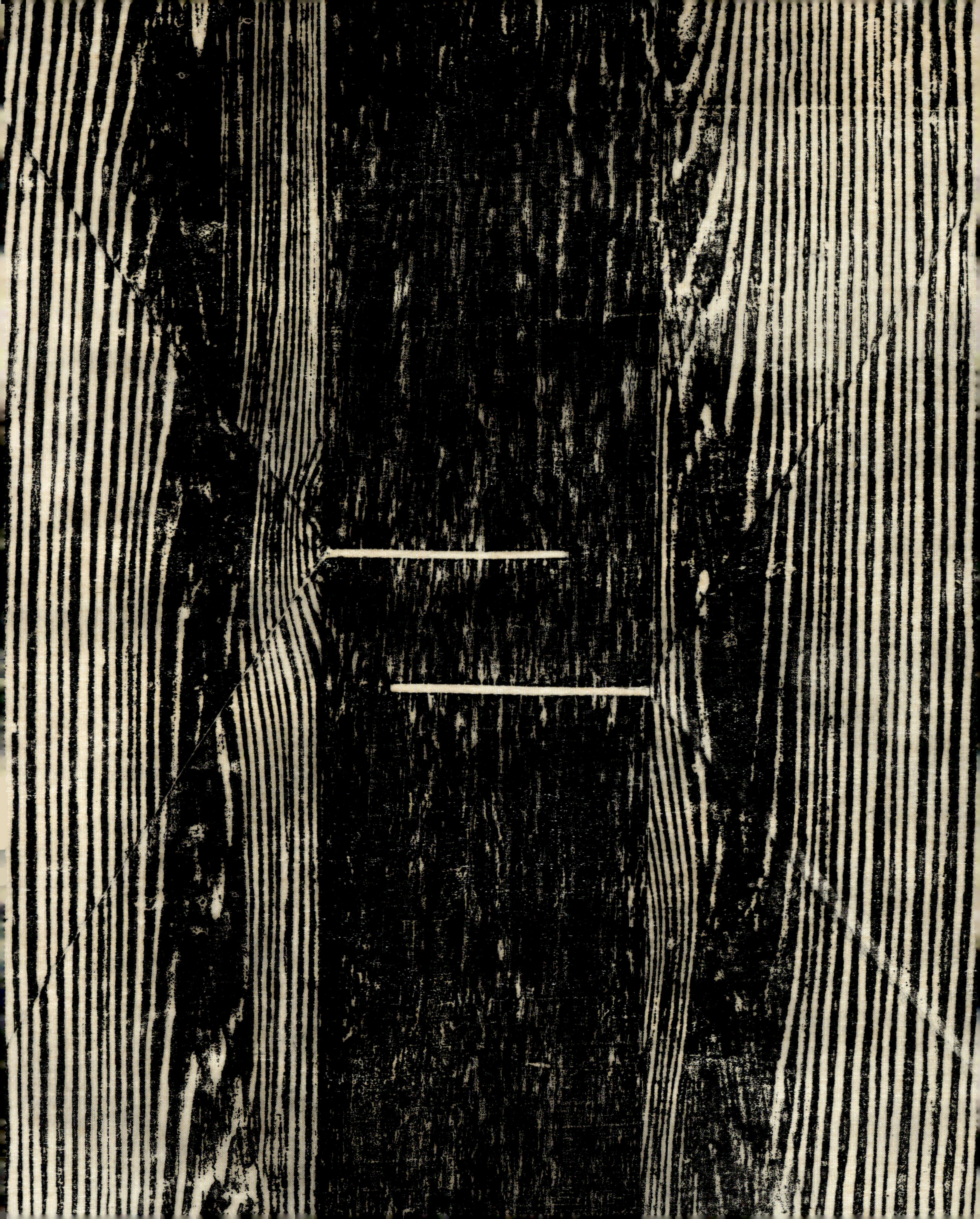

PLATES

All works by Lygia Pape
(Brazilian, 1927–2004)

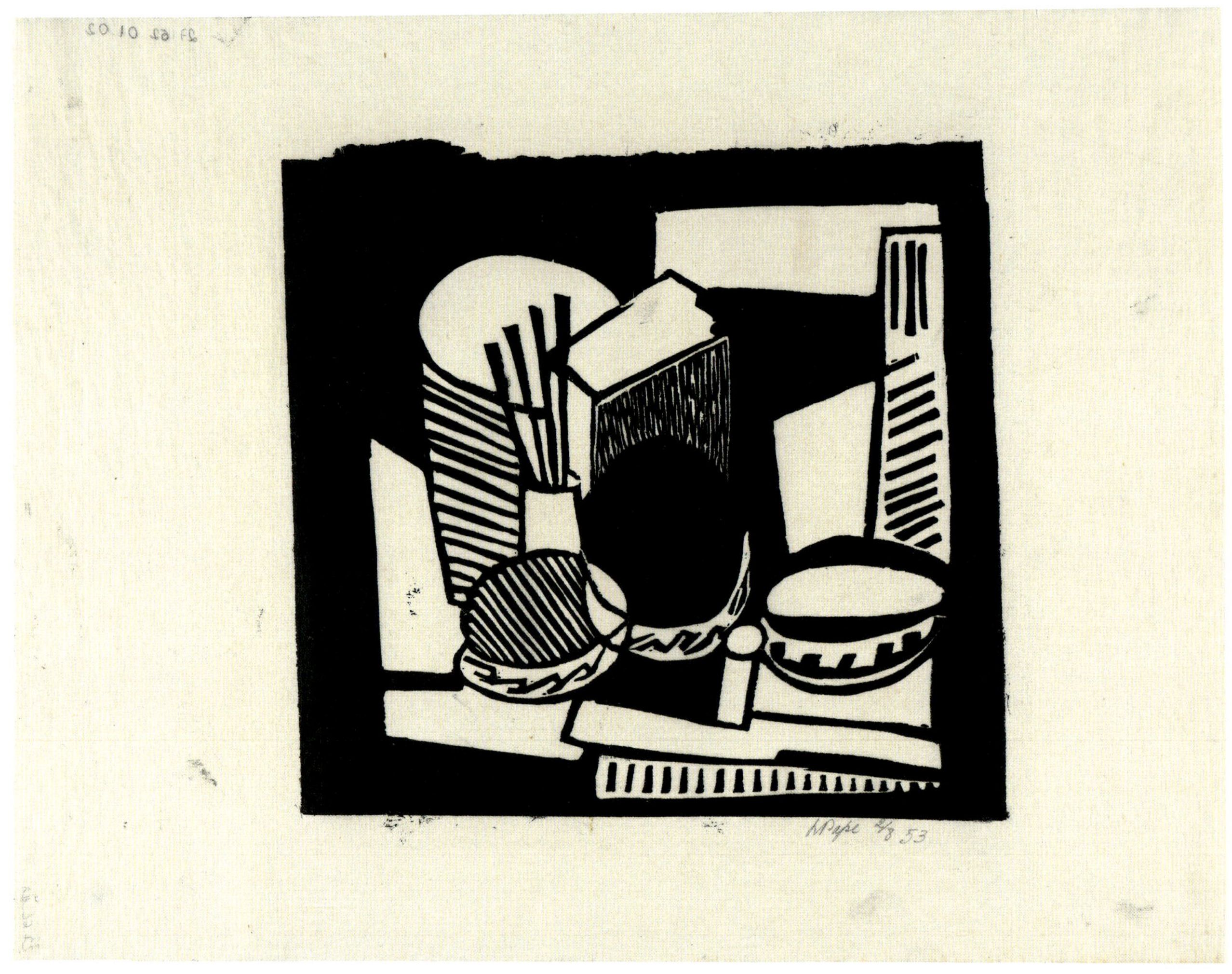

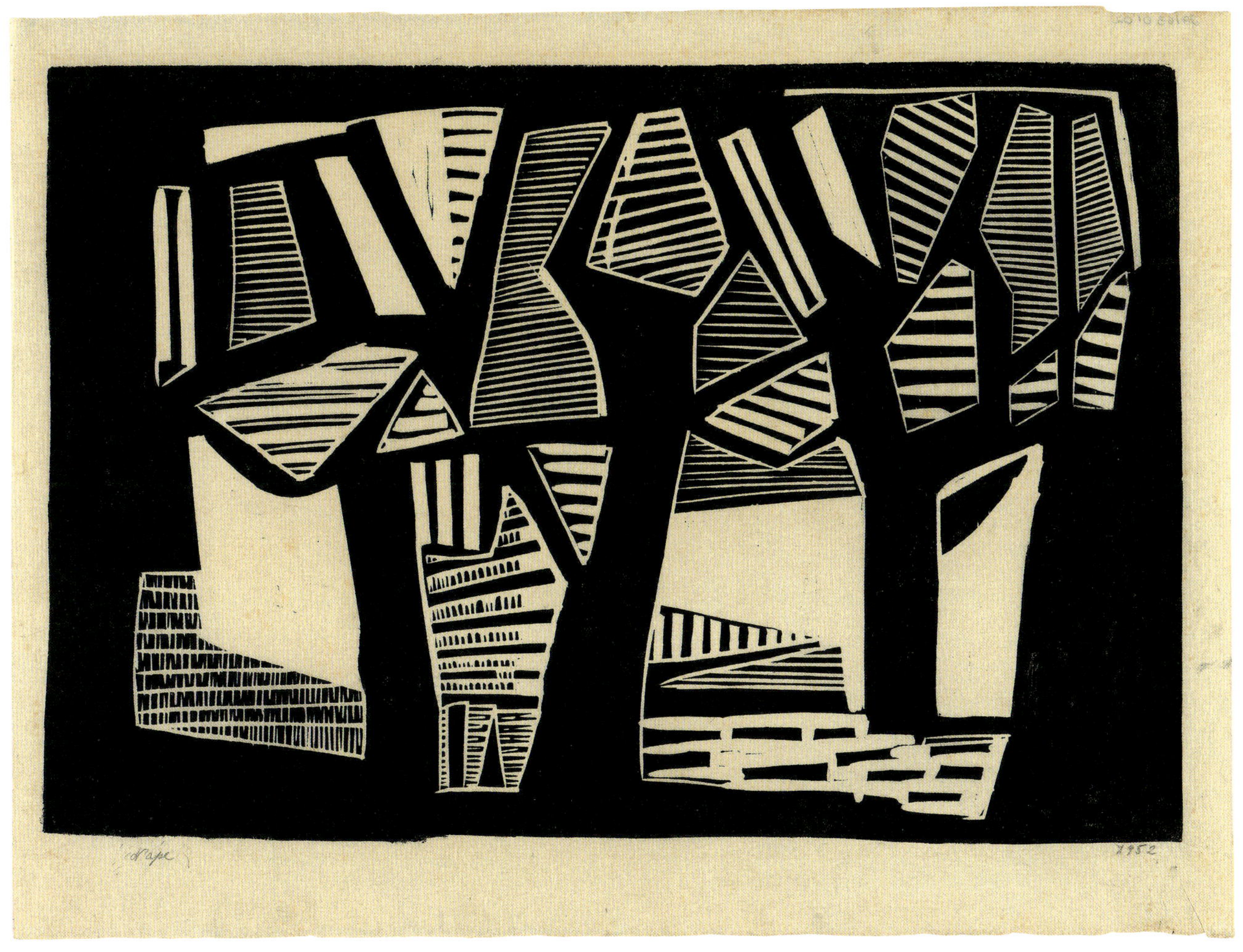

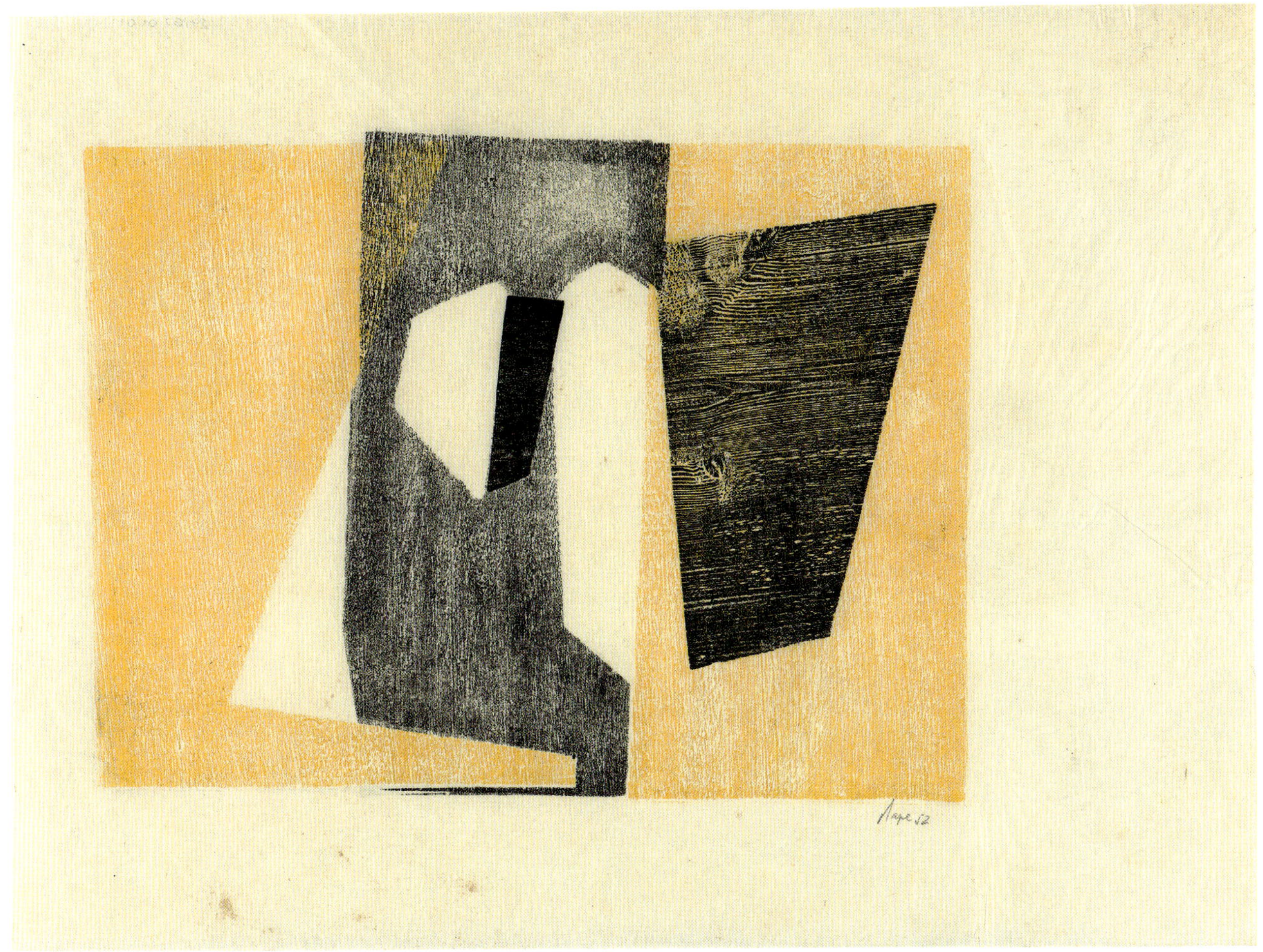

4 *TECELAR* (WEAVING), 1952

5 *TECELAR* (WEAVING), 1952

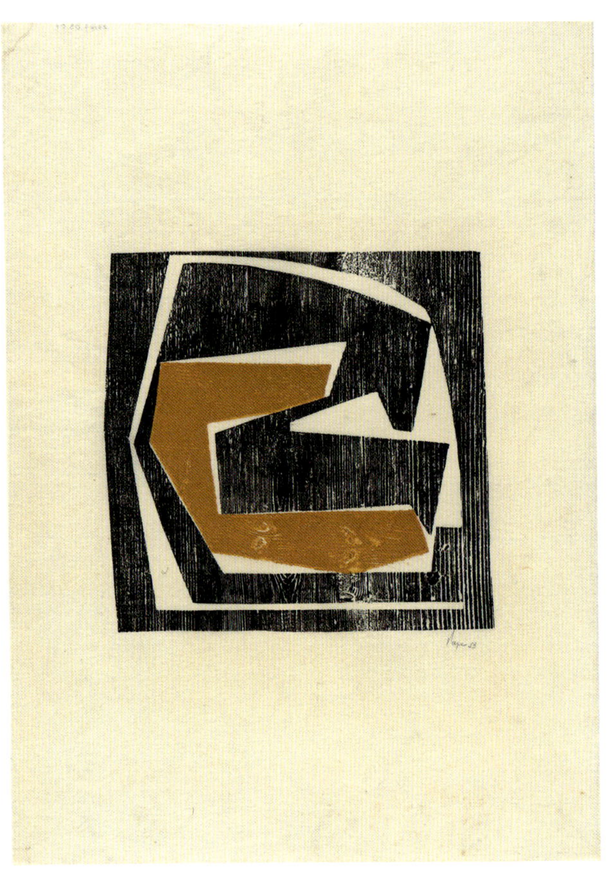

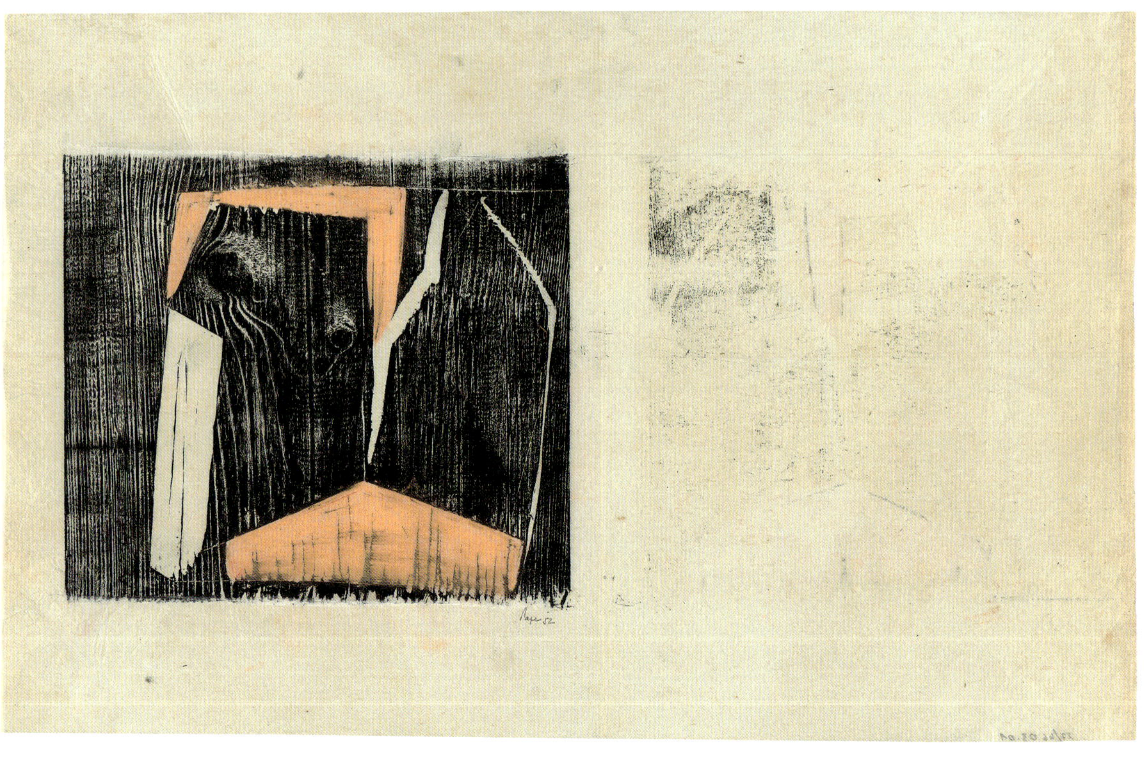

6 *TECELAR* (WEAVING), 1952

7 *TECELAR* (WEAVING), 1952

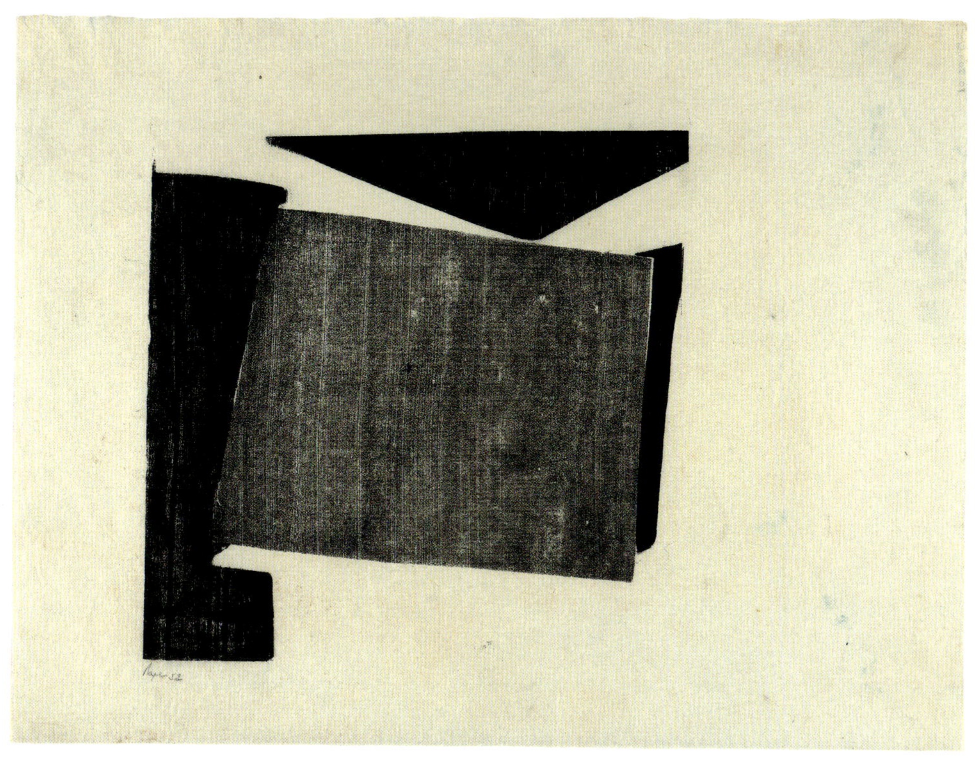

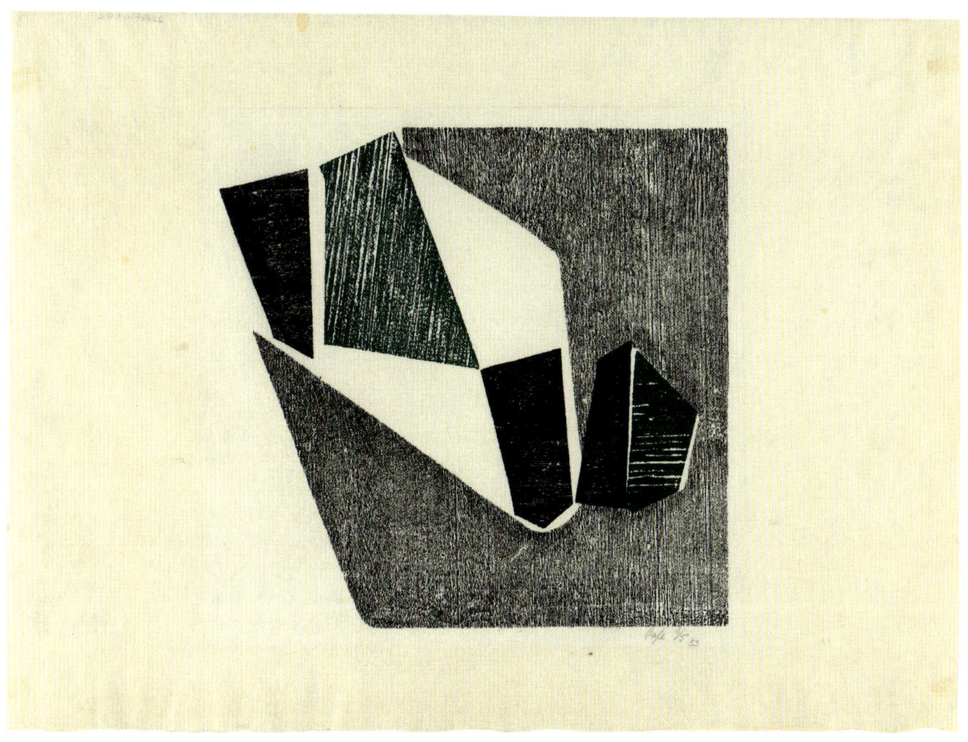

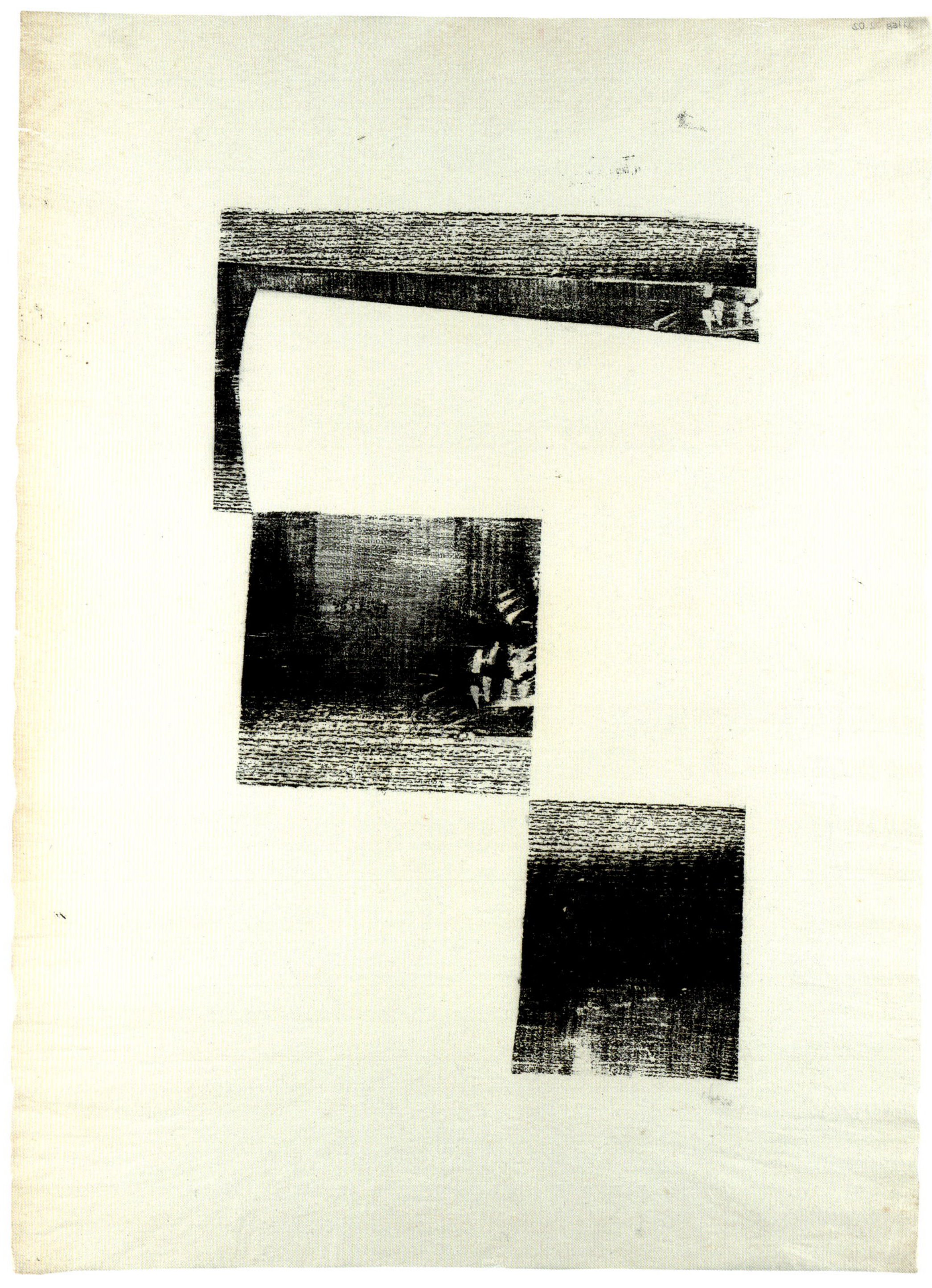

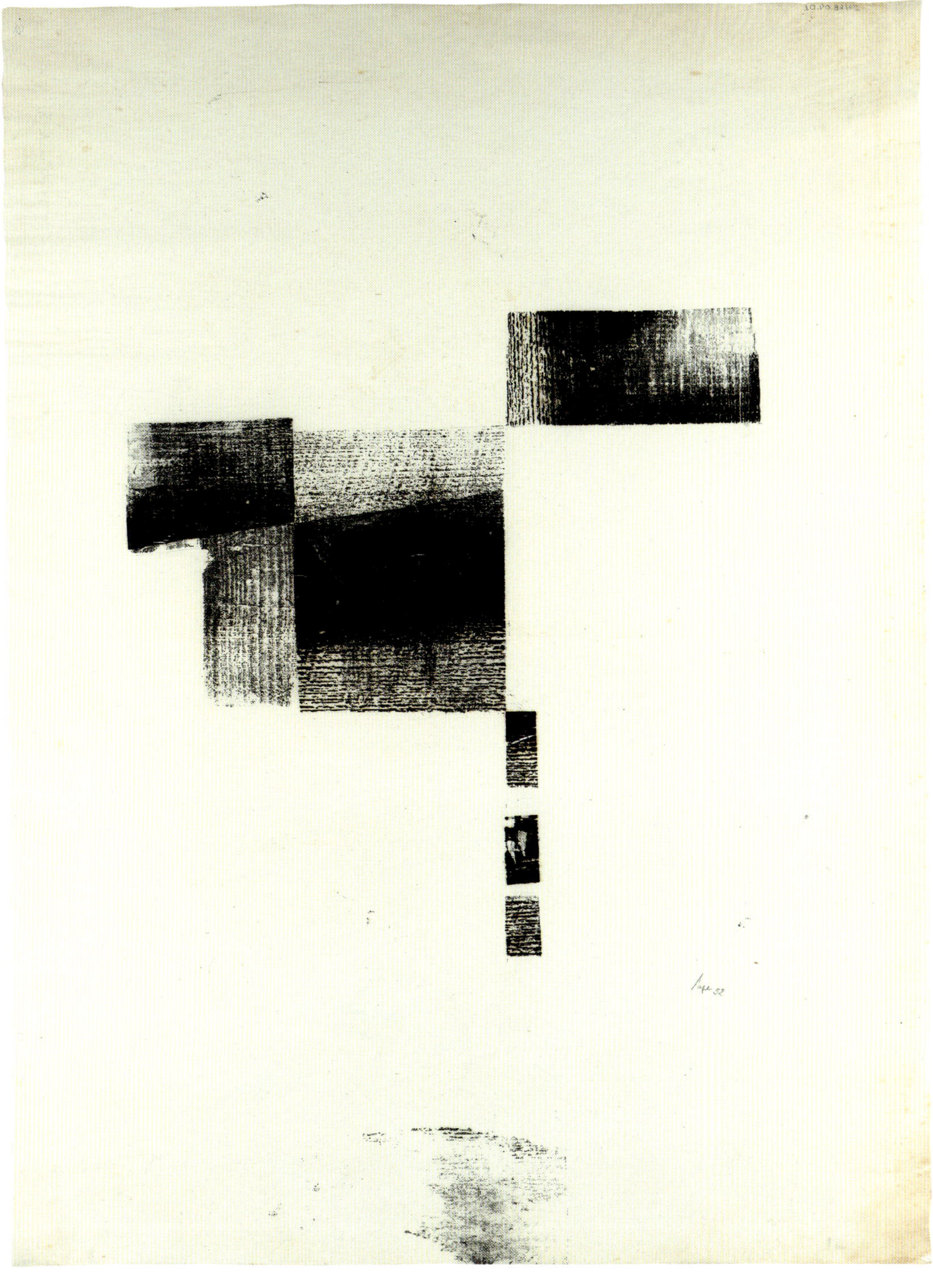

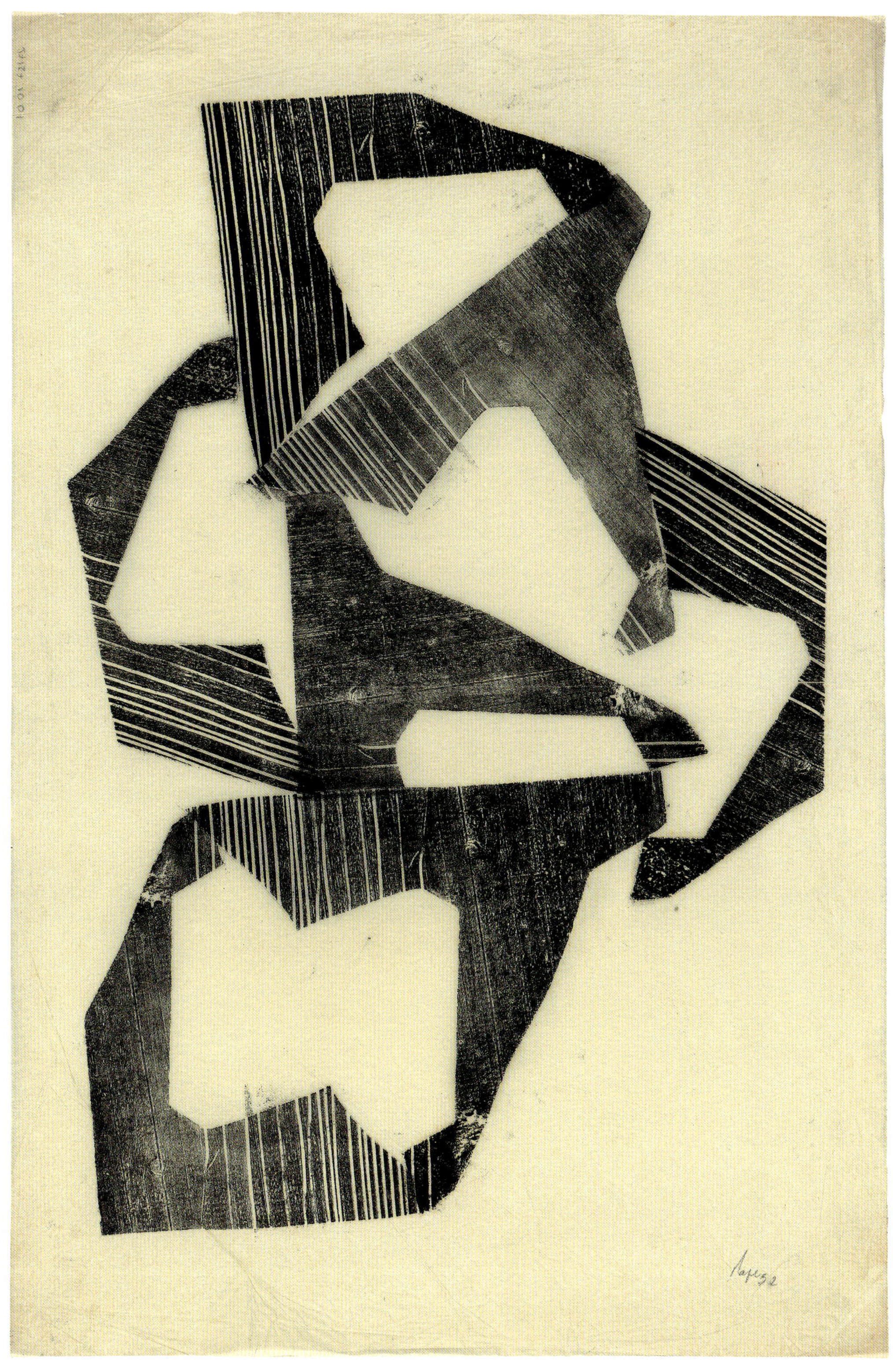

11 *TECELAR* (WEAVING), 1953

12 *TECELAR* (WEAVING), 1953

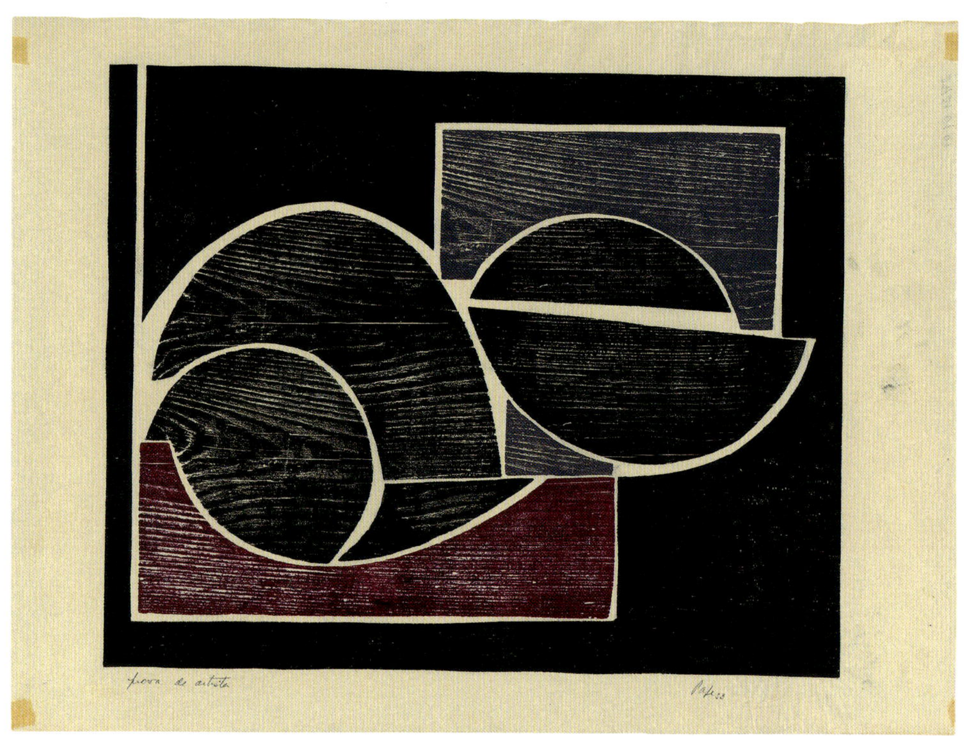

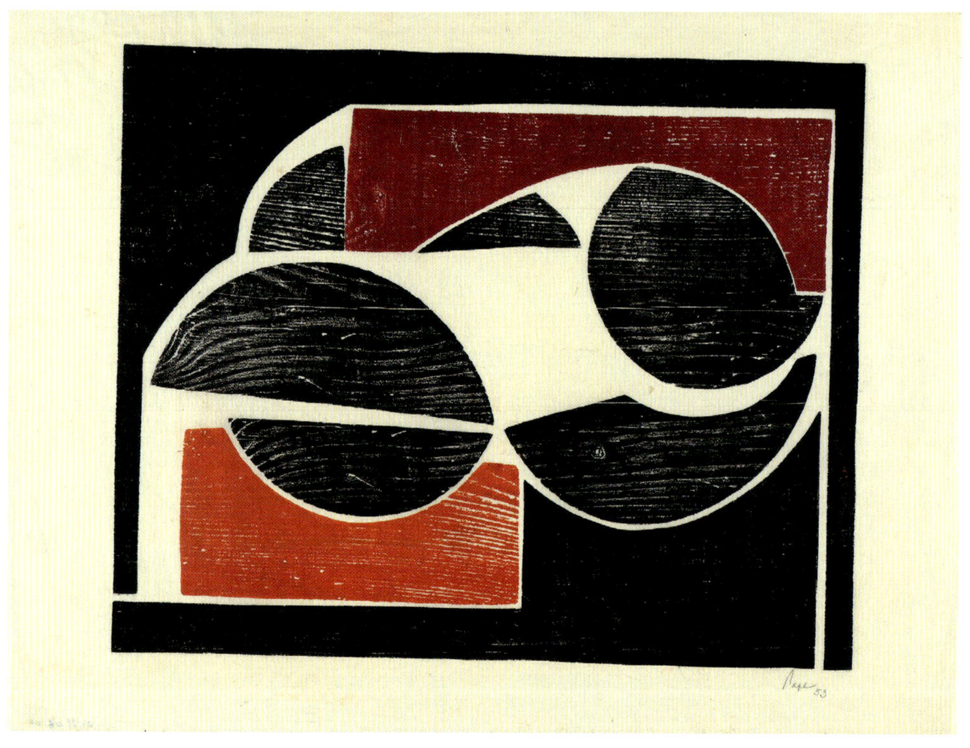

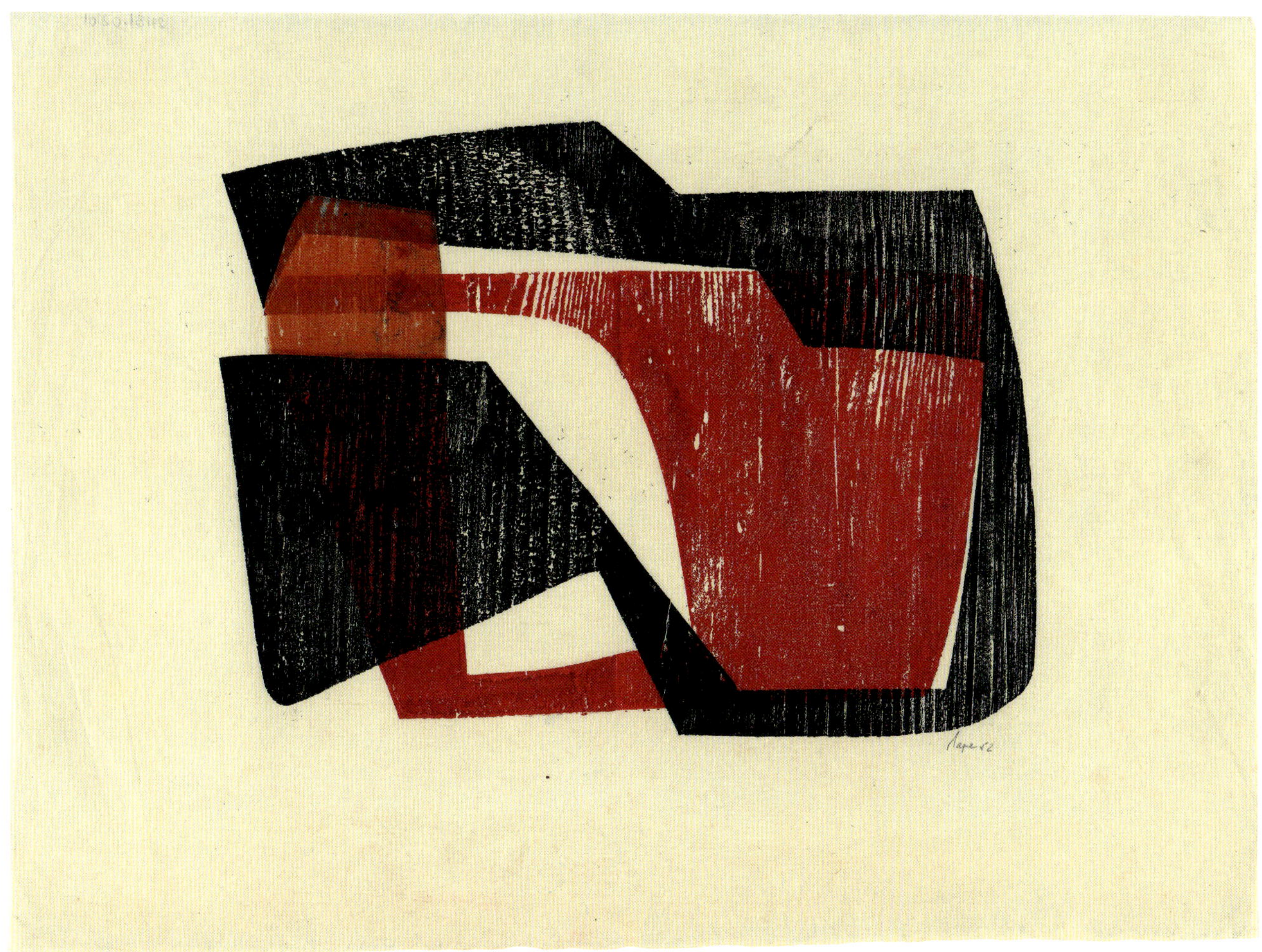

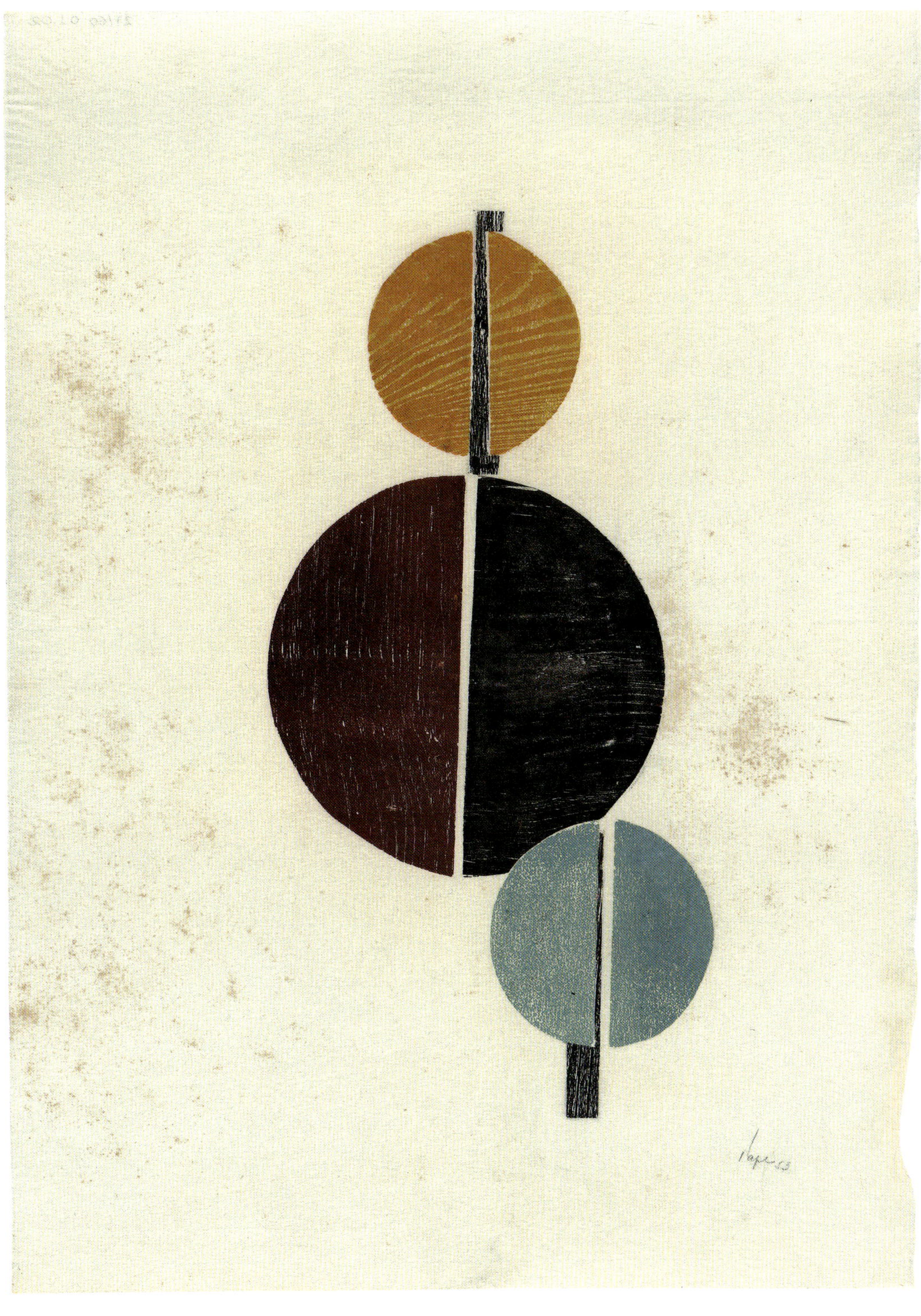

15 *TECELAR* (WEAVING), 1953

16 *TECELAR* (WEAVING), 1953

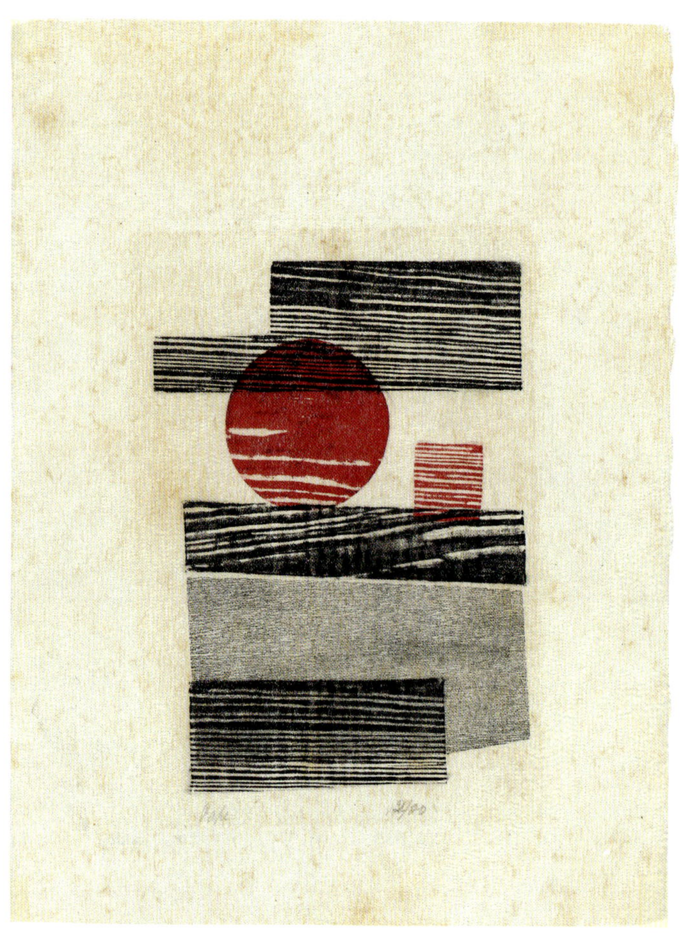

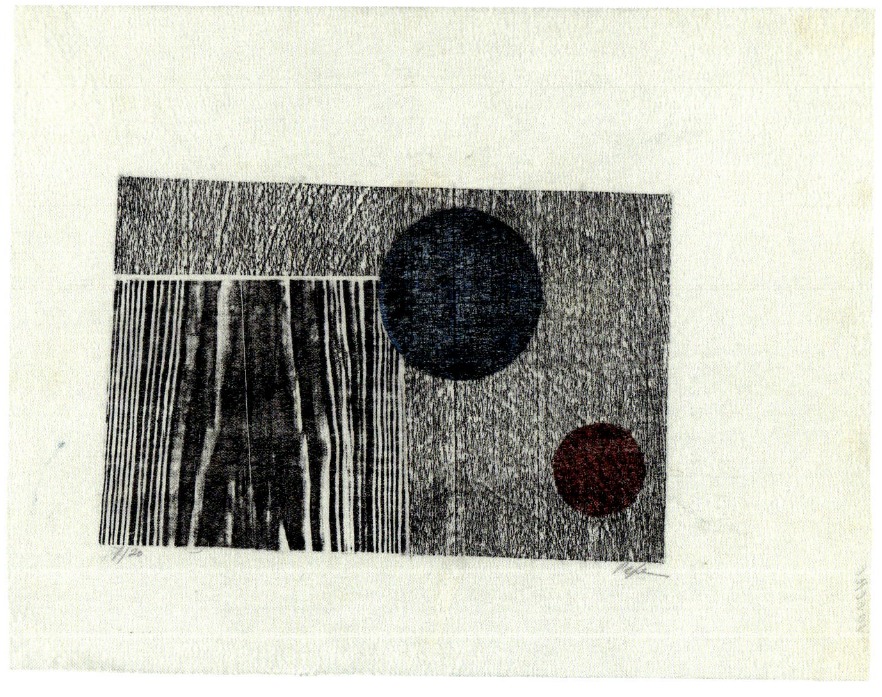

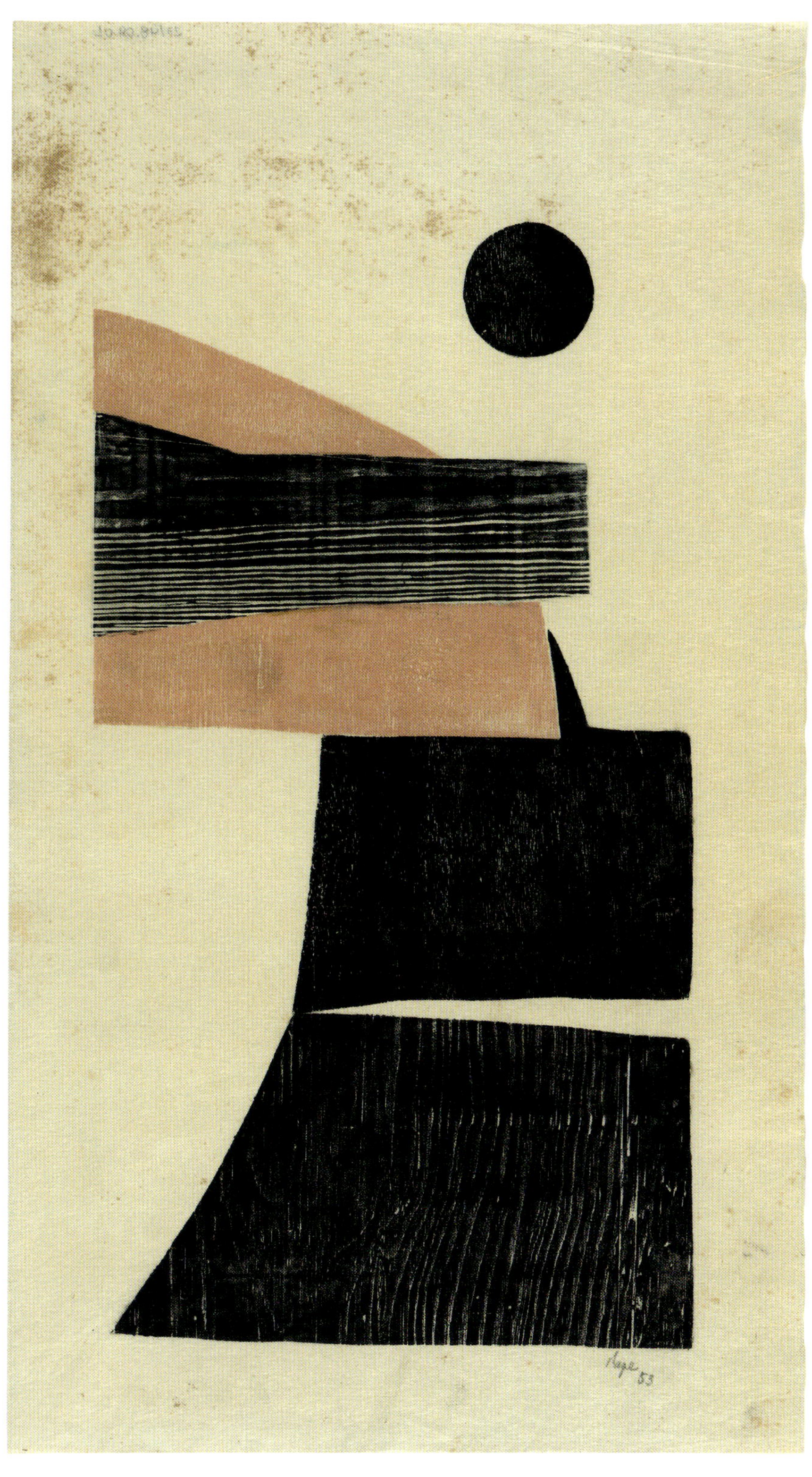

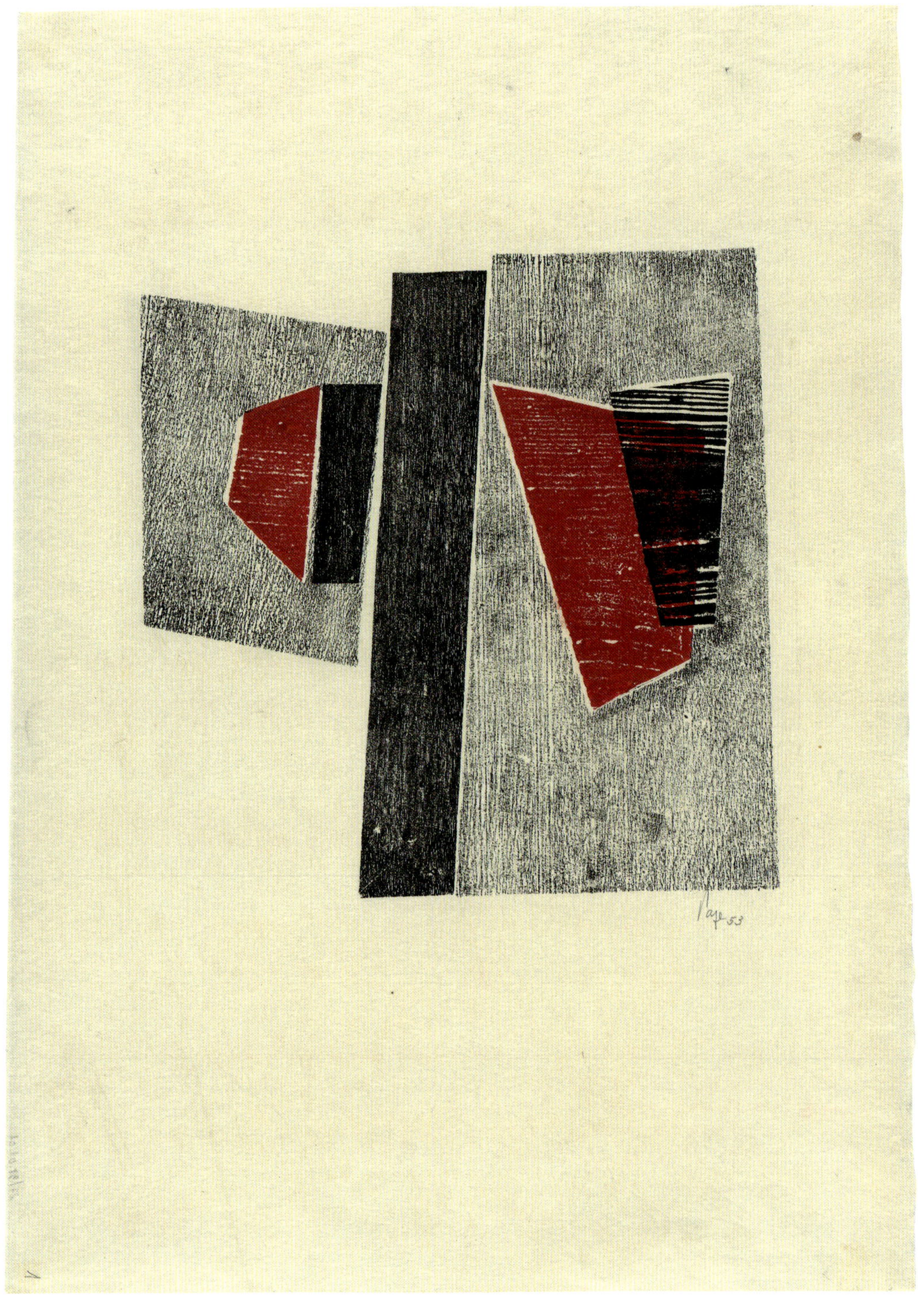

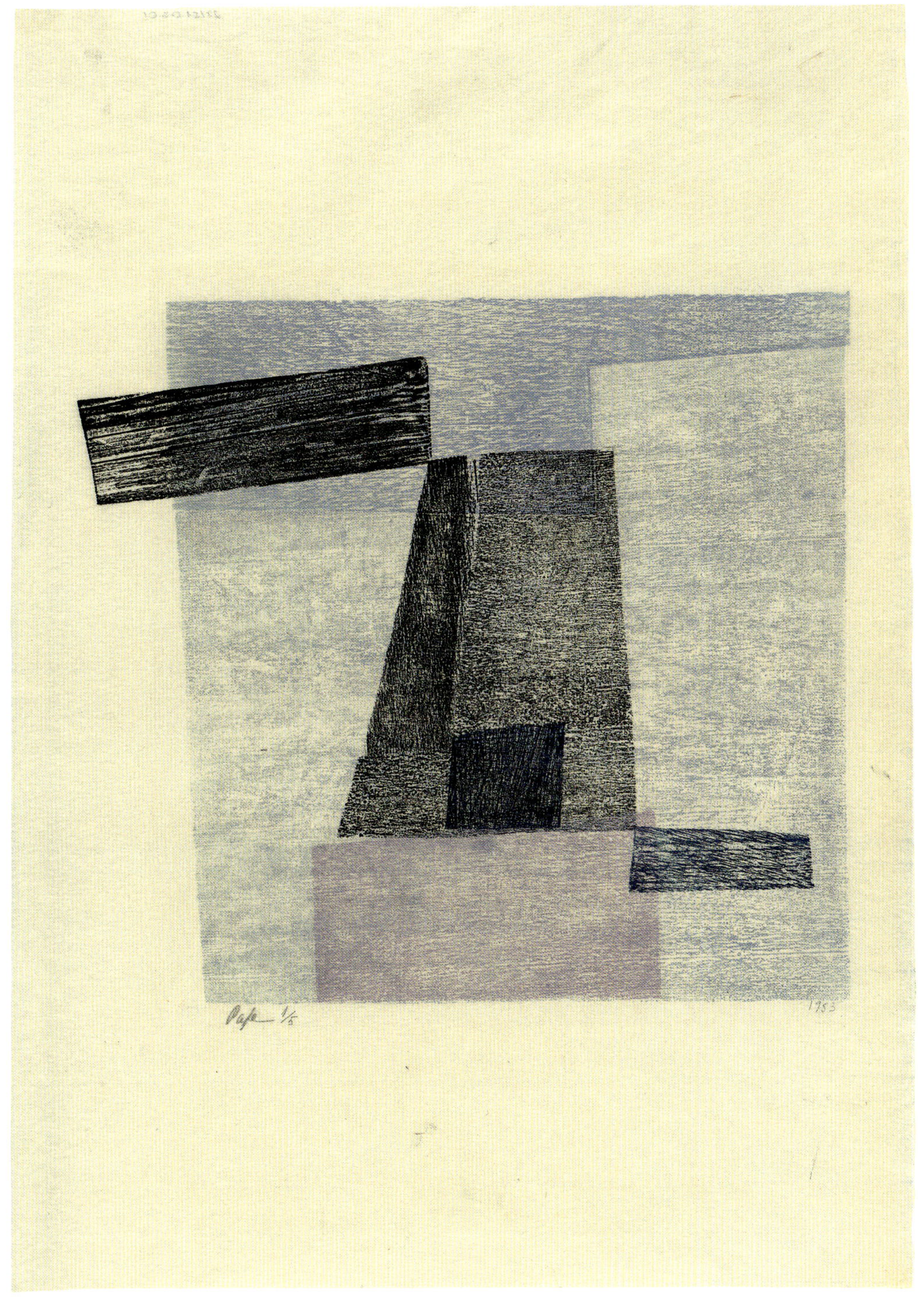

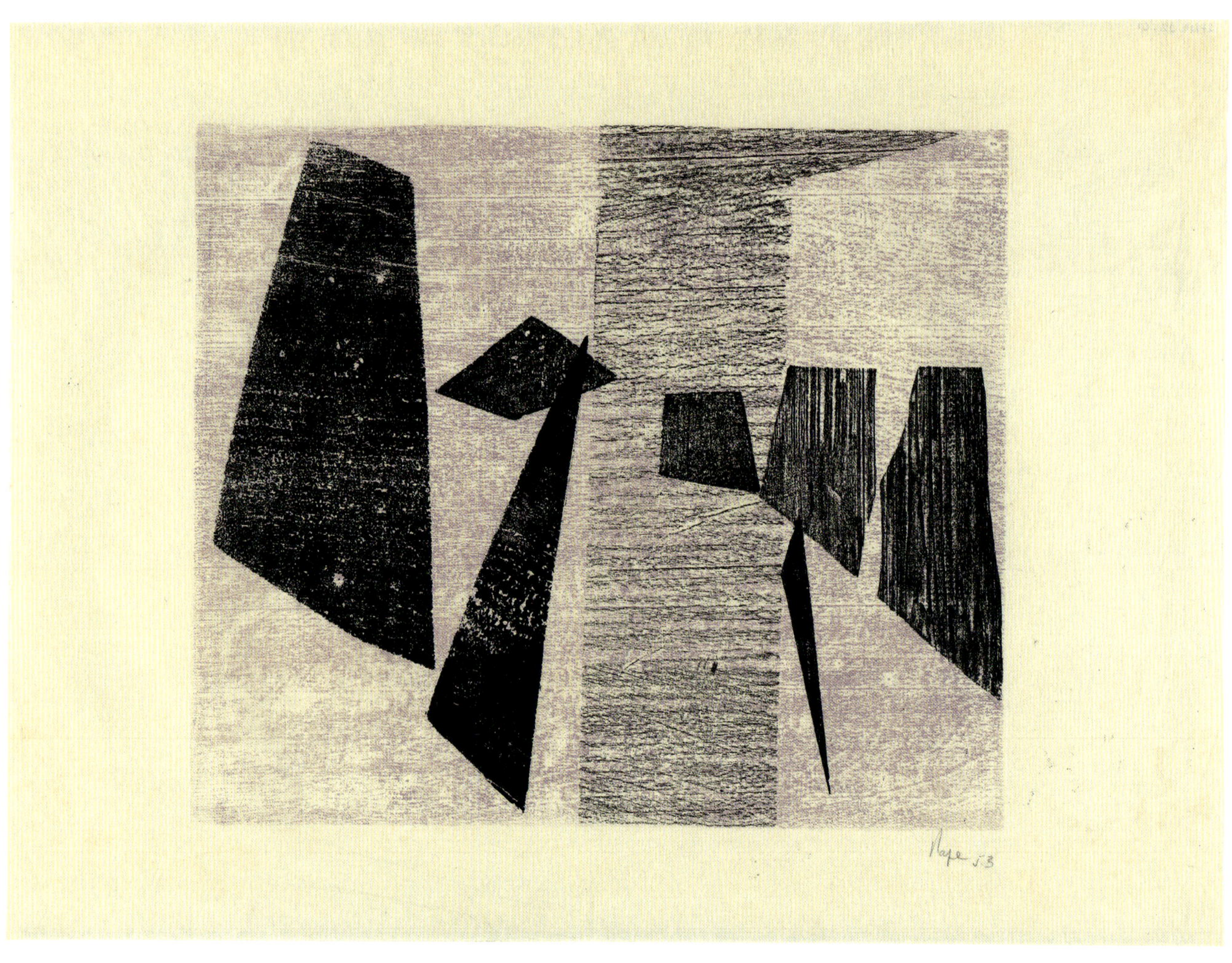

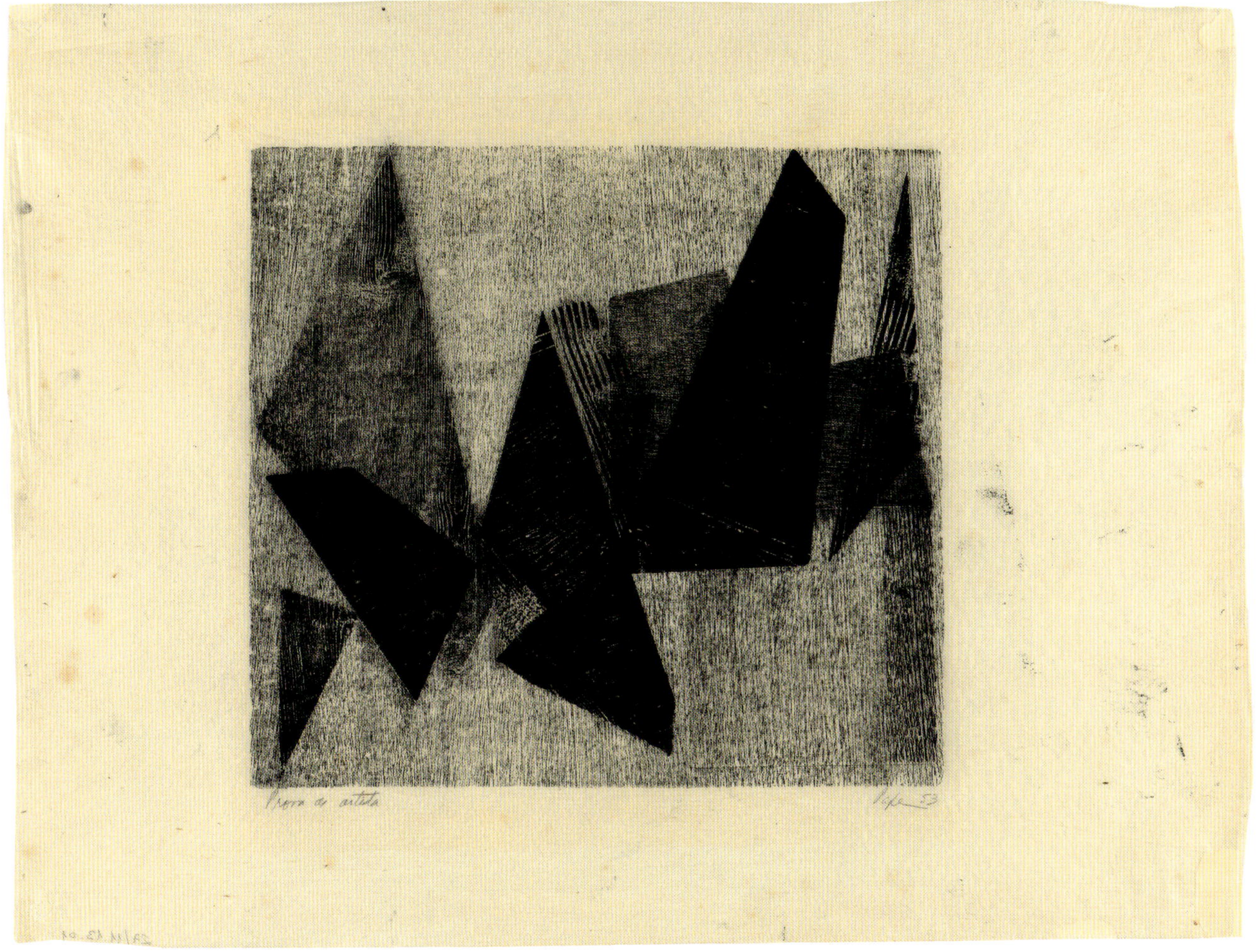

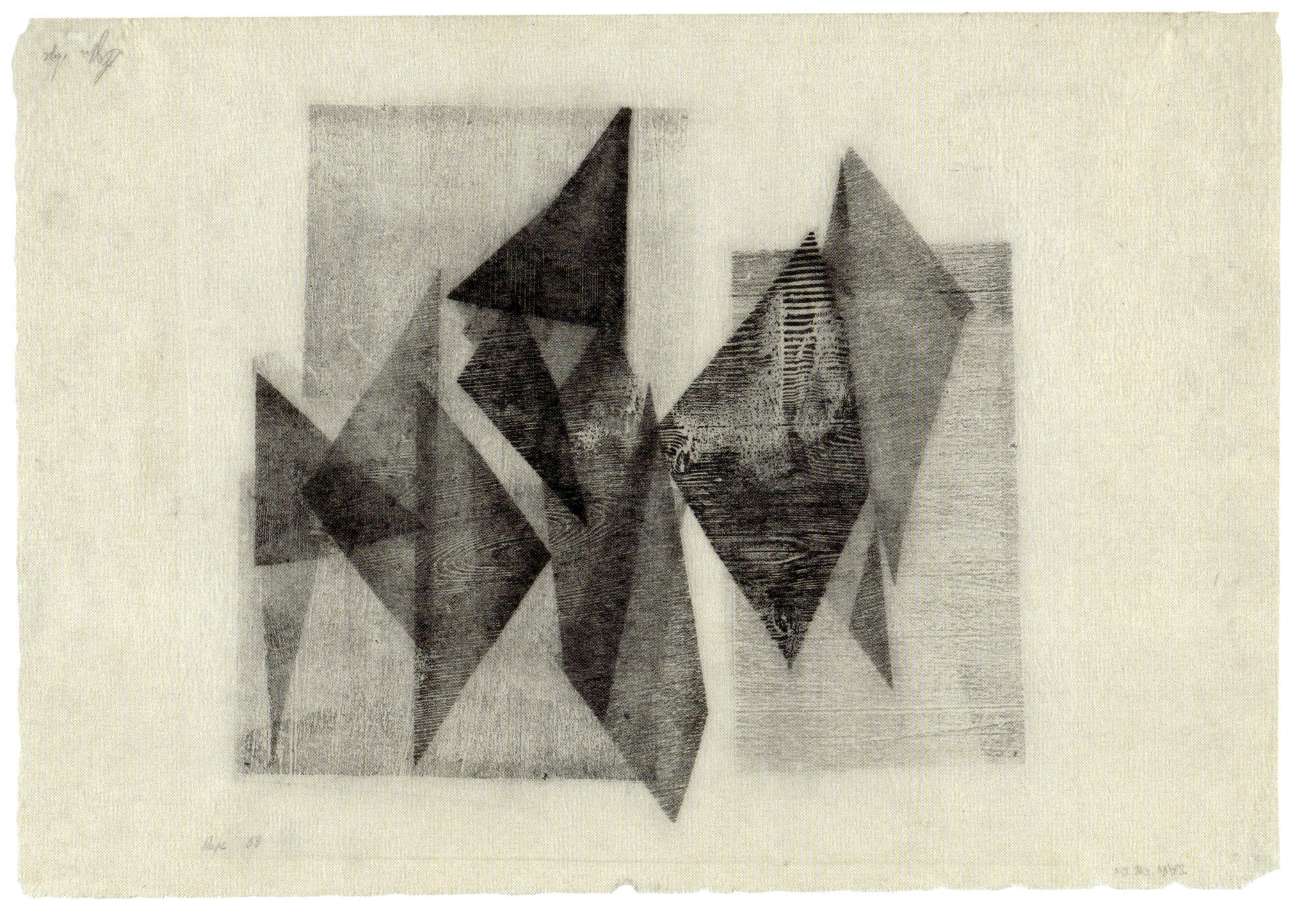

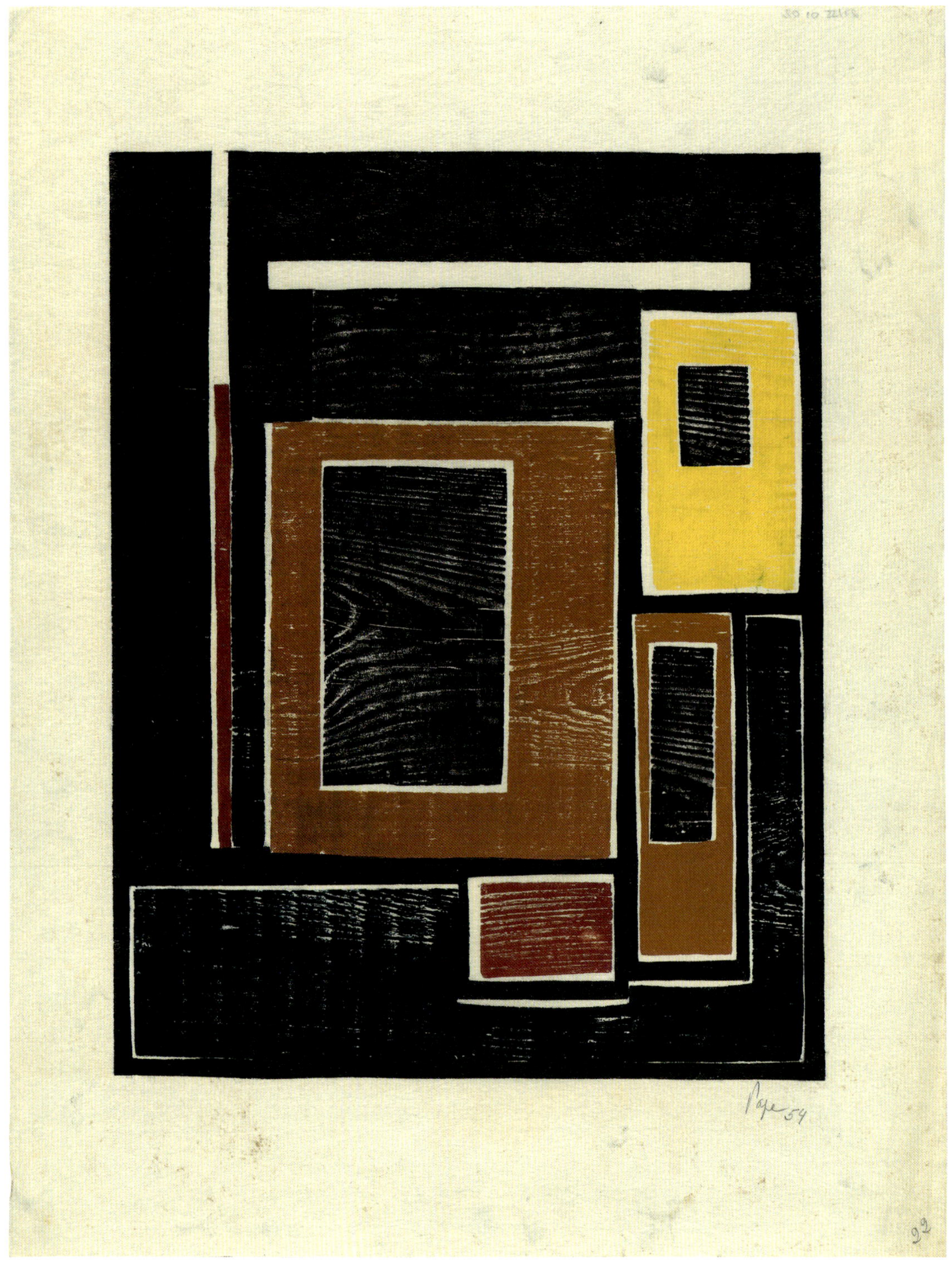

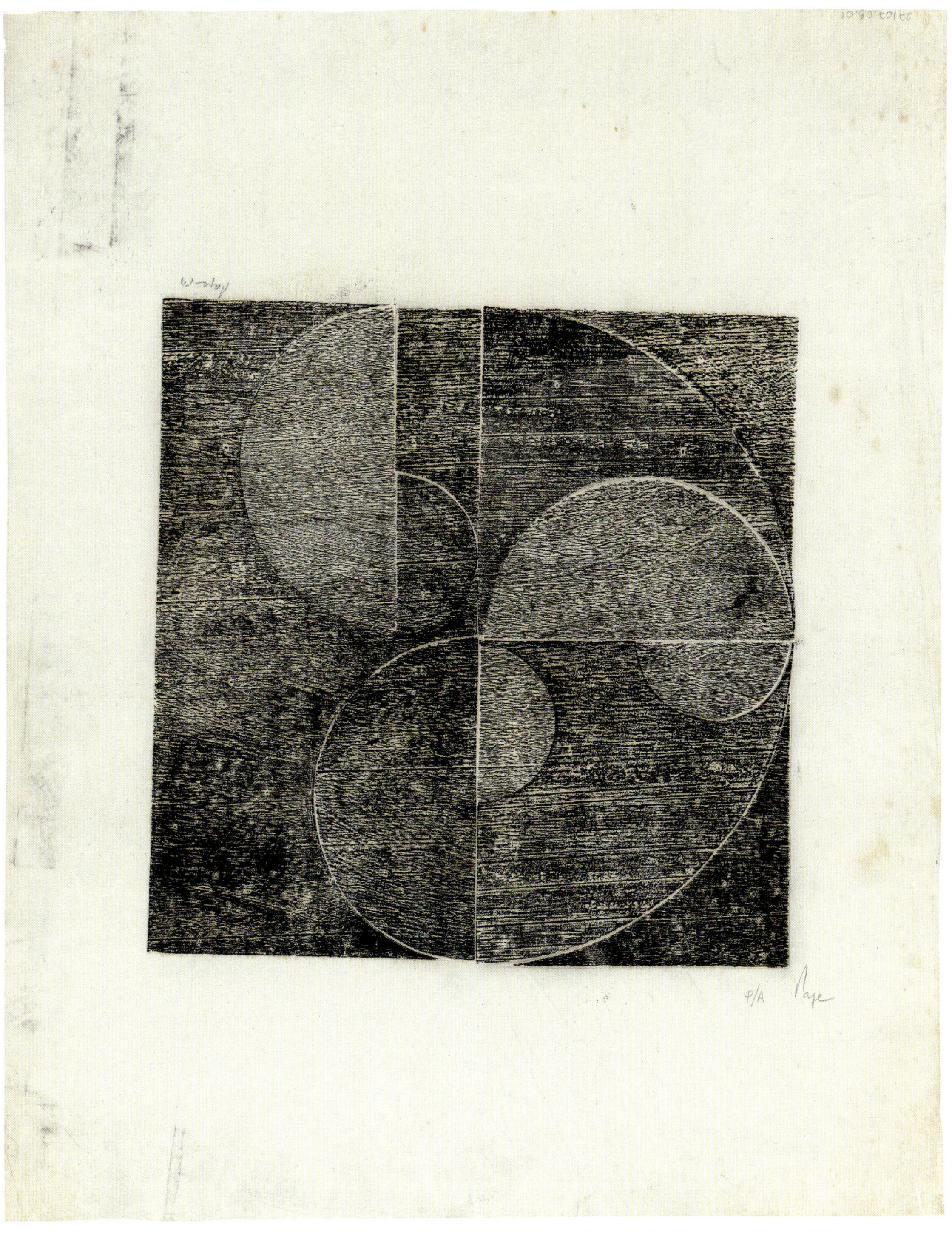

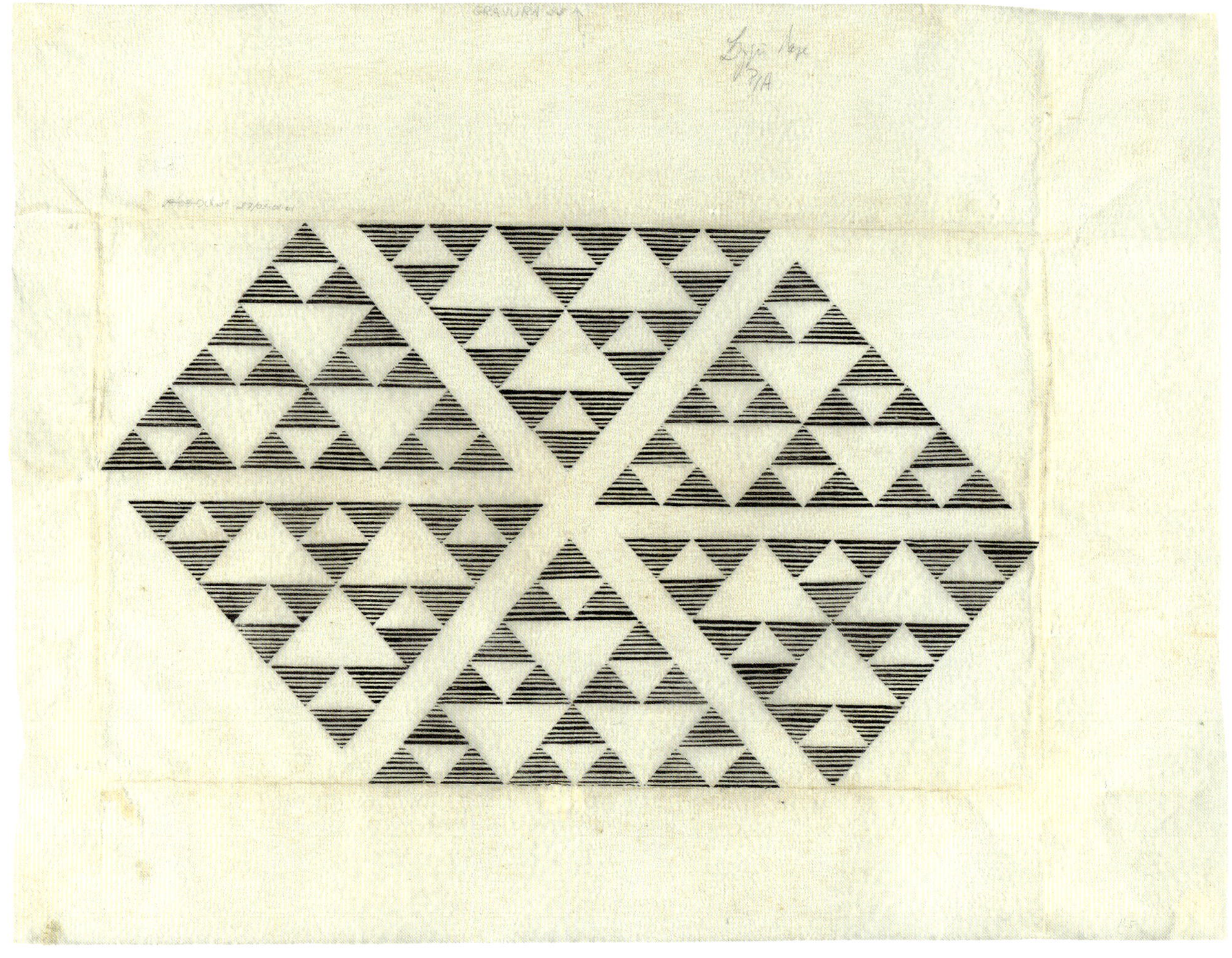

26 *TECELAR* (WEAVING), 1955

27 *TECELAR* (WEAVING), 1955

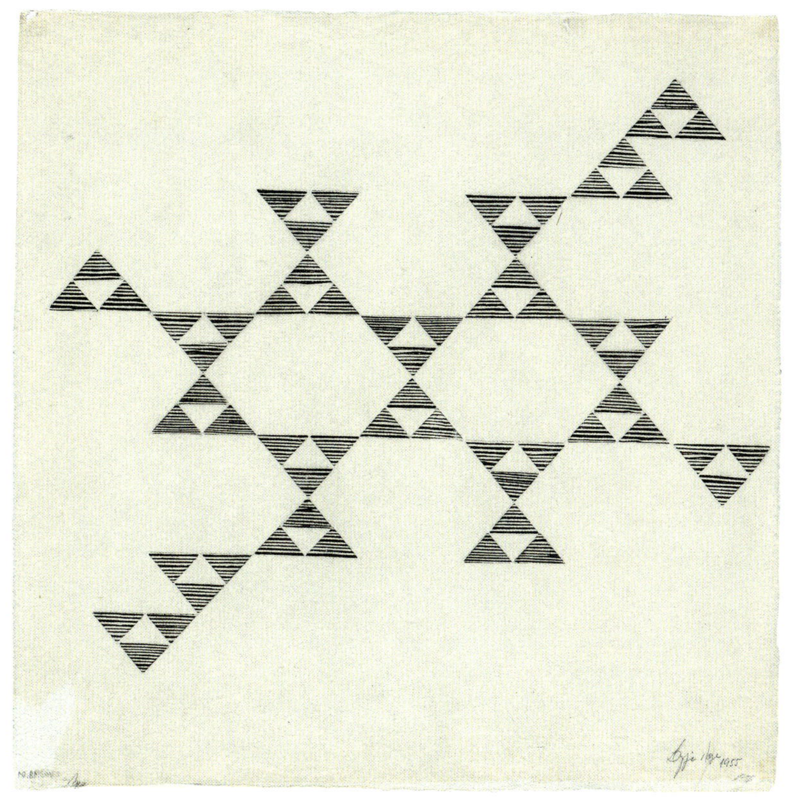

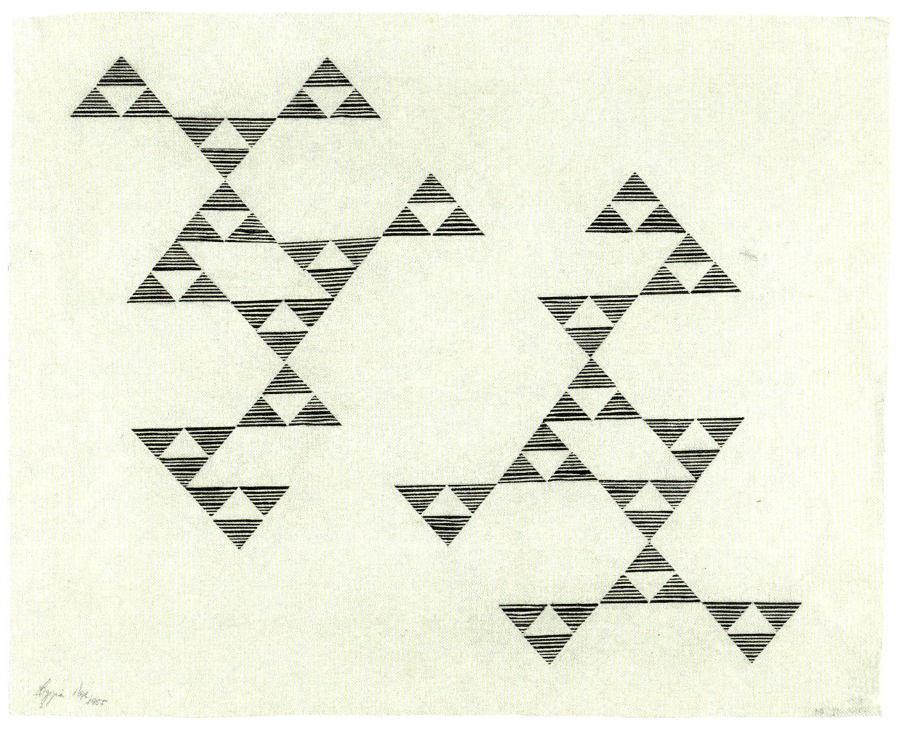

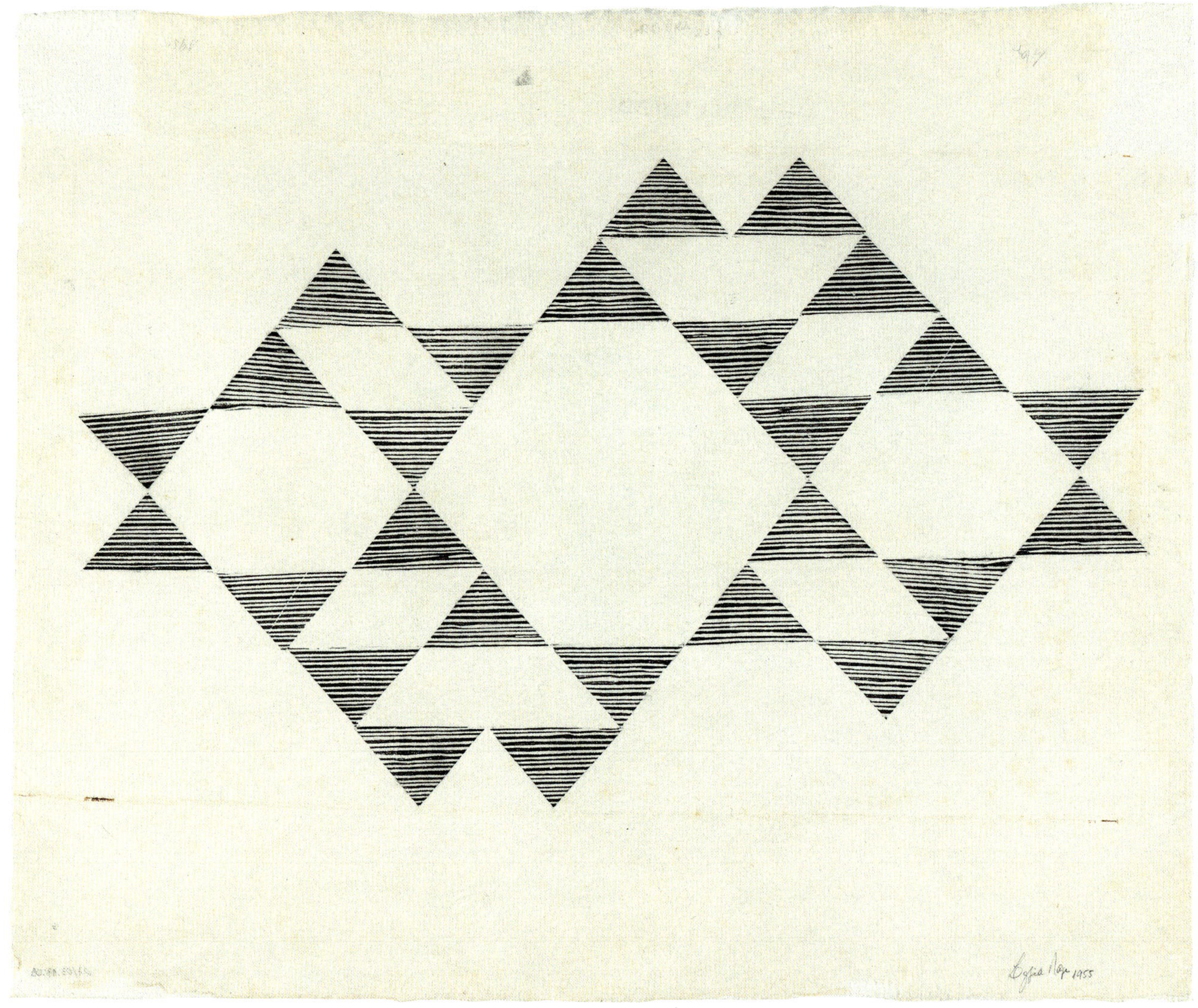

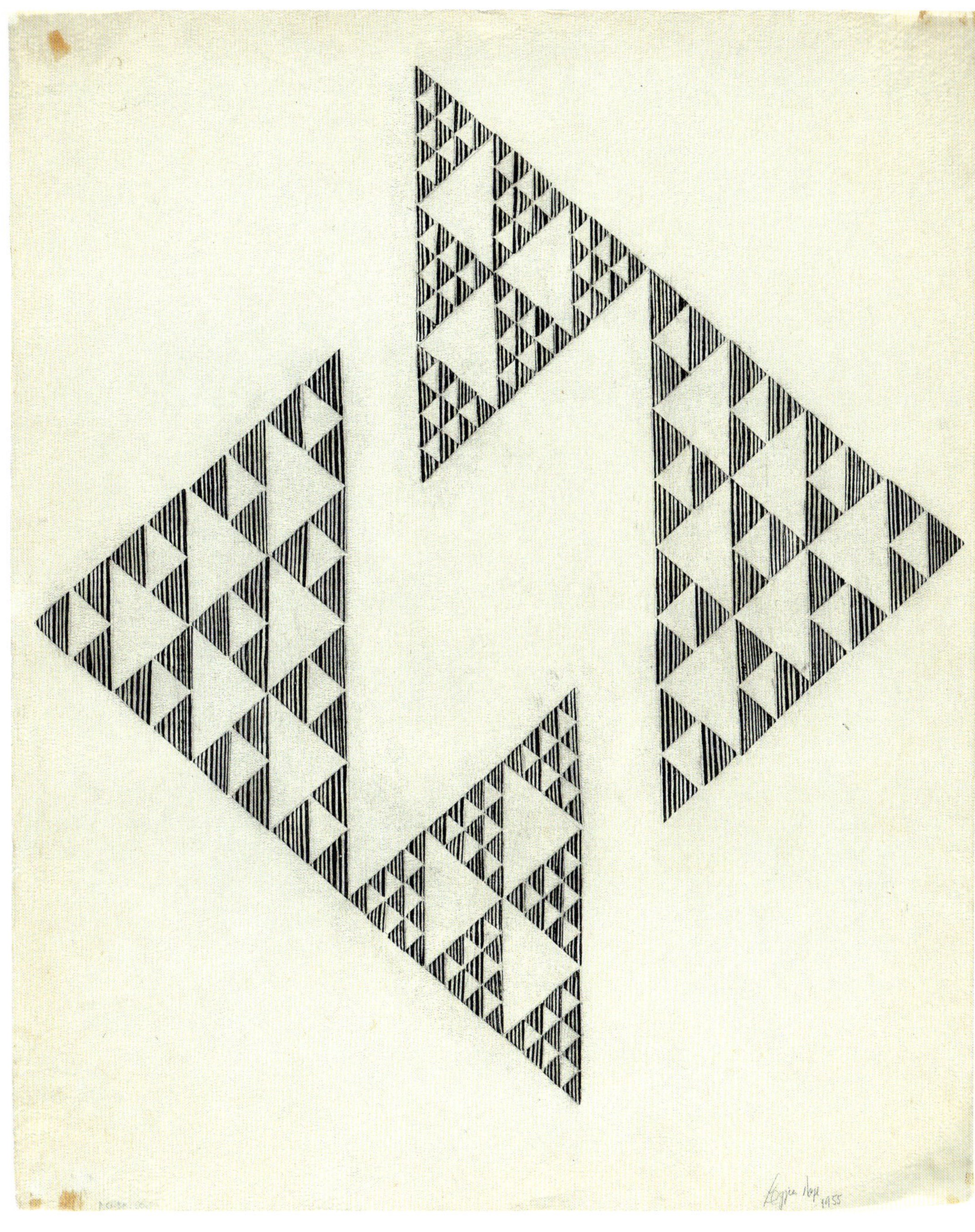

30 *TECELAR* (WEAVING), 1956

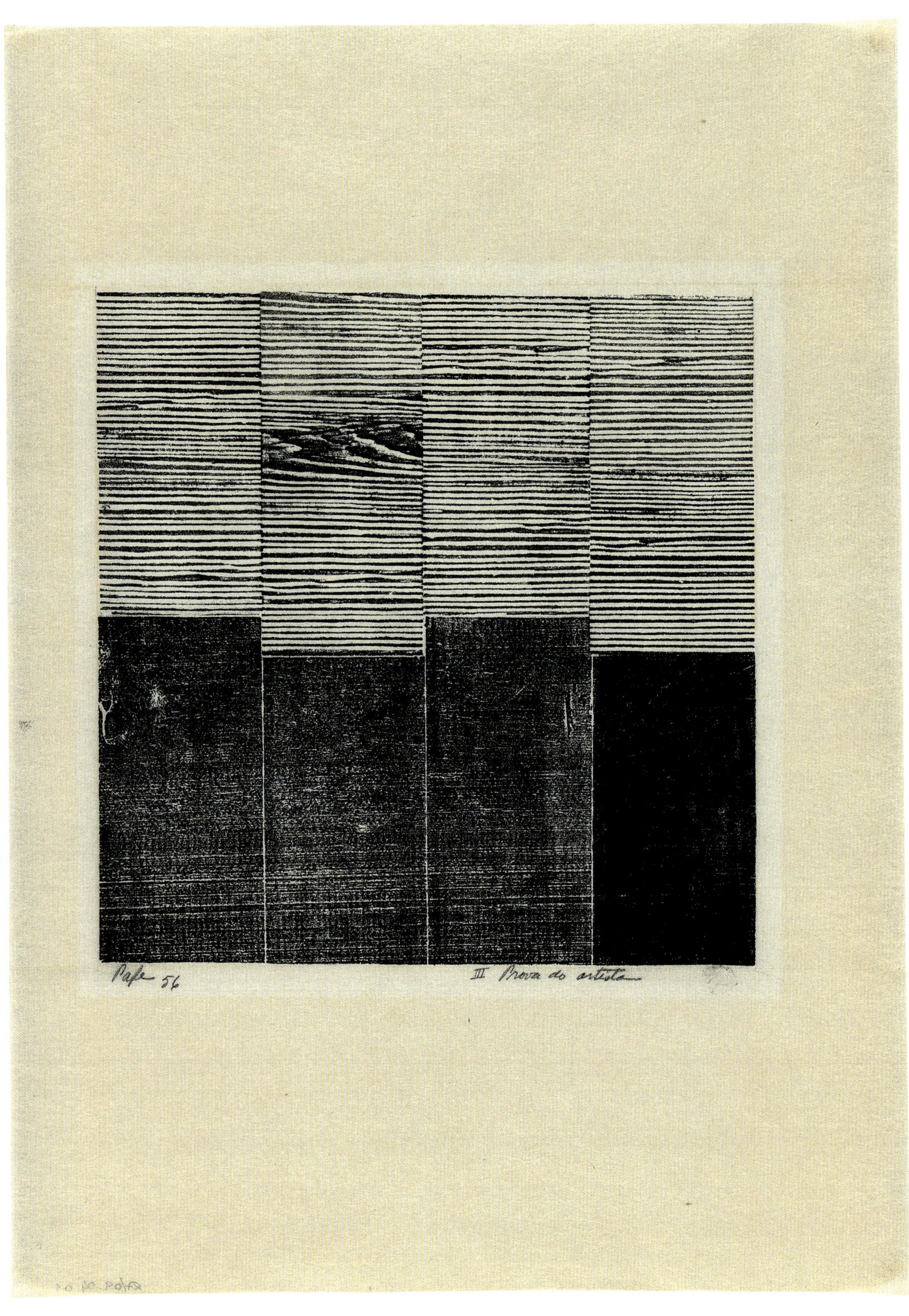

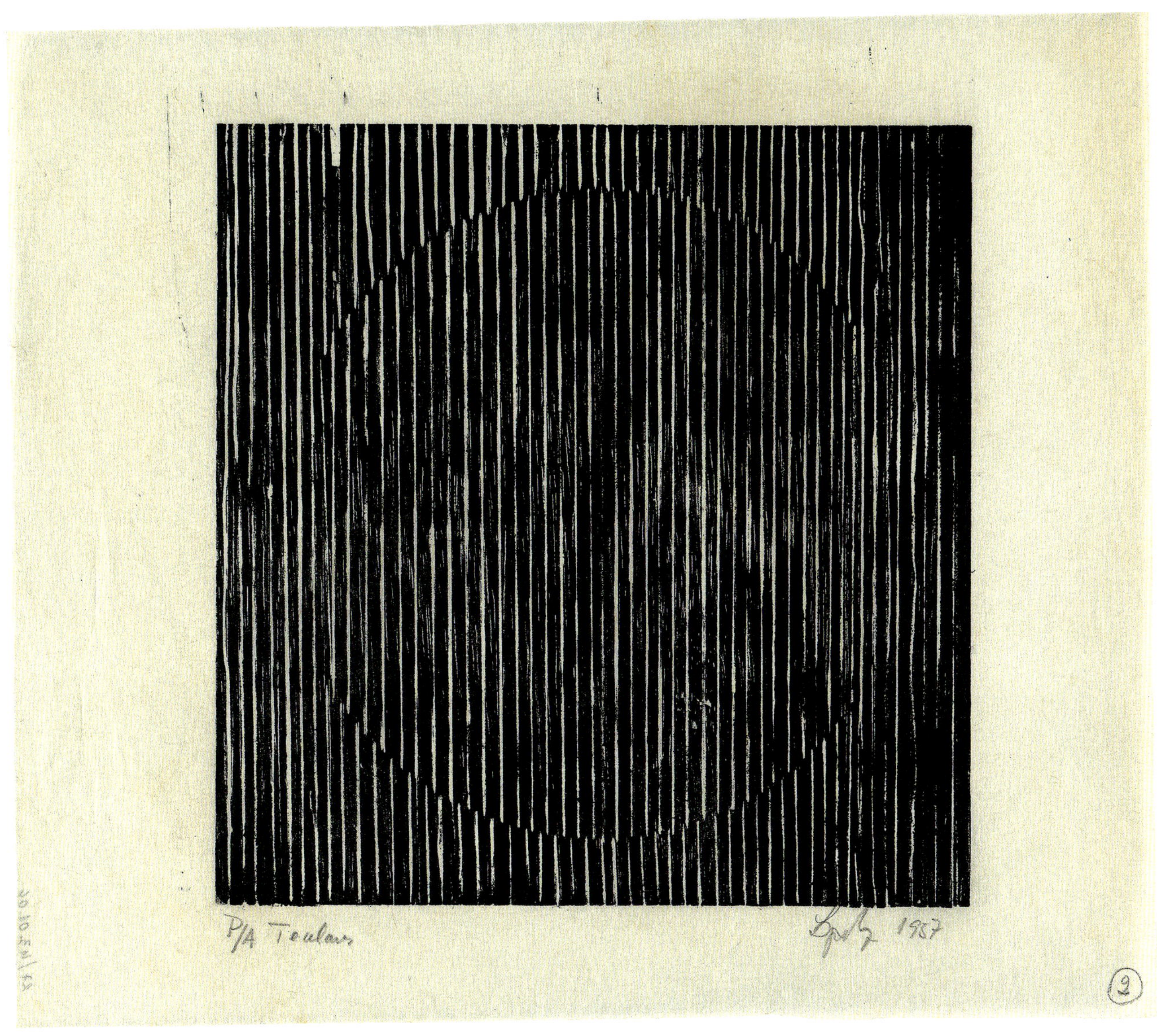
P/A Tecelar
1957

32 WOOD BLOCK FOR CAT. 33, 1957

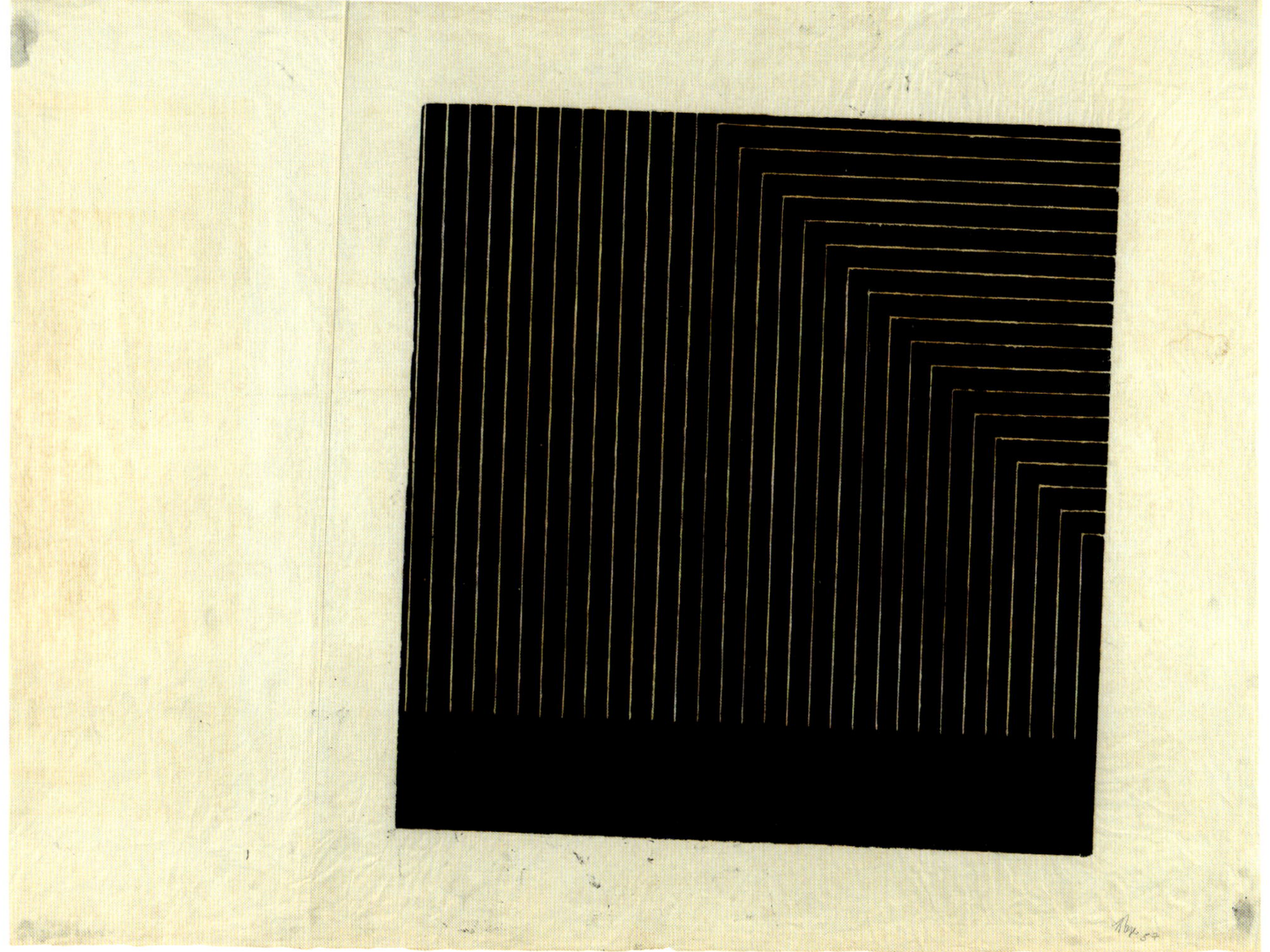

34 RECTO OF WOOD BLOCK FOR CATS. 35 (SHOWN) AND 36, 1957

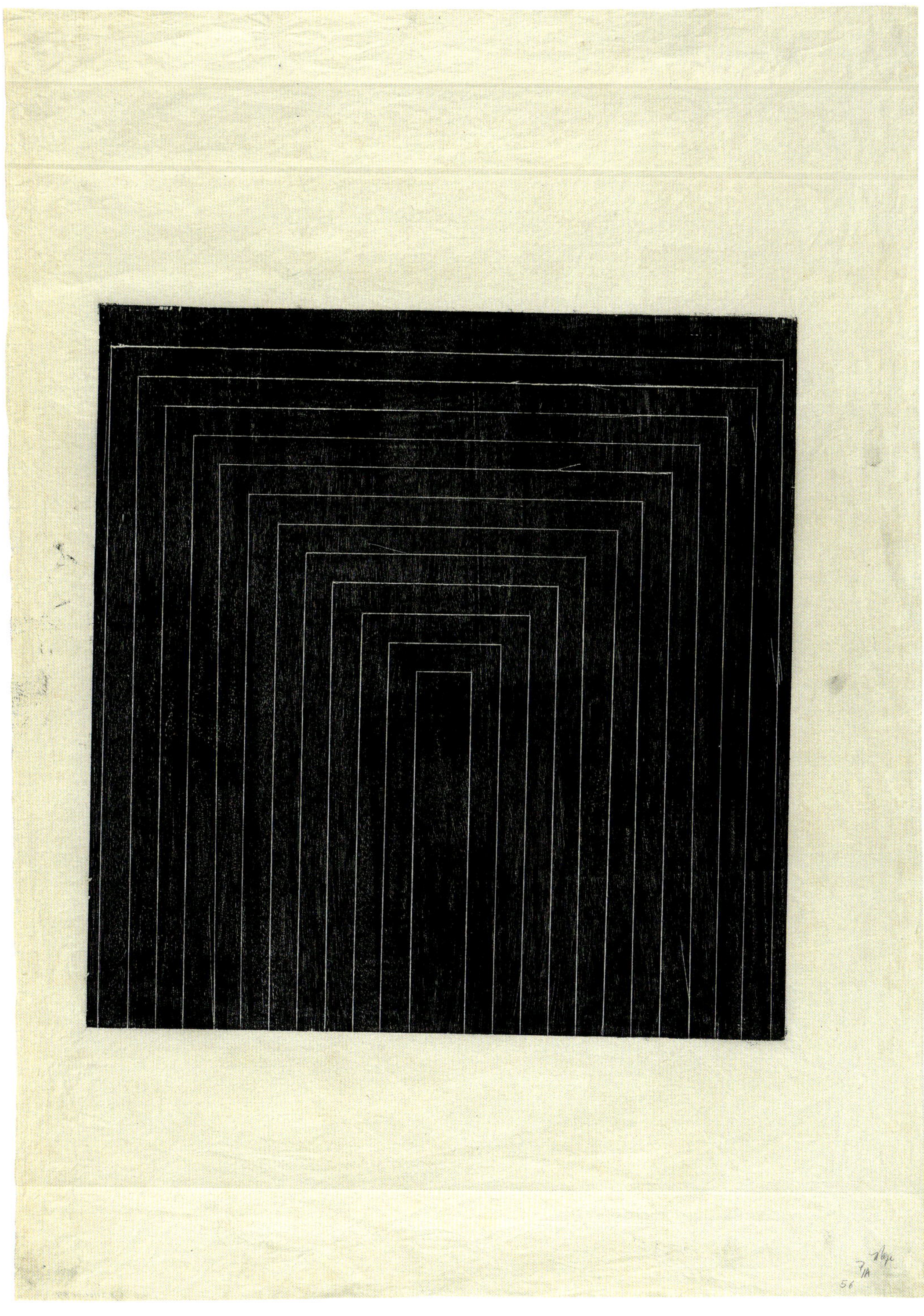

34 VERSO OF WOOD BLOCK FOR FOR CATS. 35 AND 36 (SHOWN), 1957

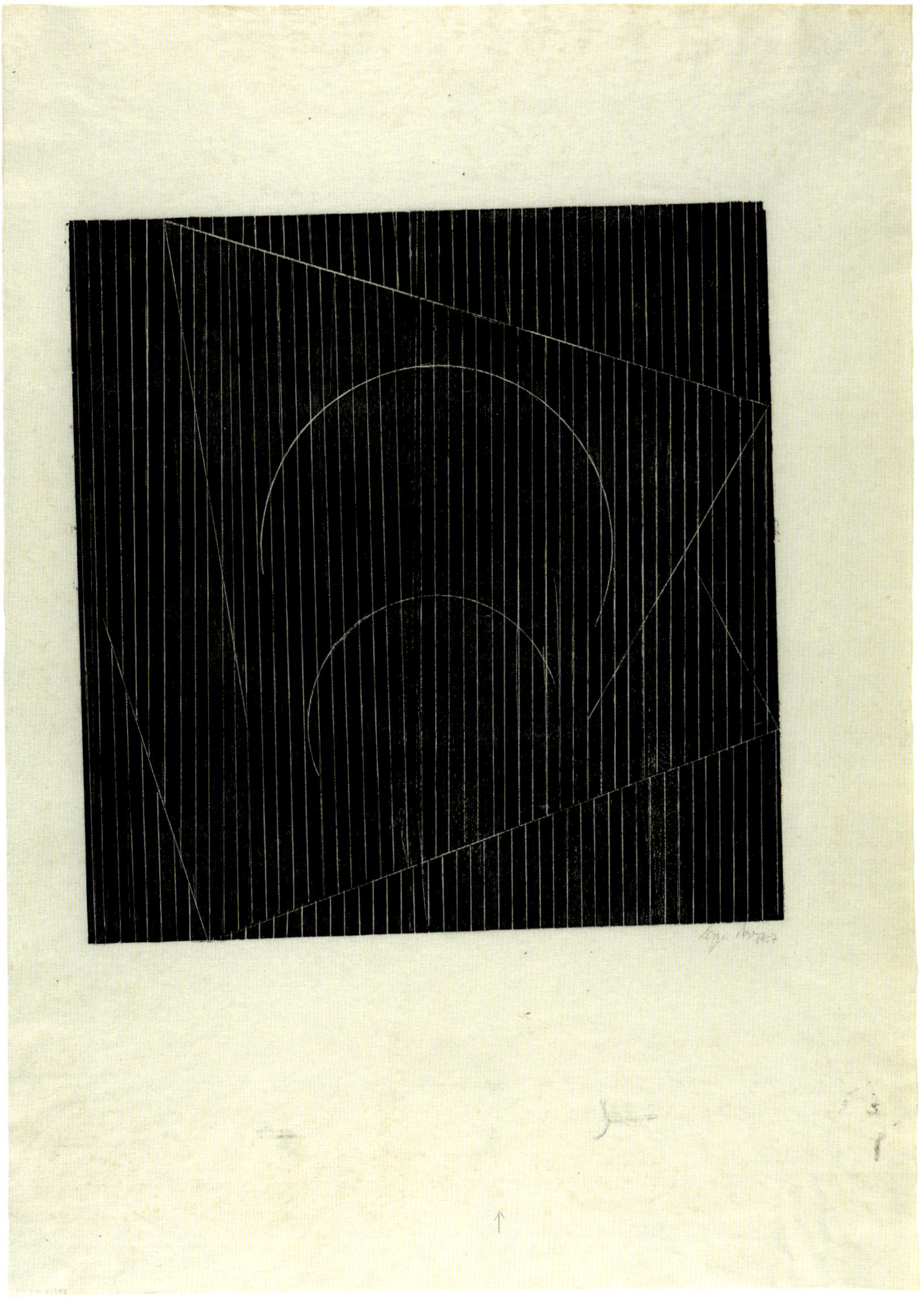

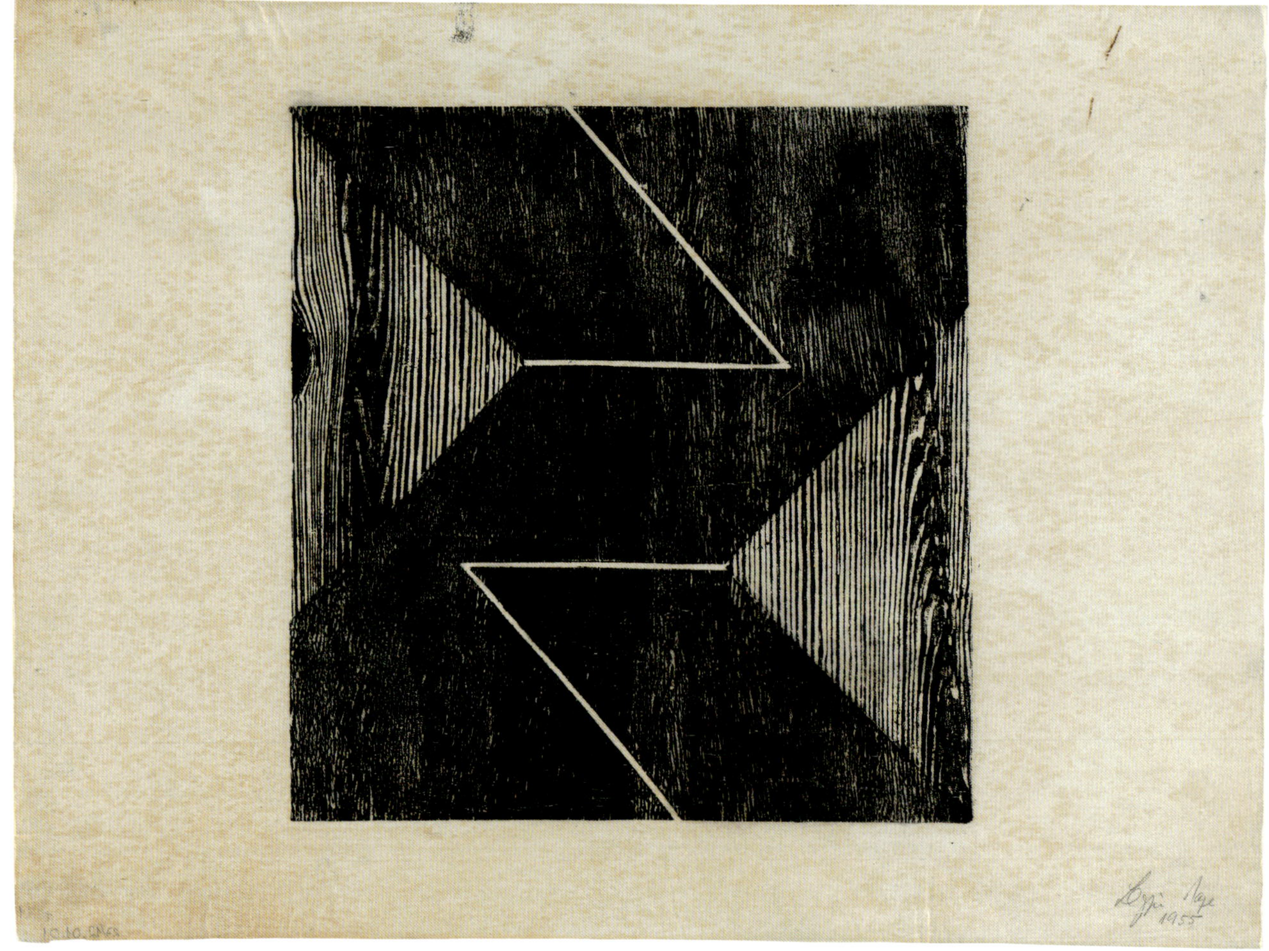

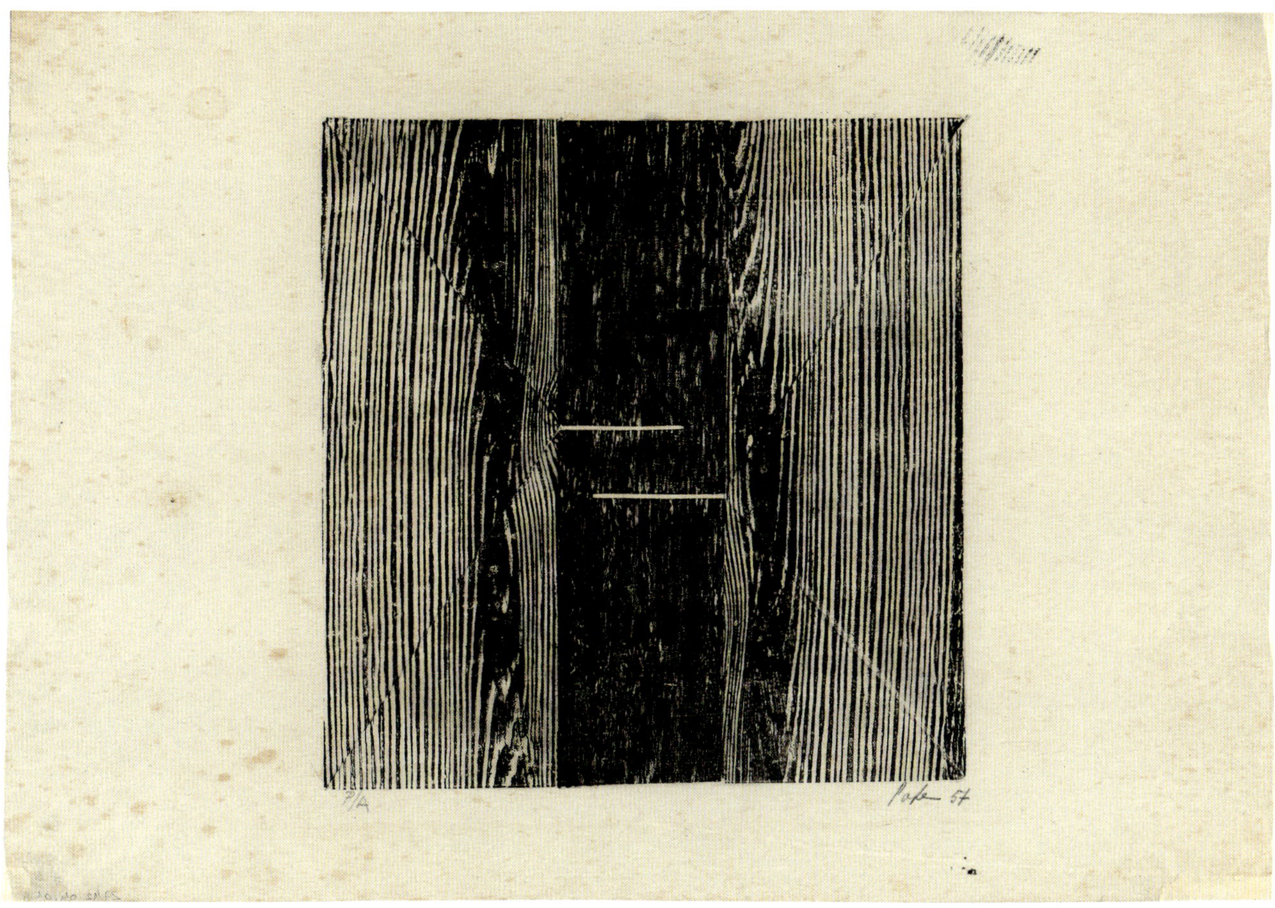

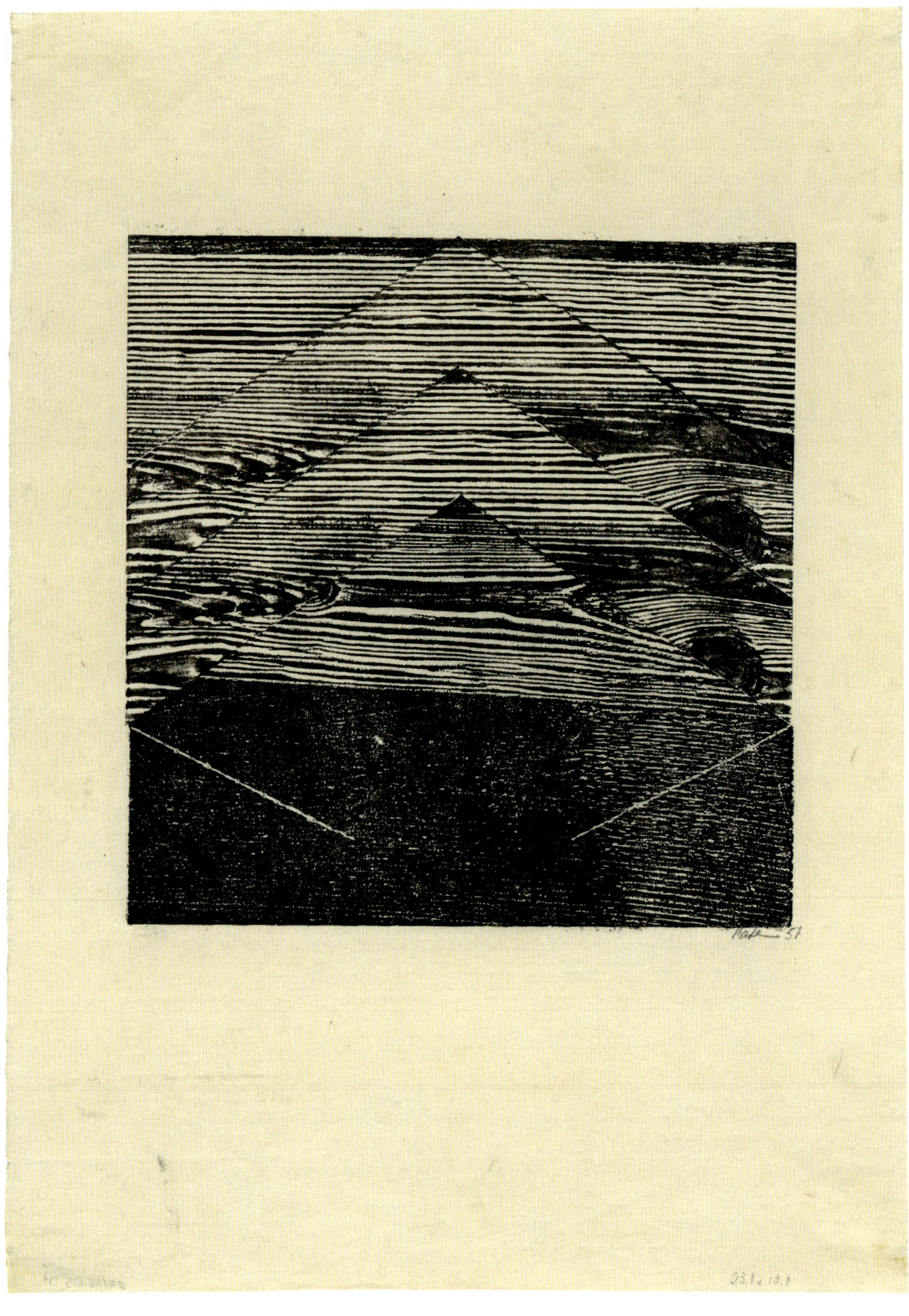

40 *TECELAR* (WEAVING), 1957

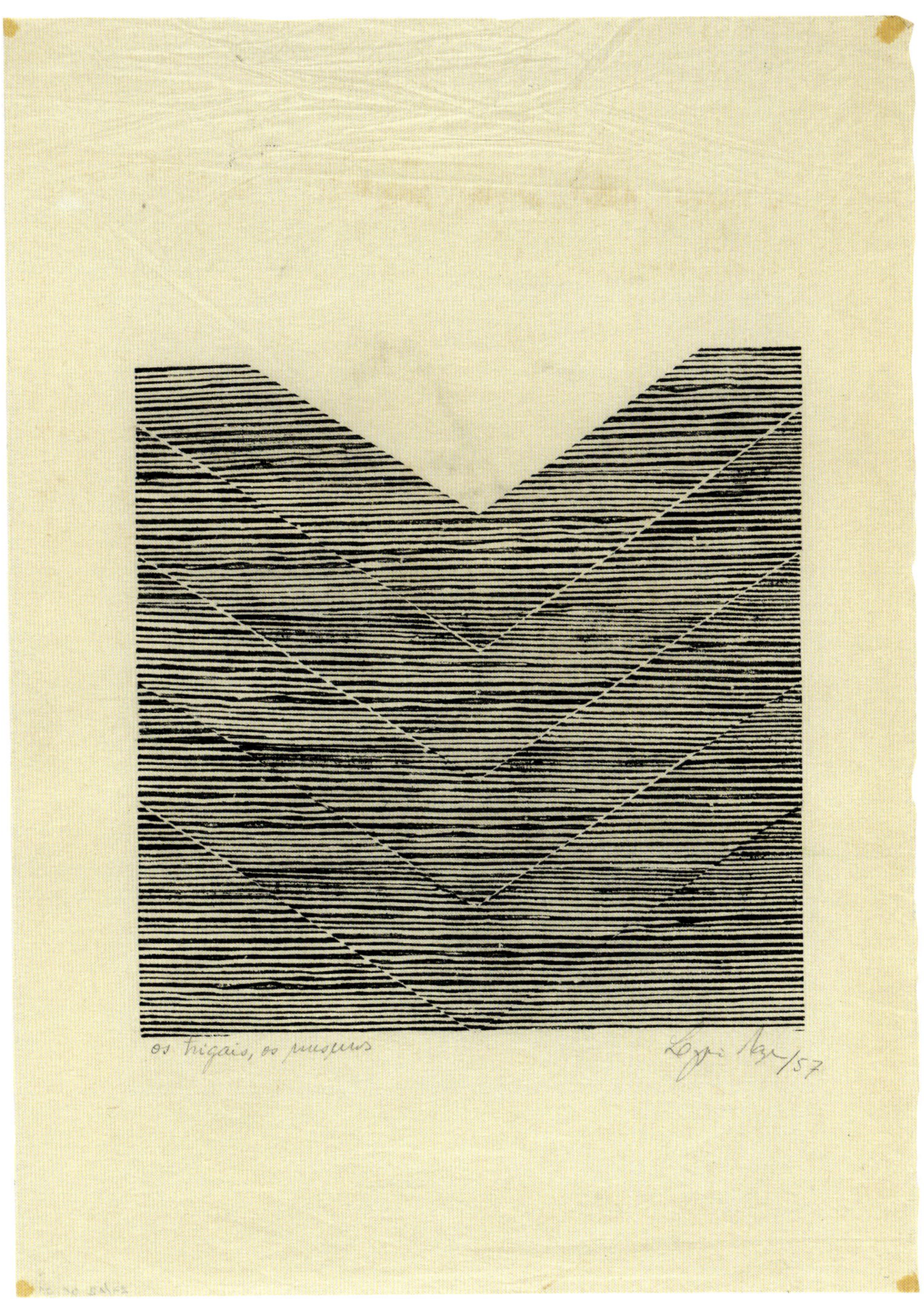

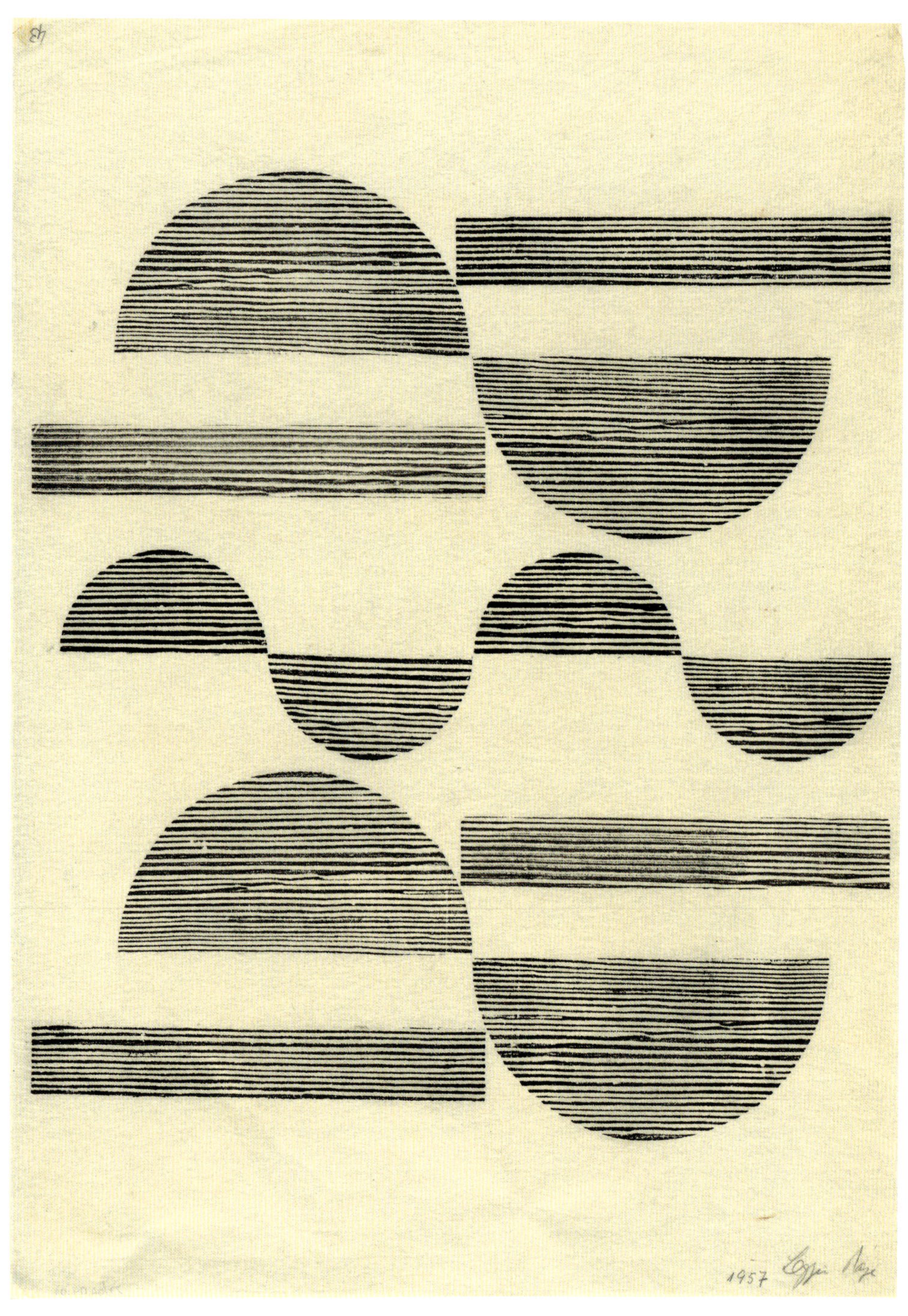
1957

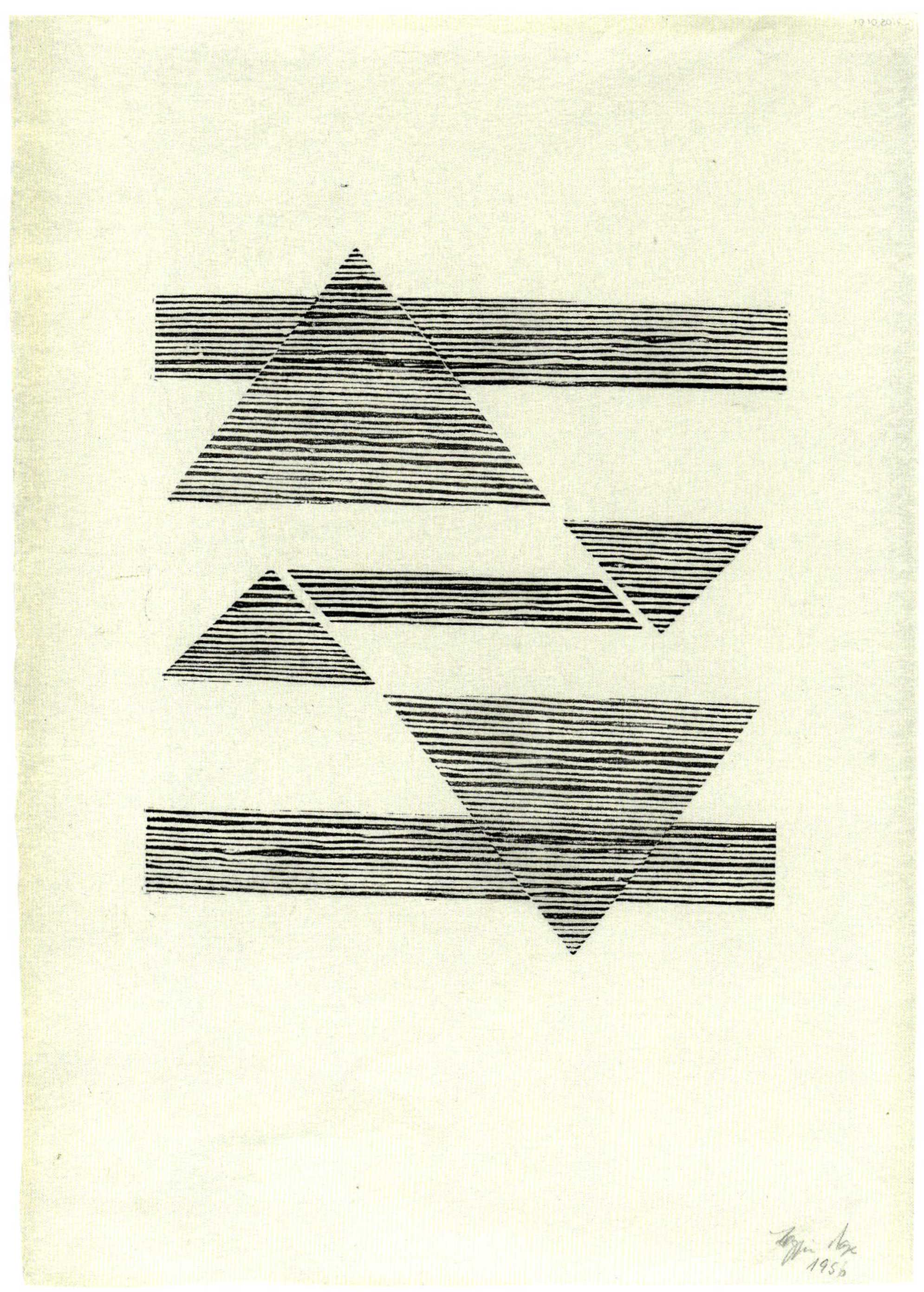

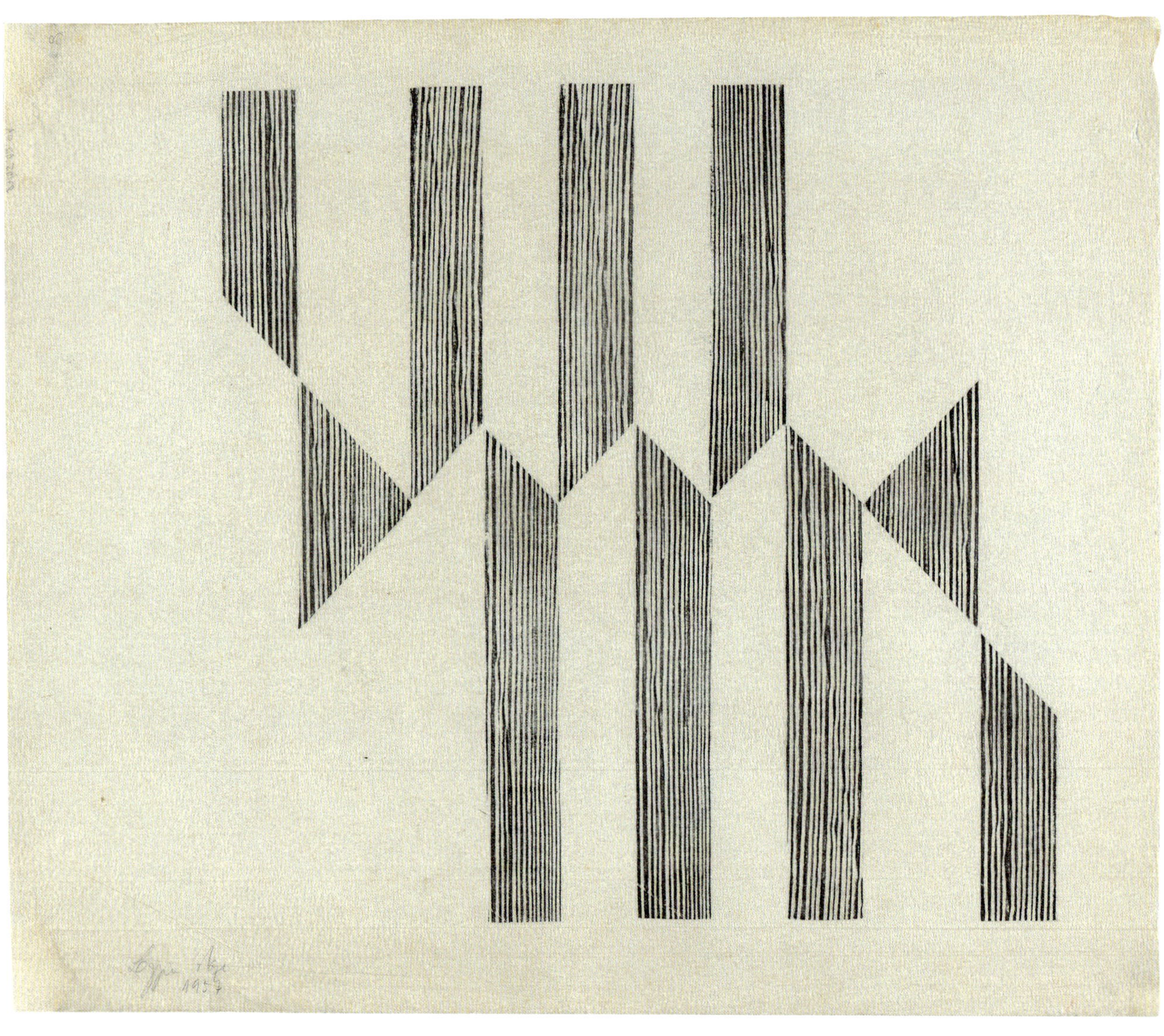

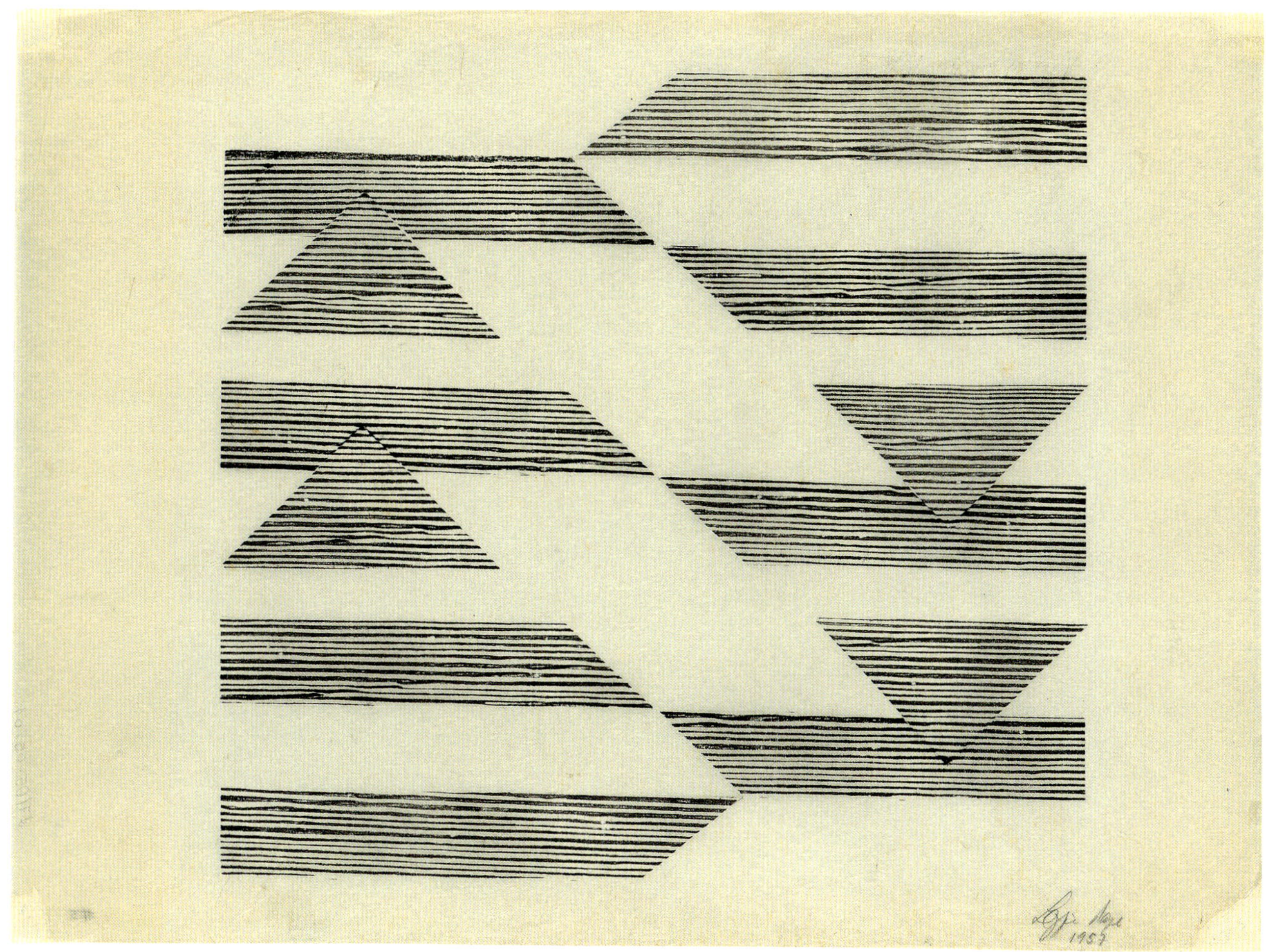

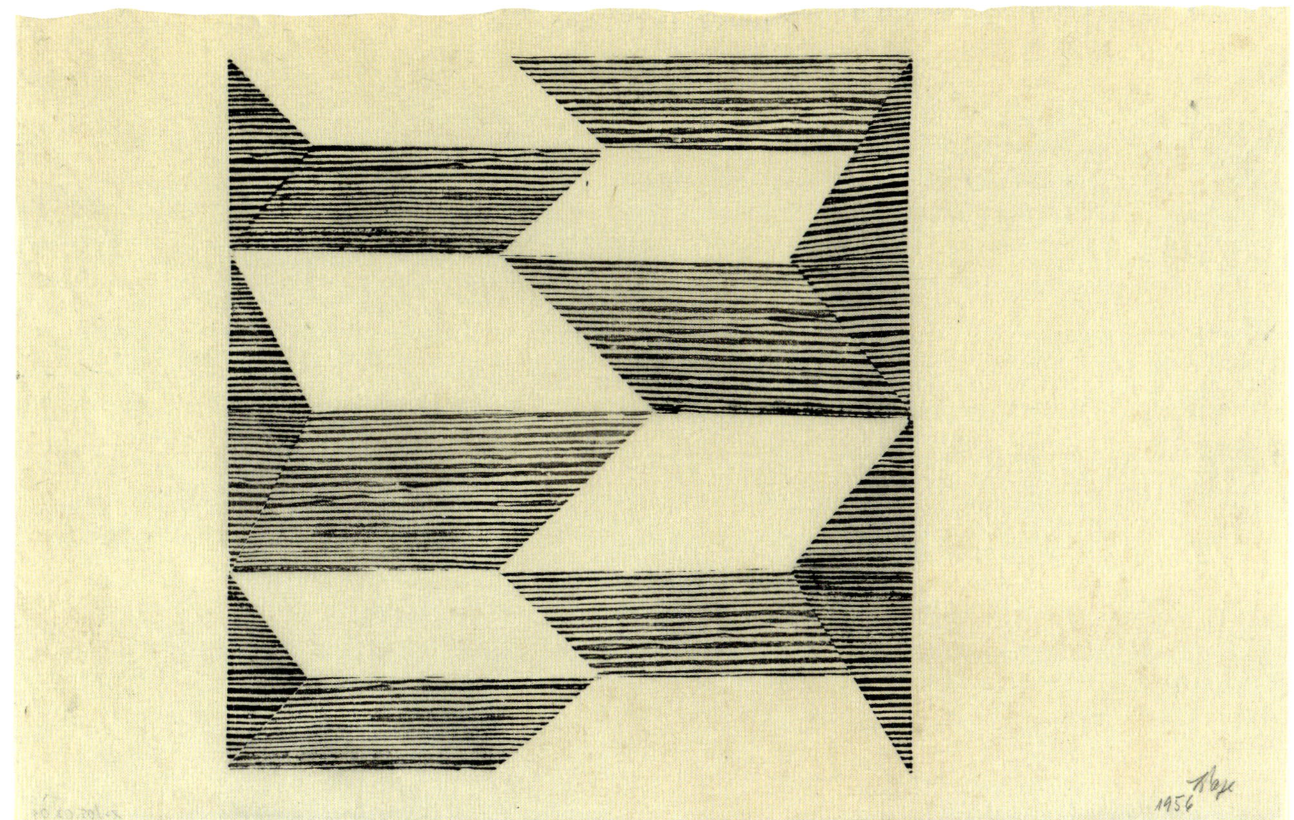

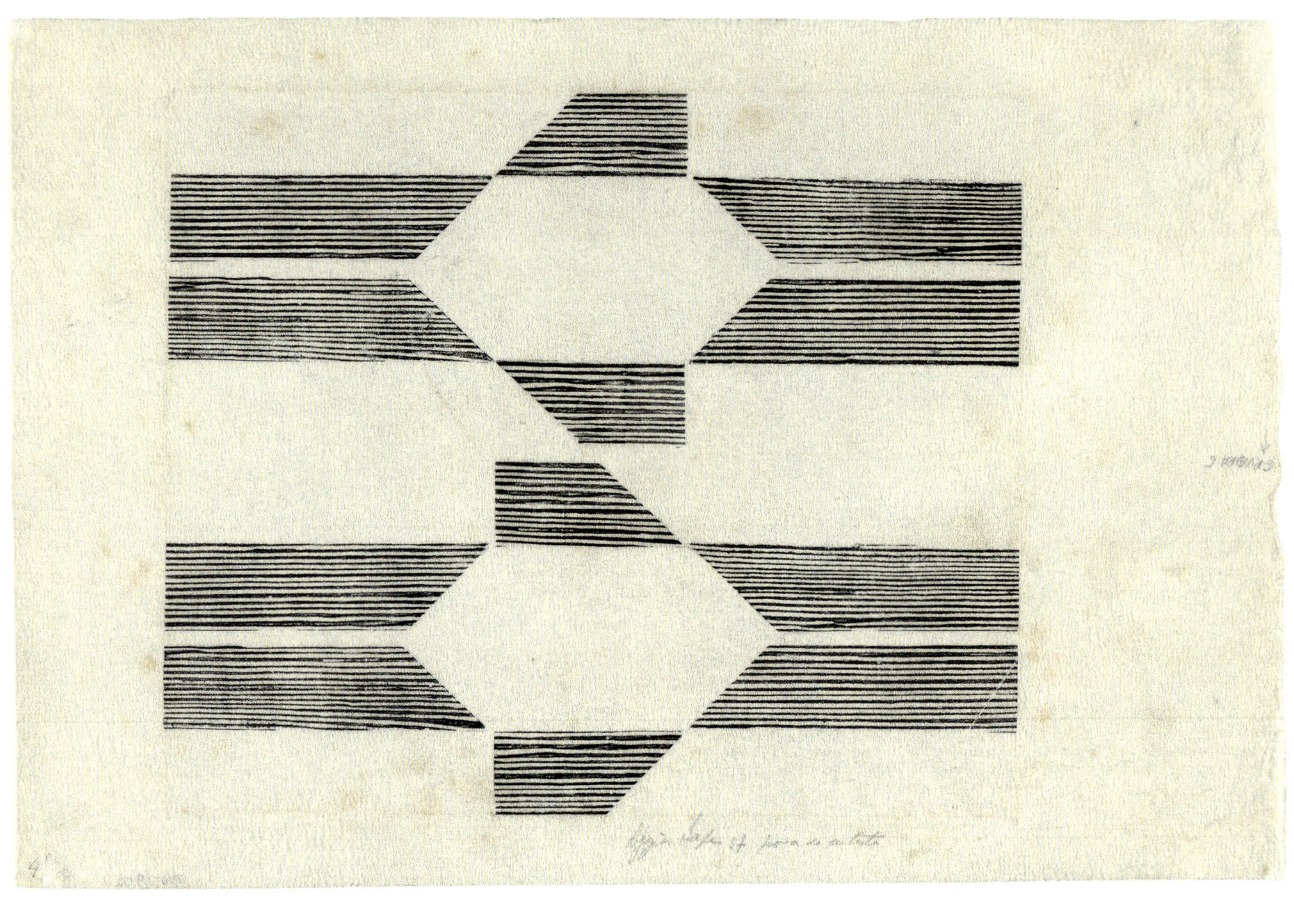

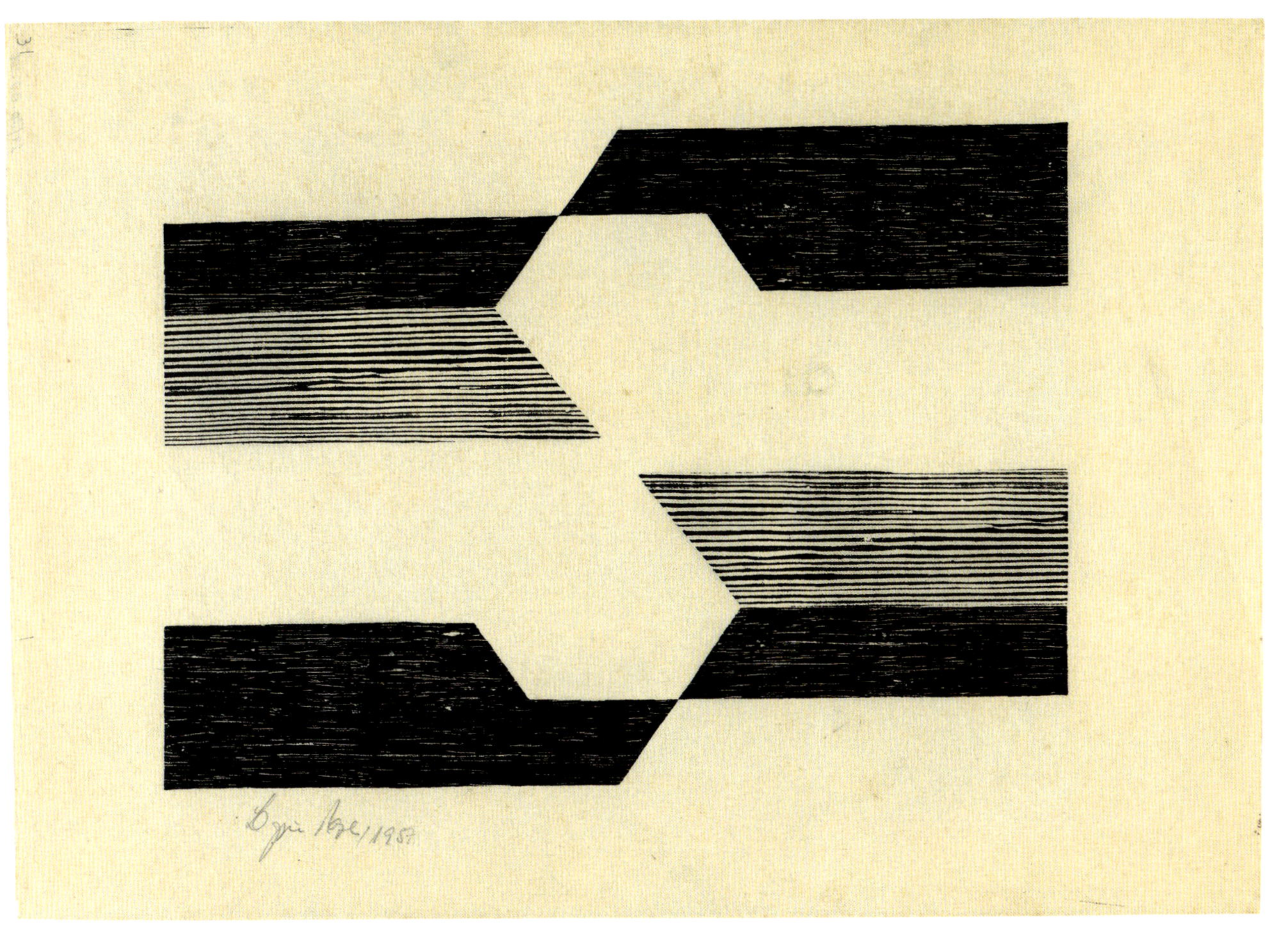

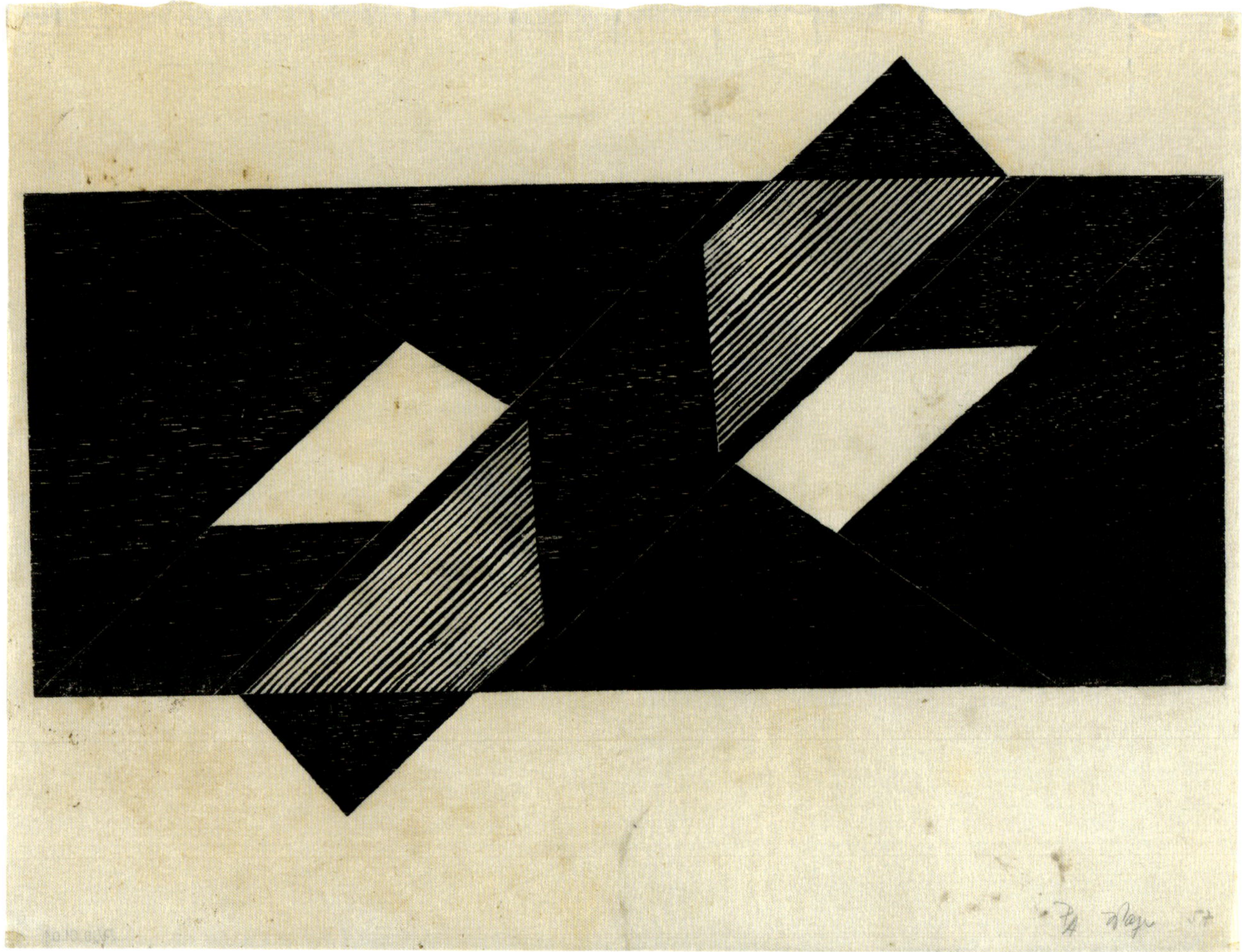

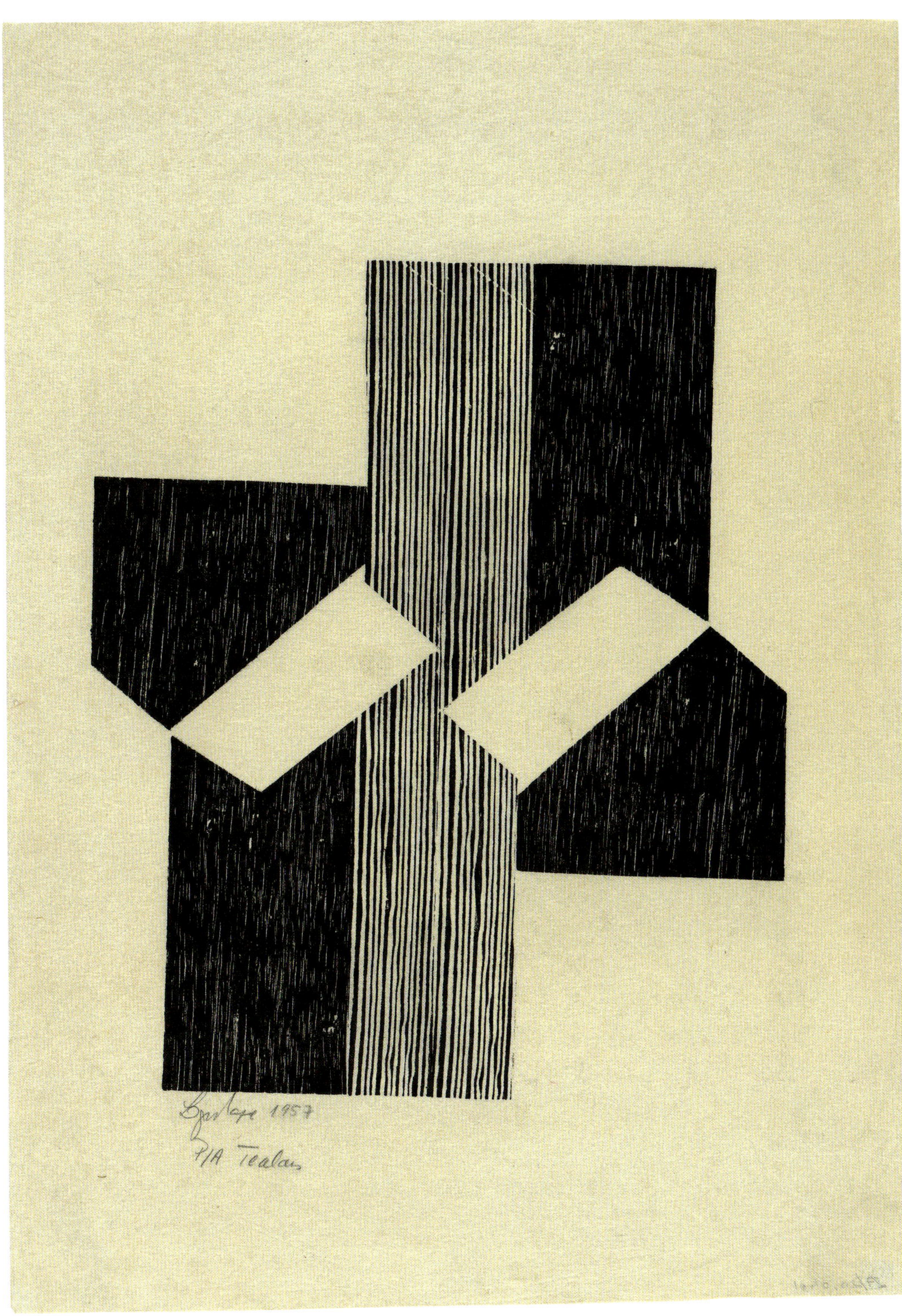

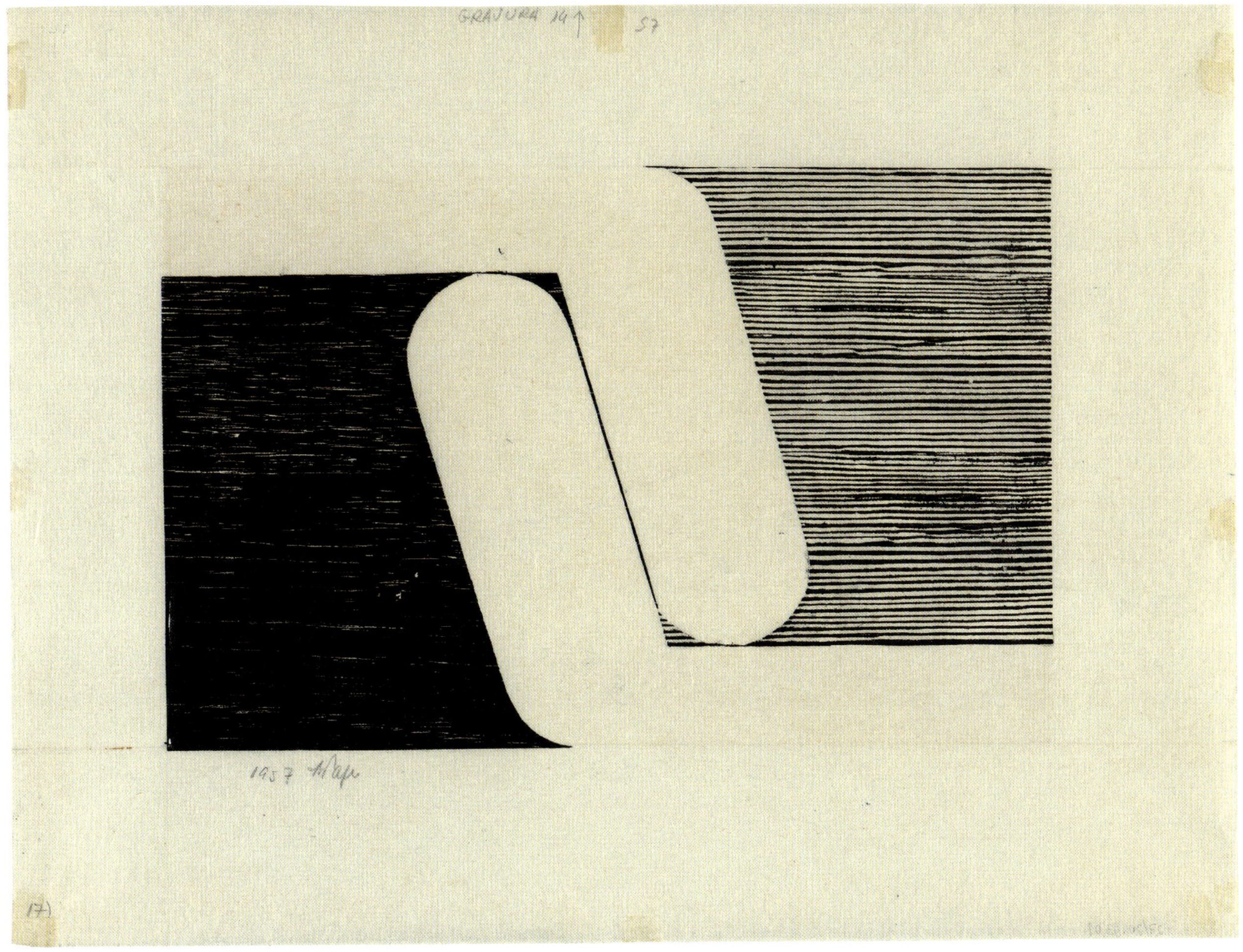

51 *TECELAR* (WEAVING), 1957

52 *TECELAR* (WEAVING), 1957

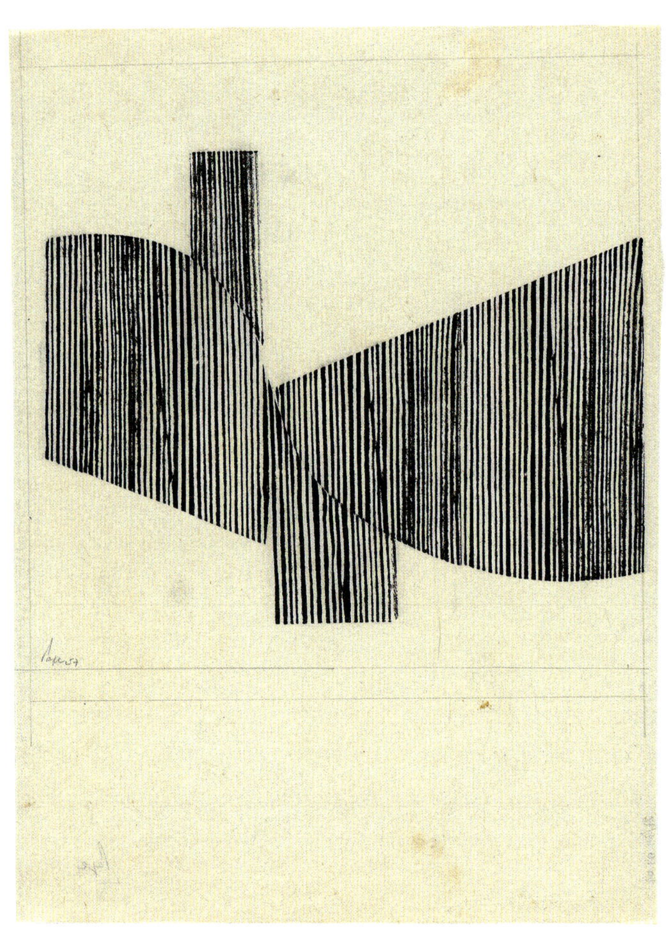

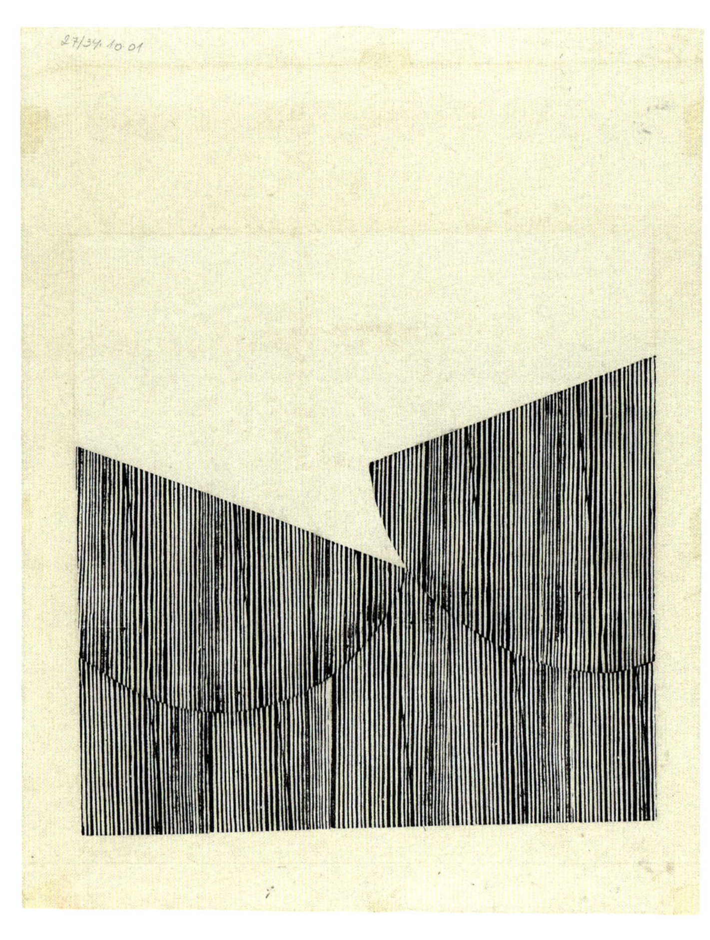

53 *TECELAR* (WEAVING), 1957

54 *TECELAR* (WEAVING), 1957

55 *TECELAR* (WEAVING), 1957

56 *TECELAR* (WEAVING), 1957

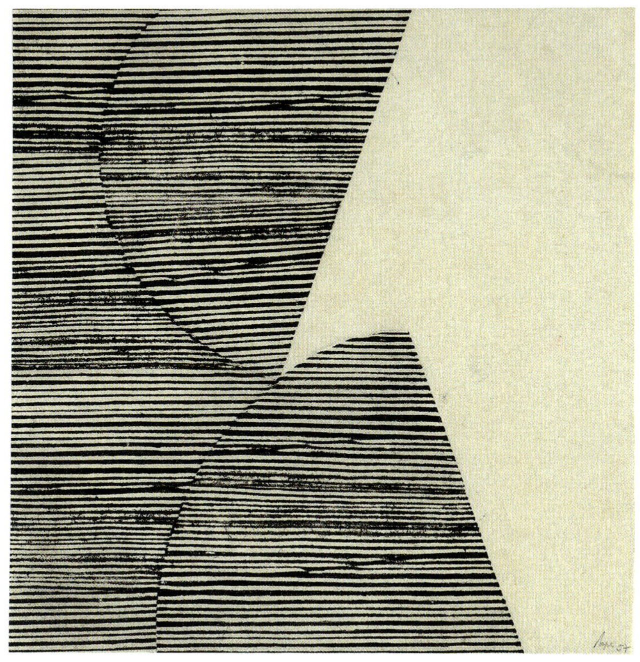

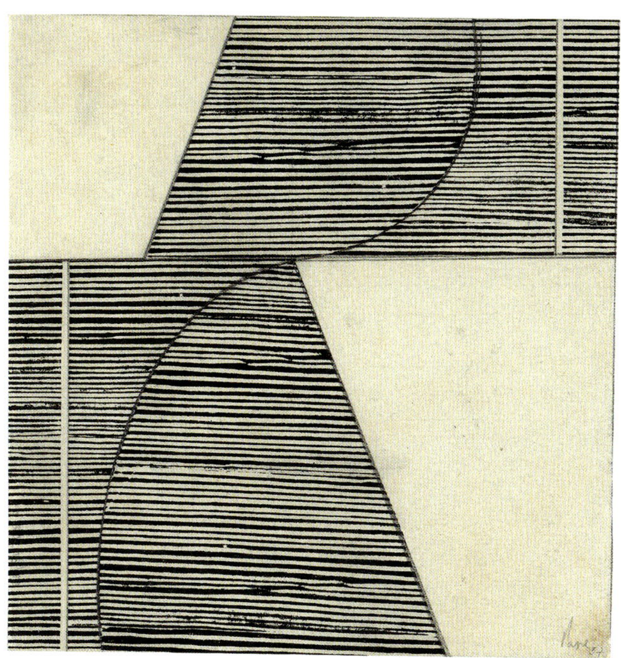

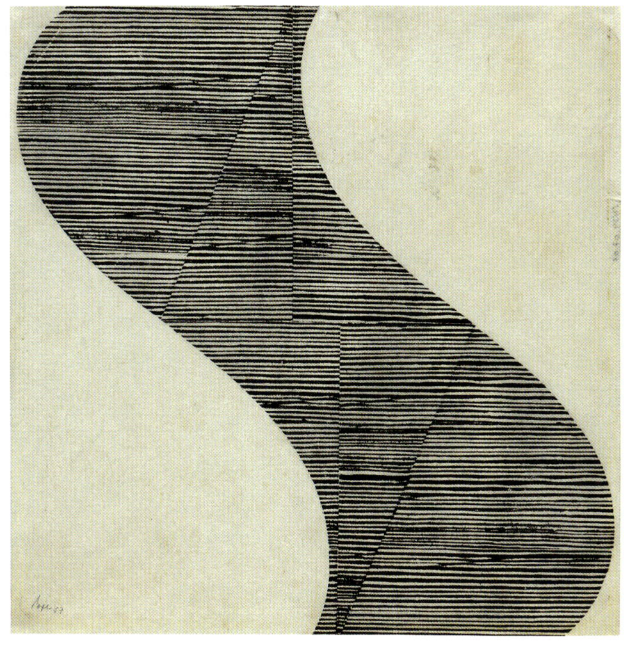

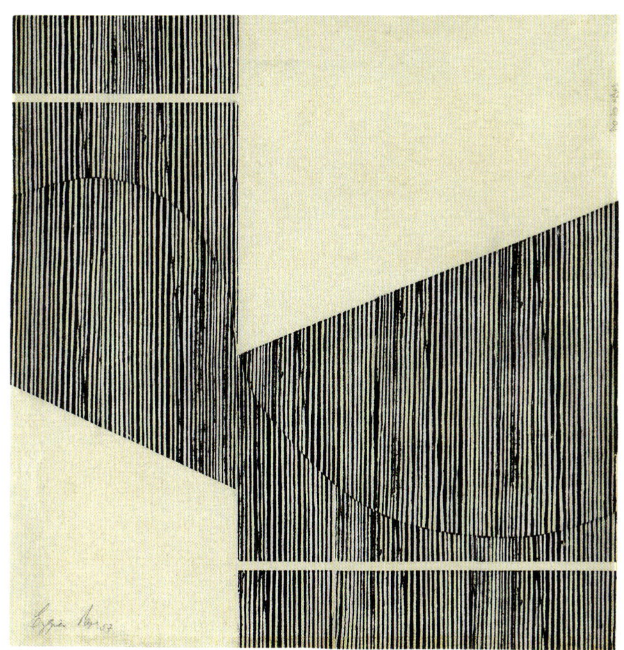

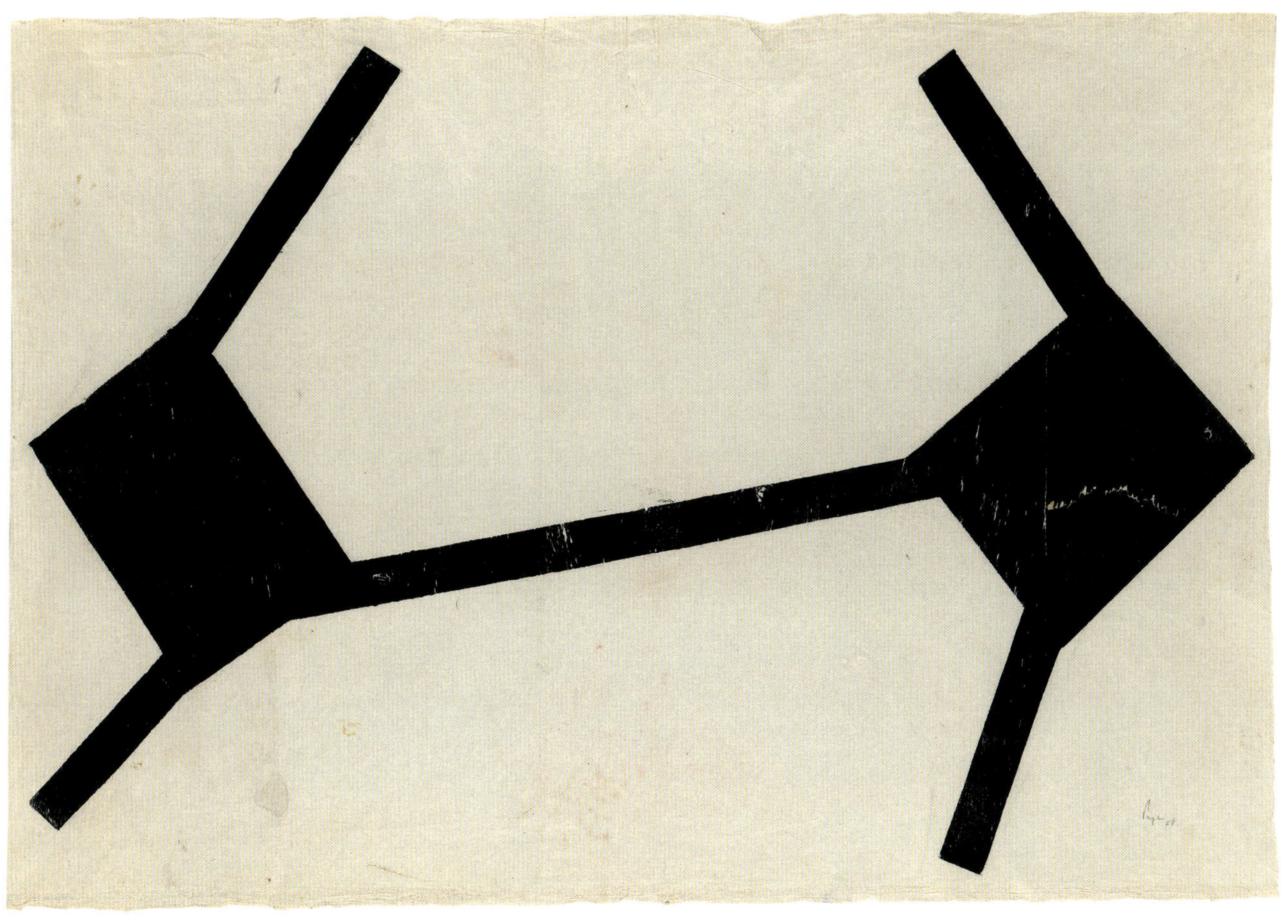

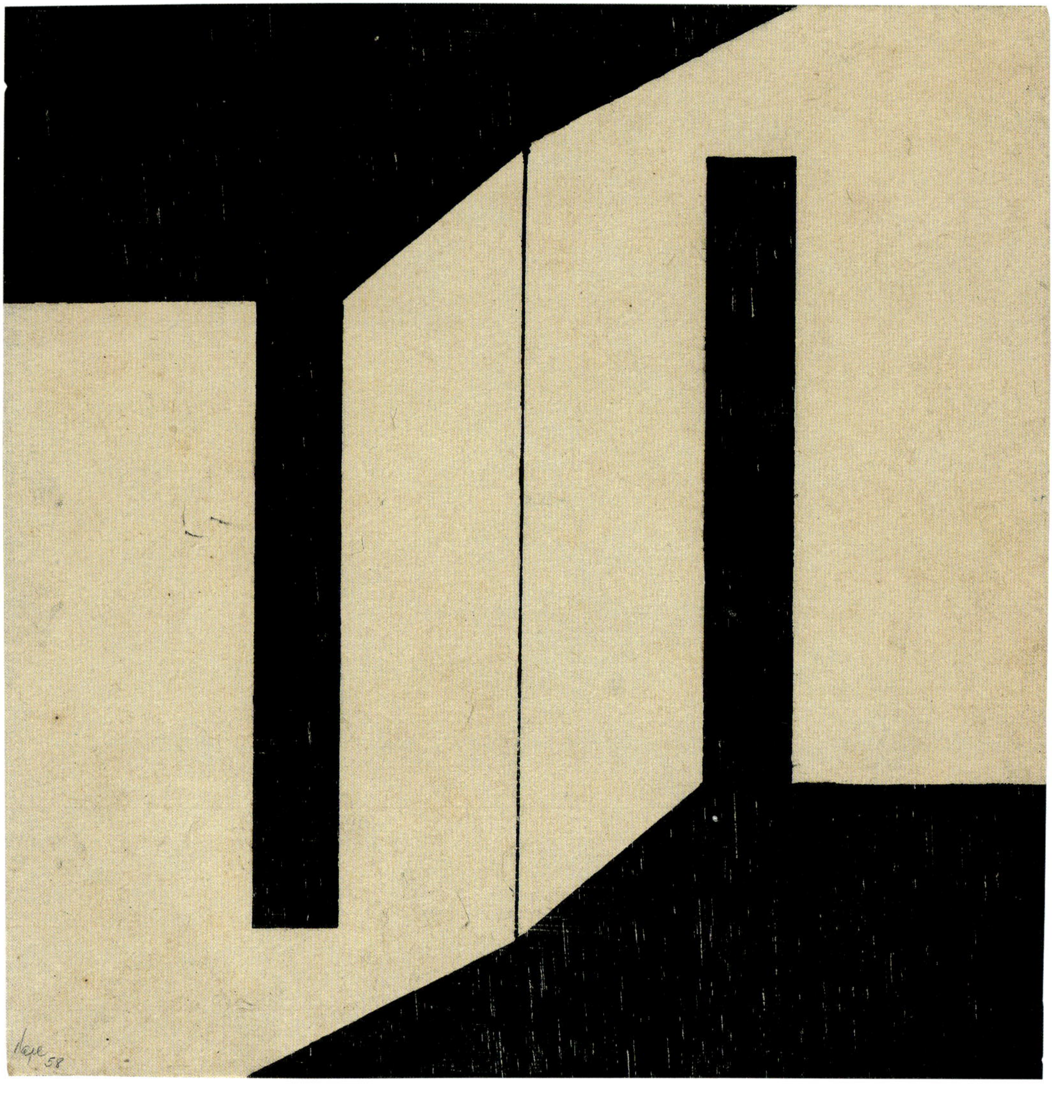

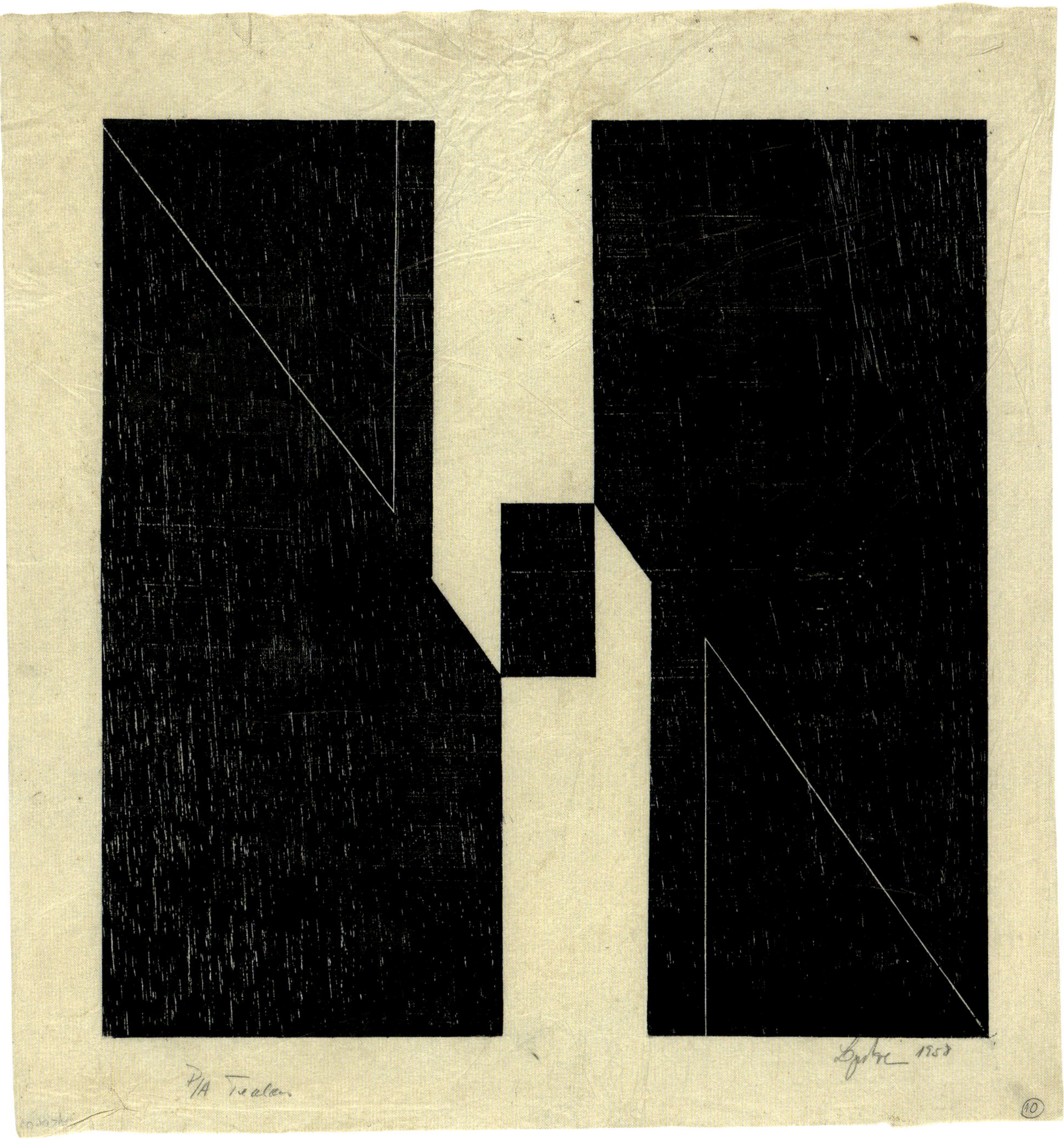

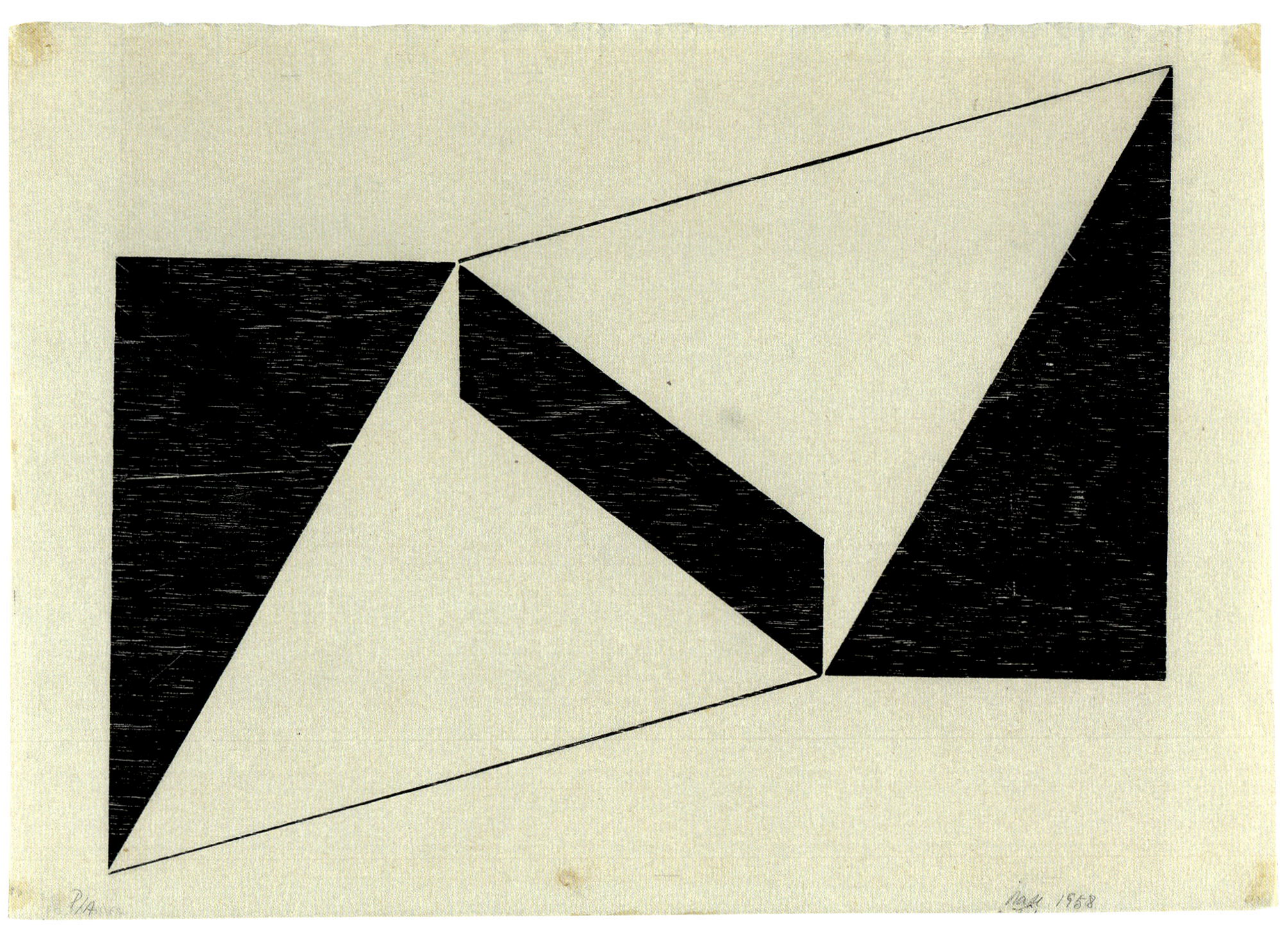

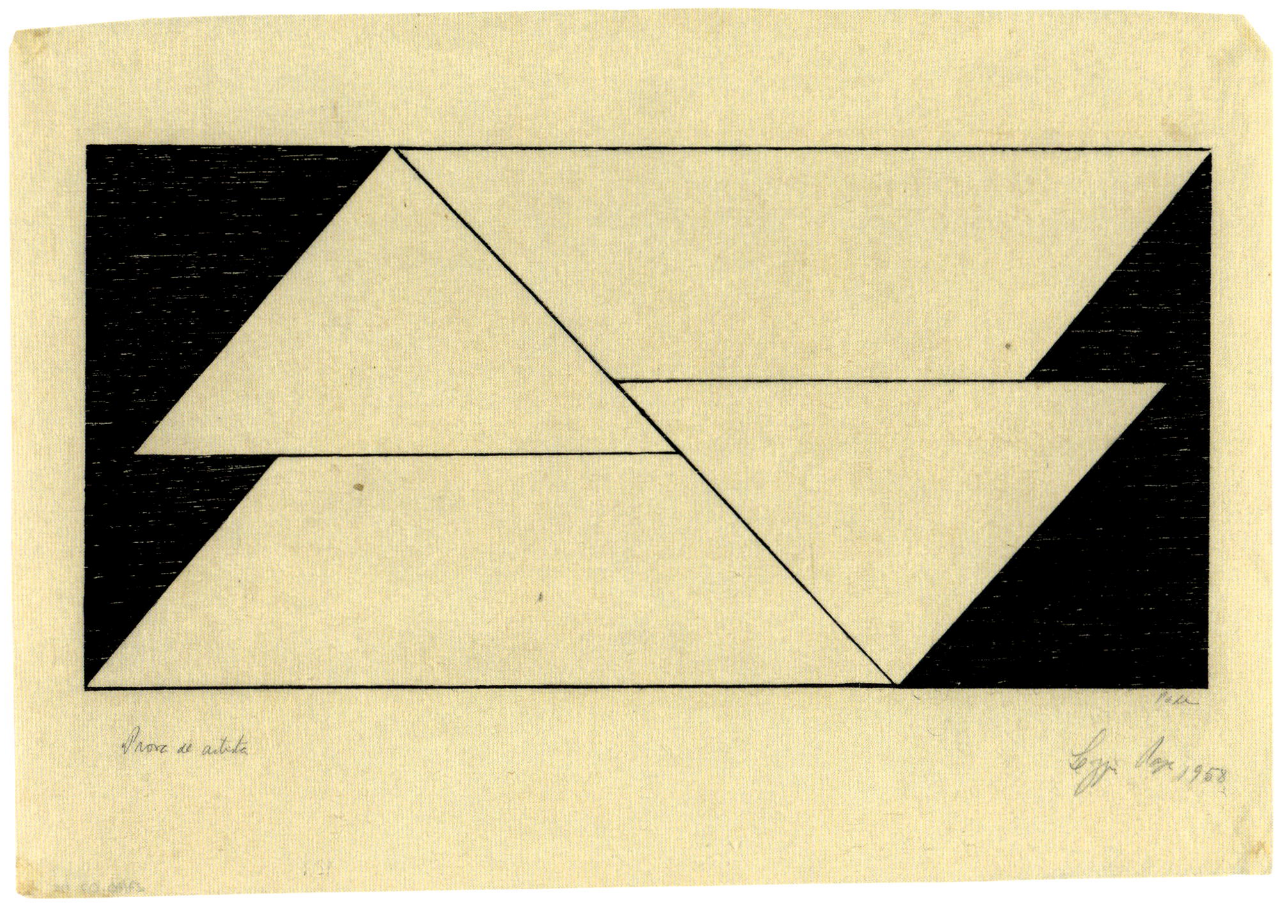

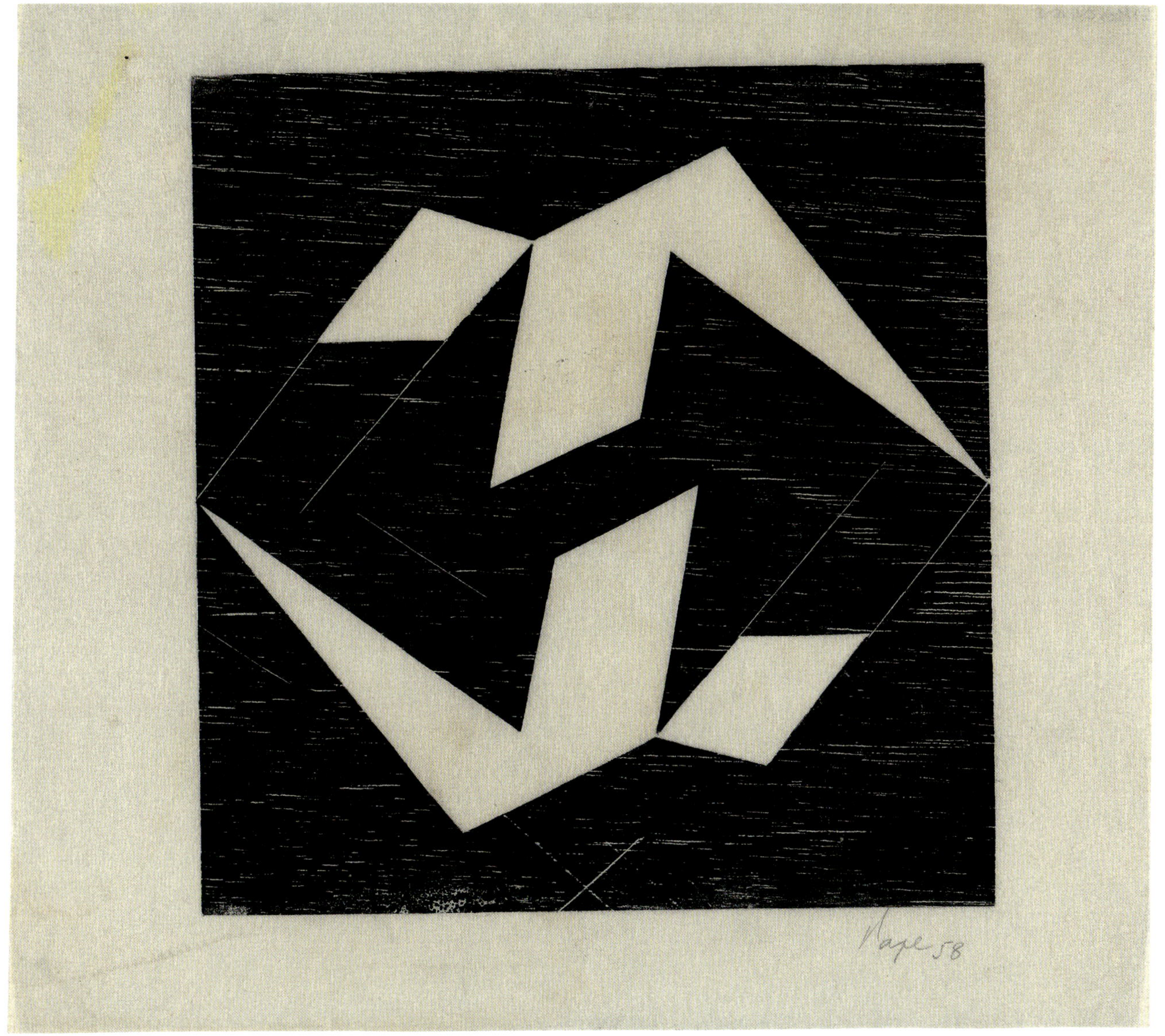

63 *TECELAR* (WEAVING), 1959

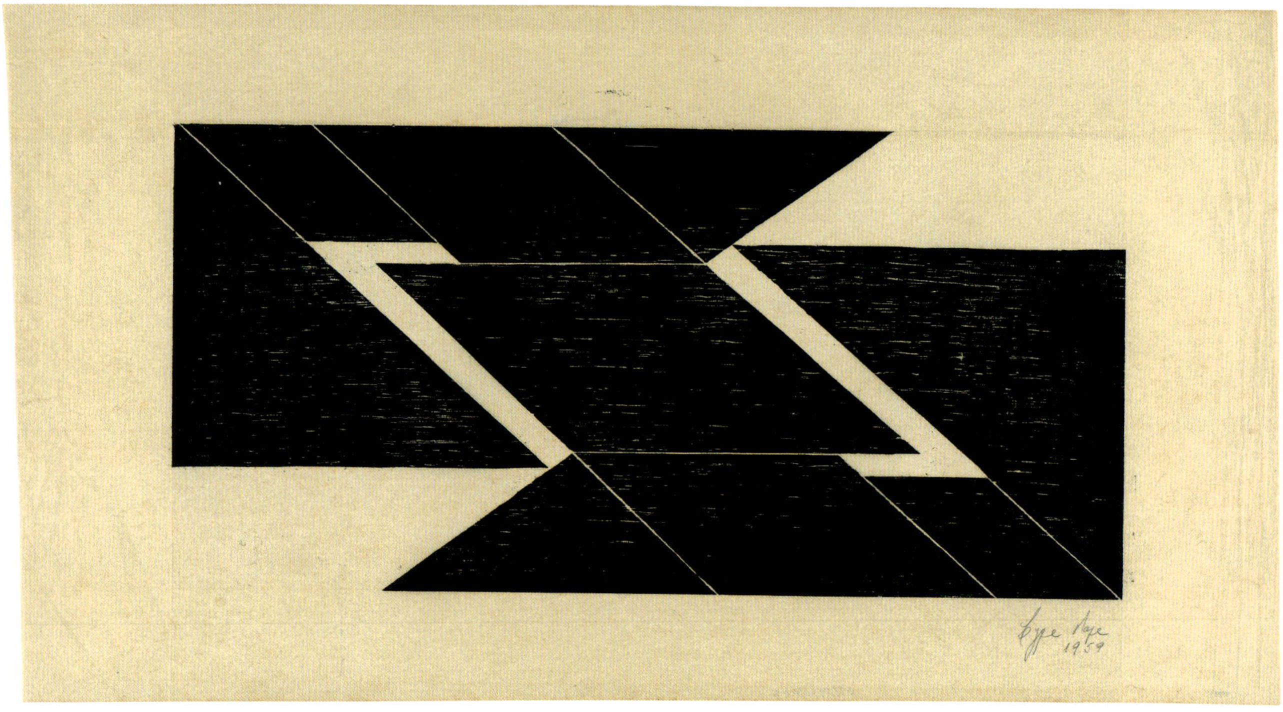

64 *TECELAR* (WEAVING), 1958

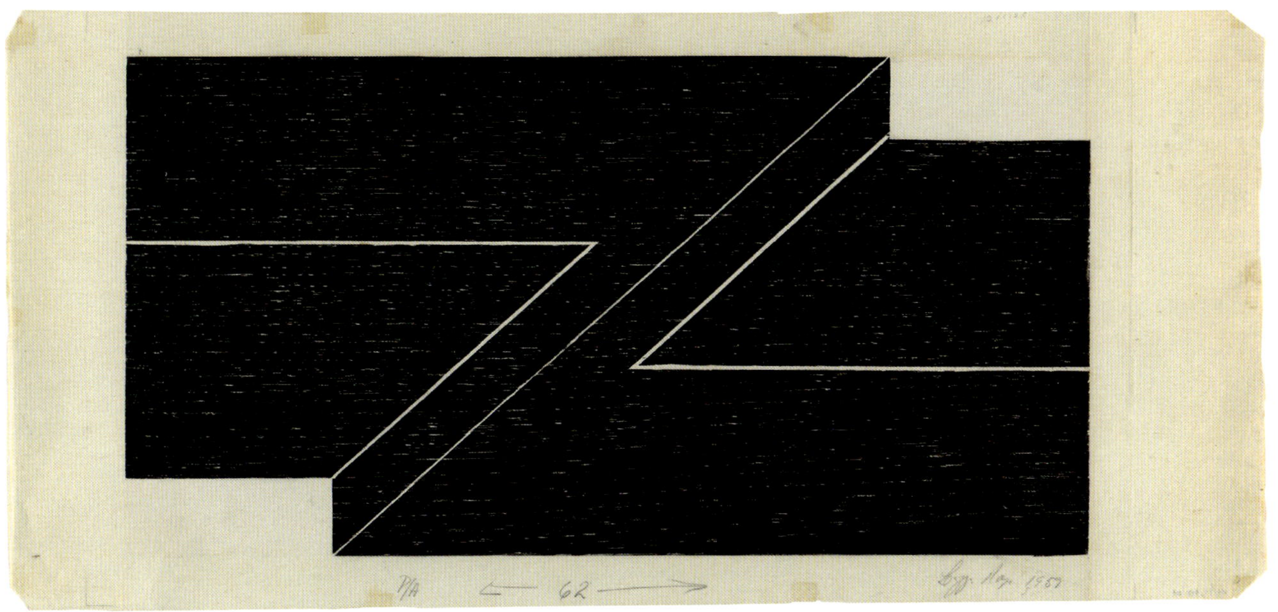

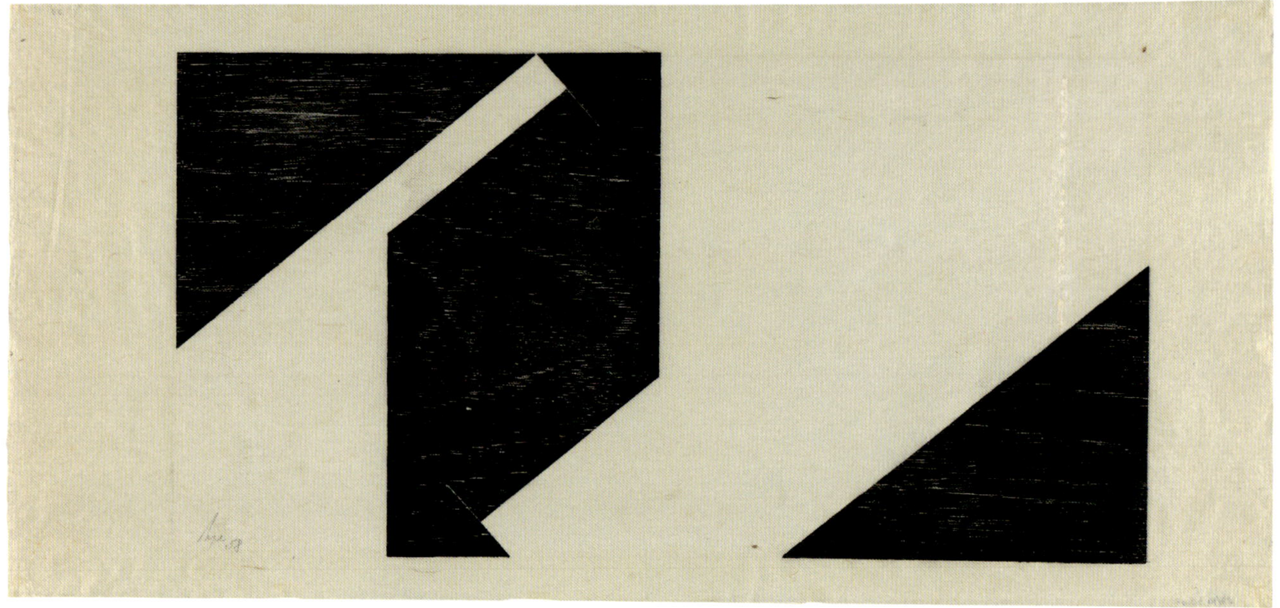

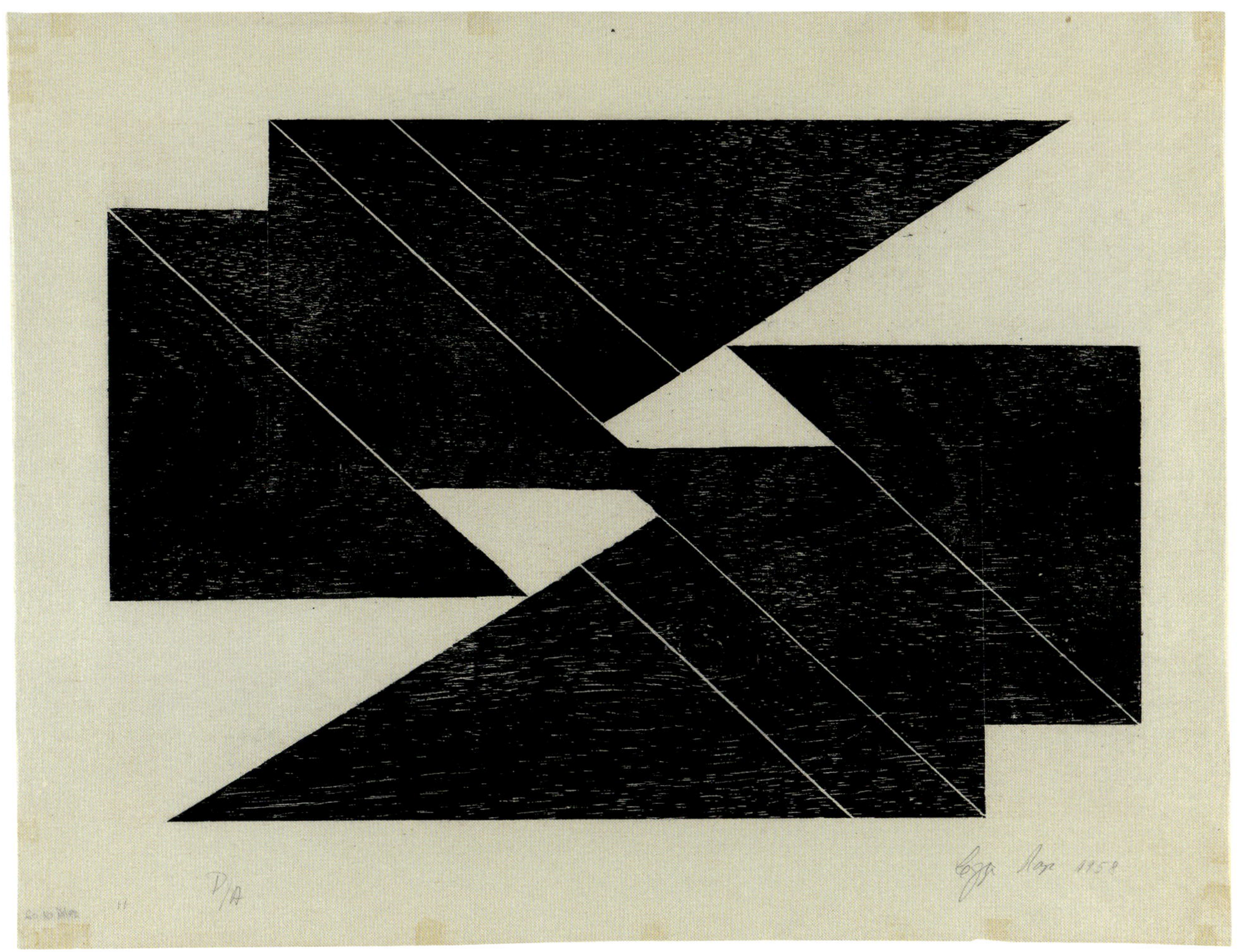

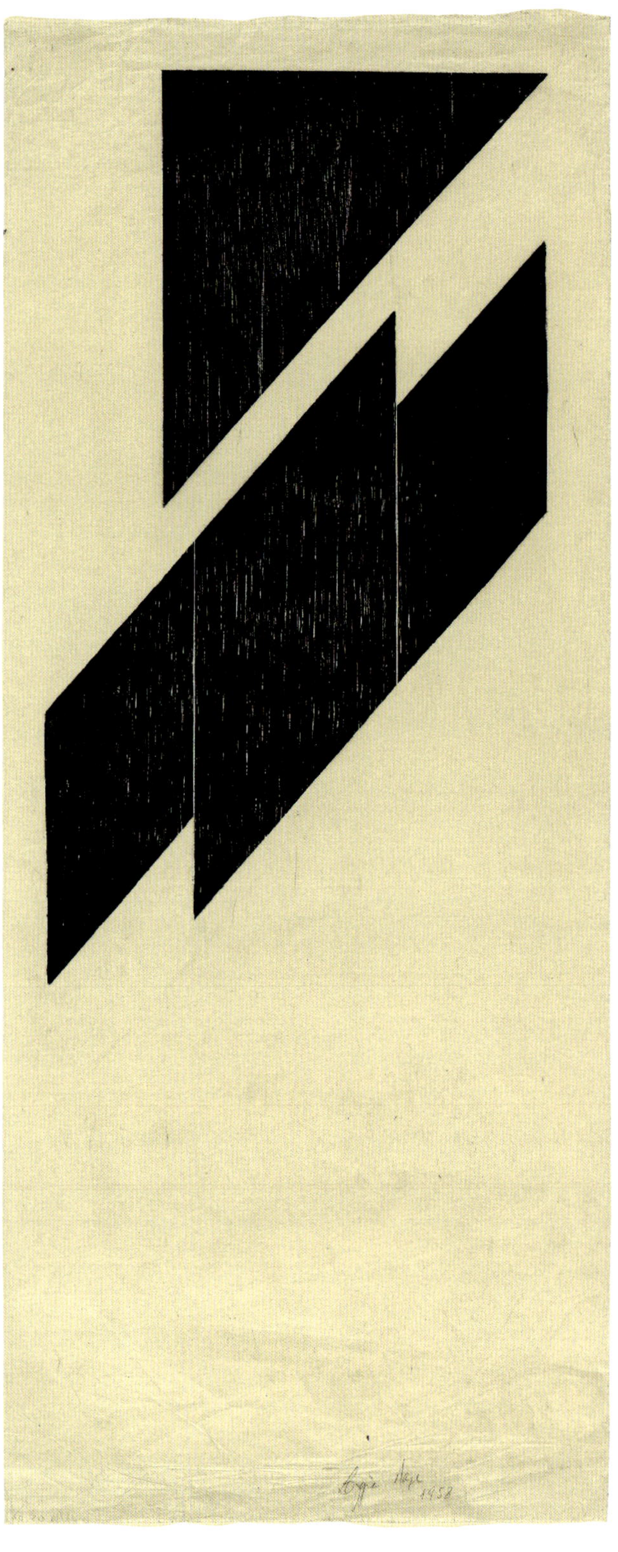

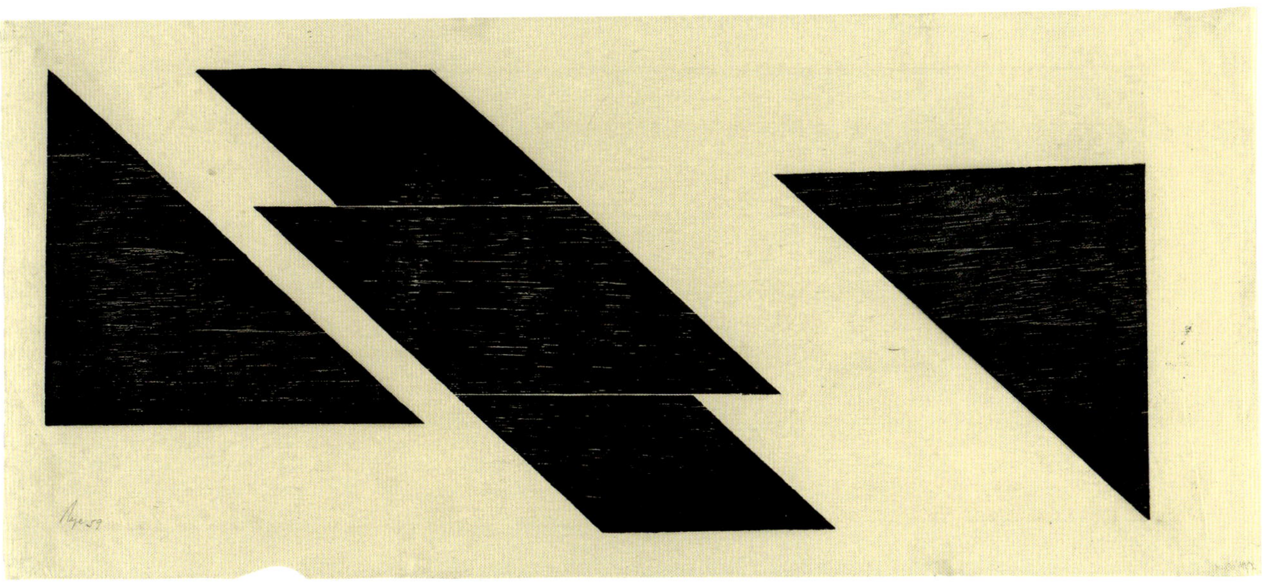

69 *TECELAR* (WEAVING), 1958

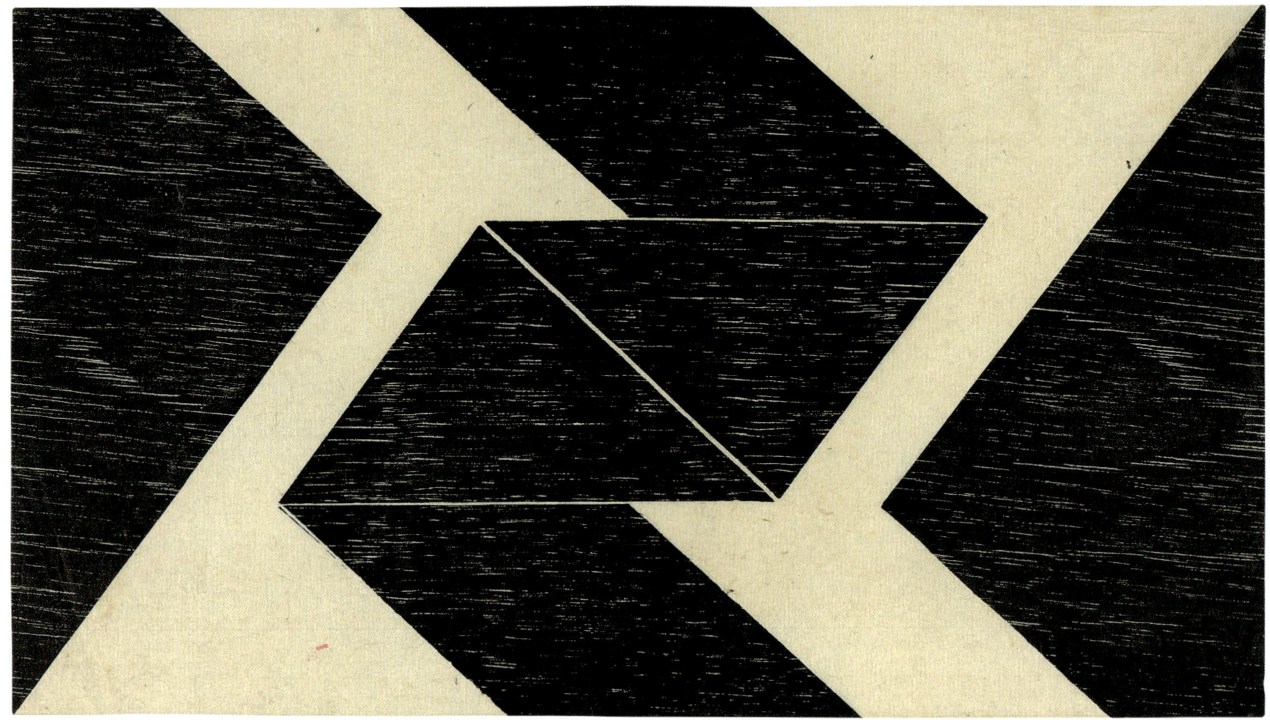

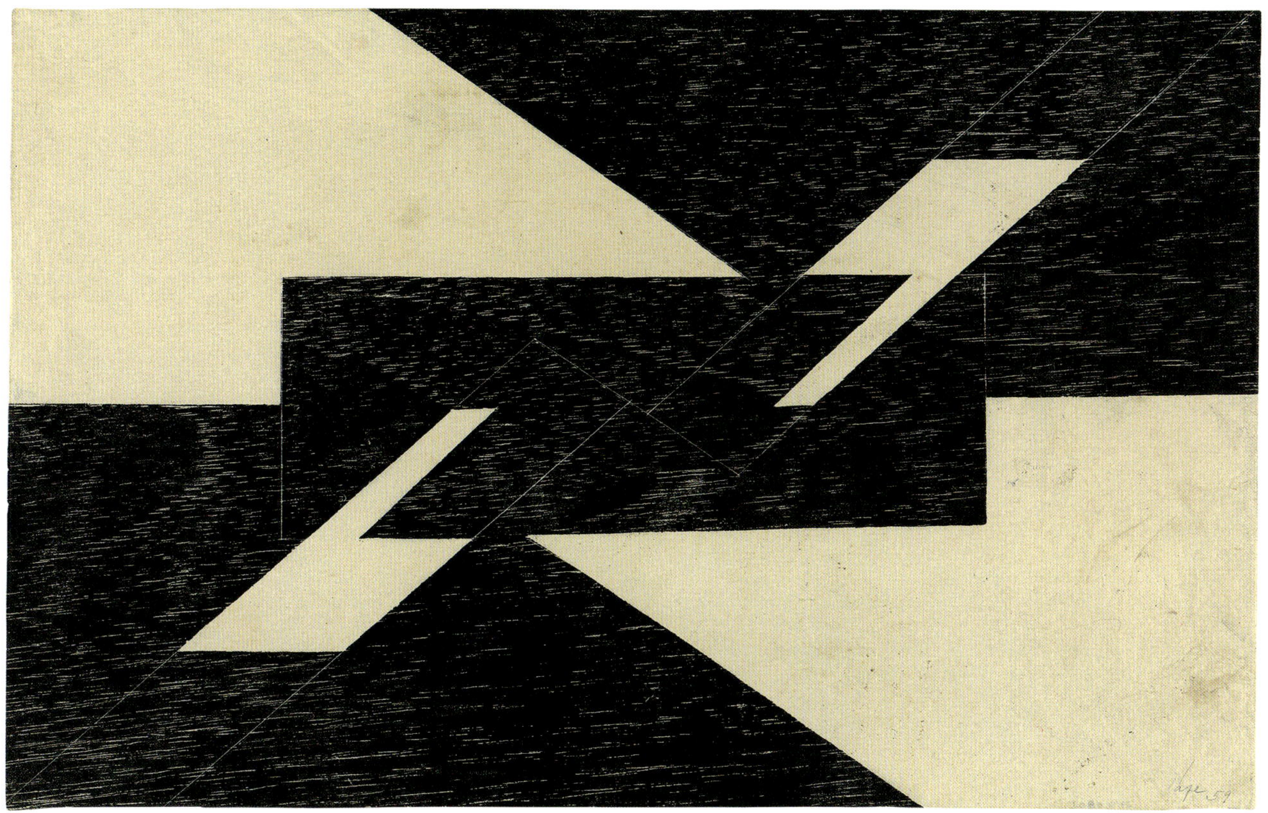

71 *TECELAR* (WEAVING), 1958

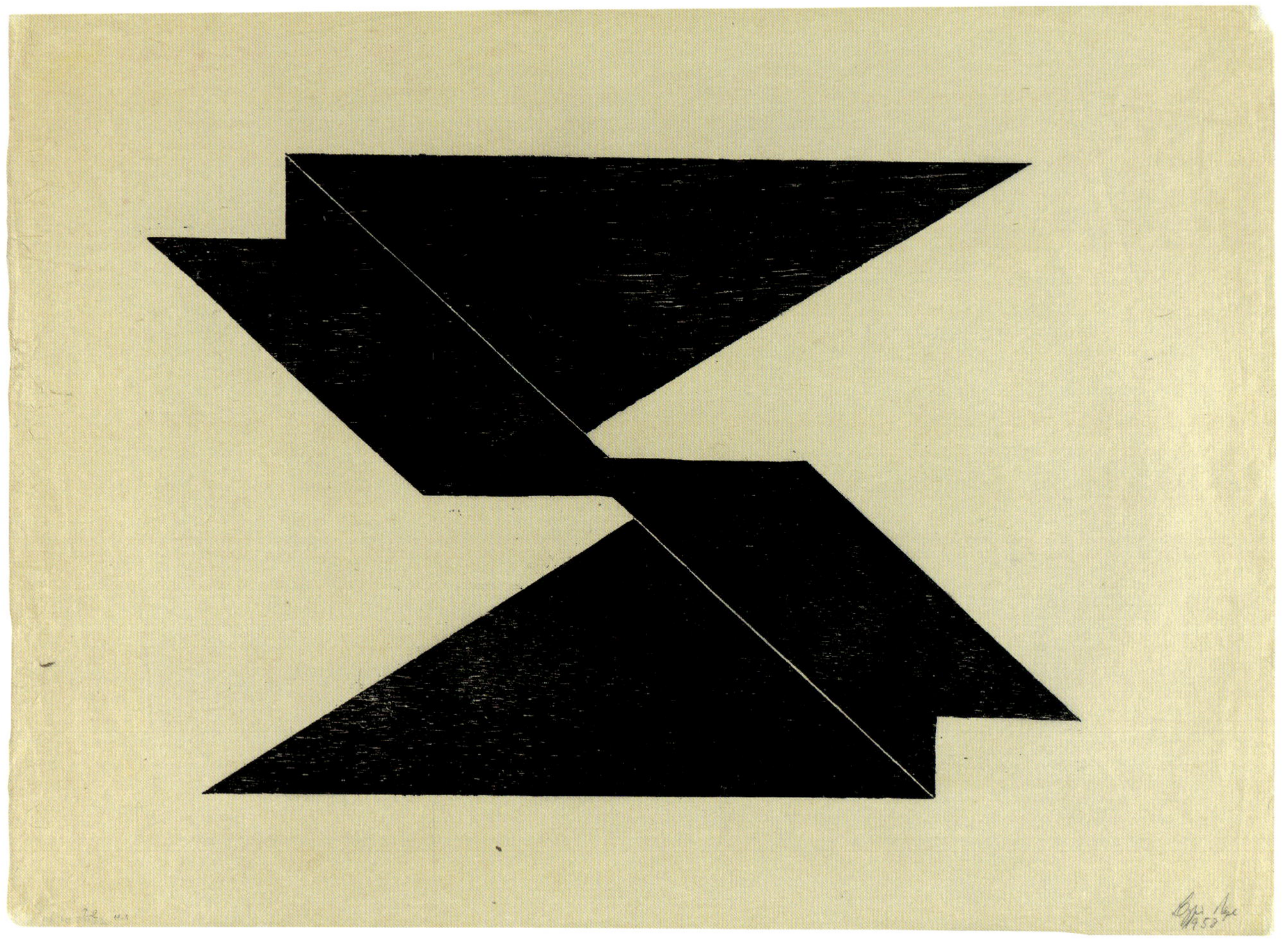

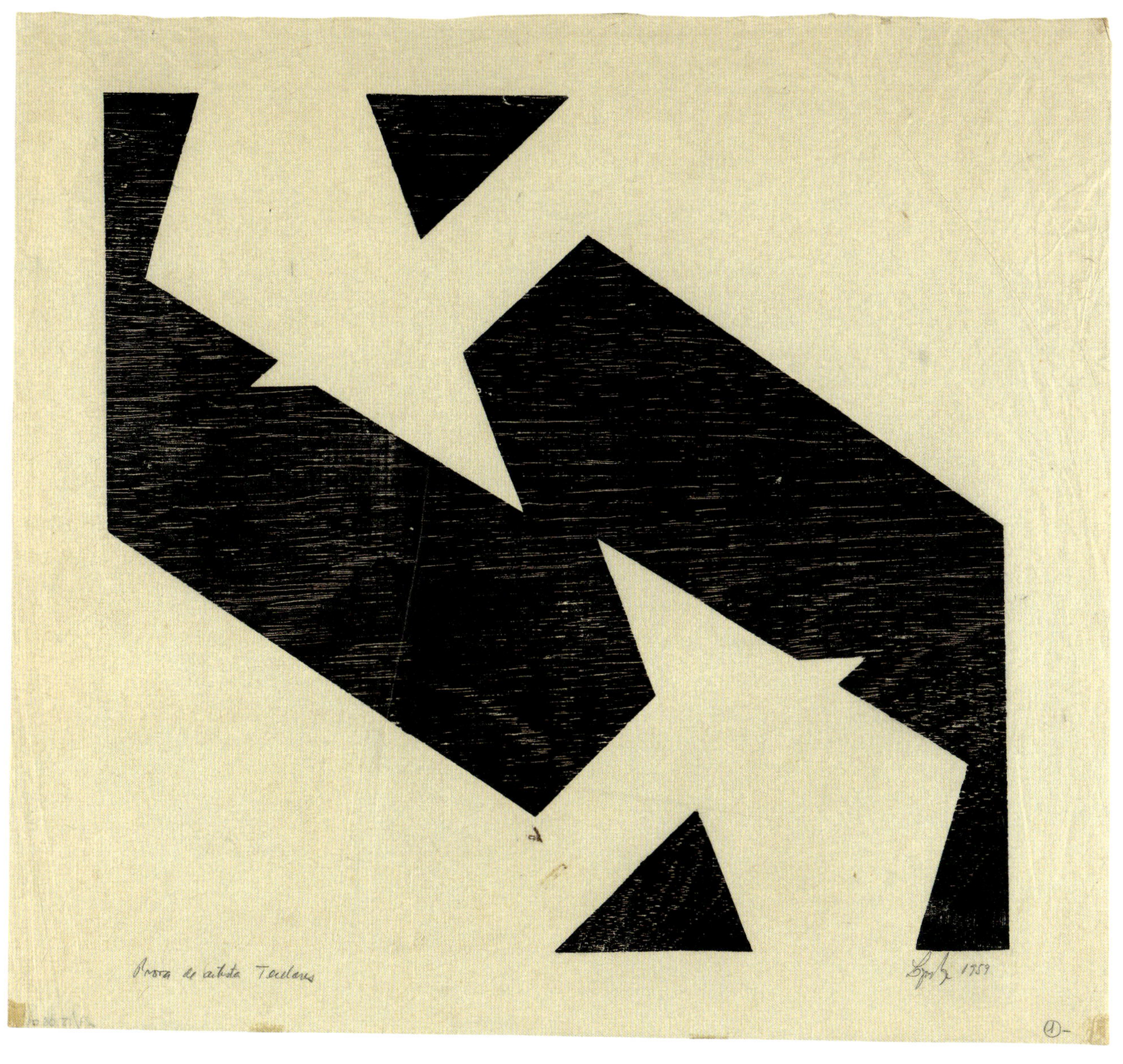

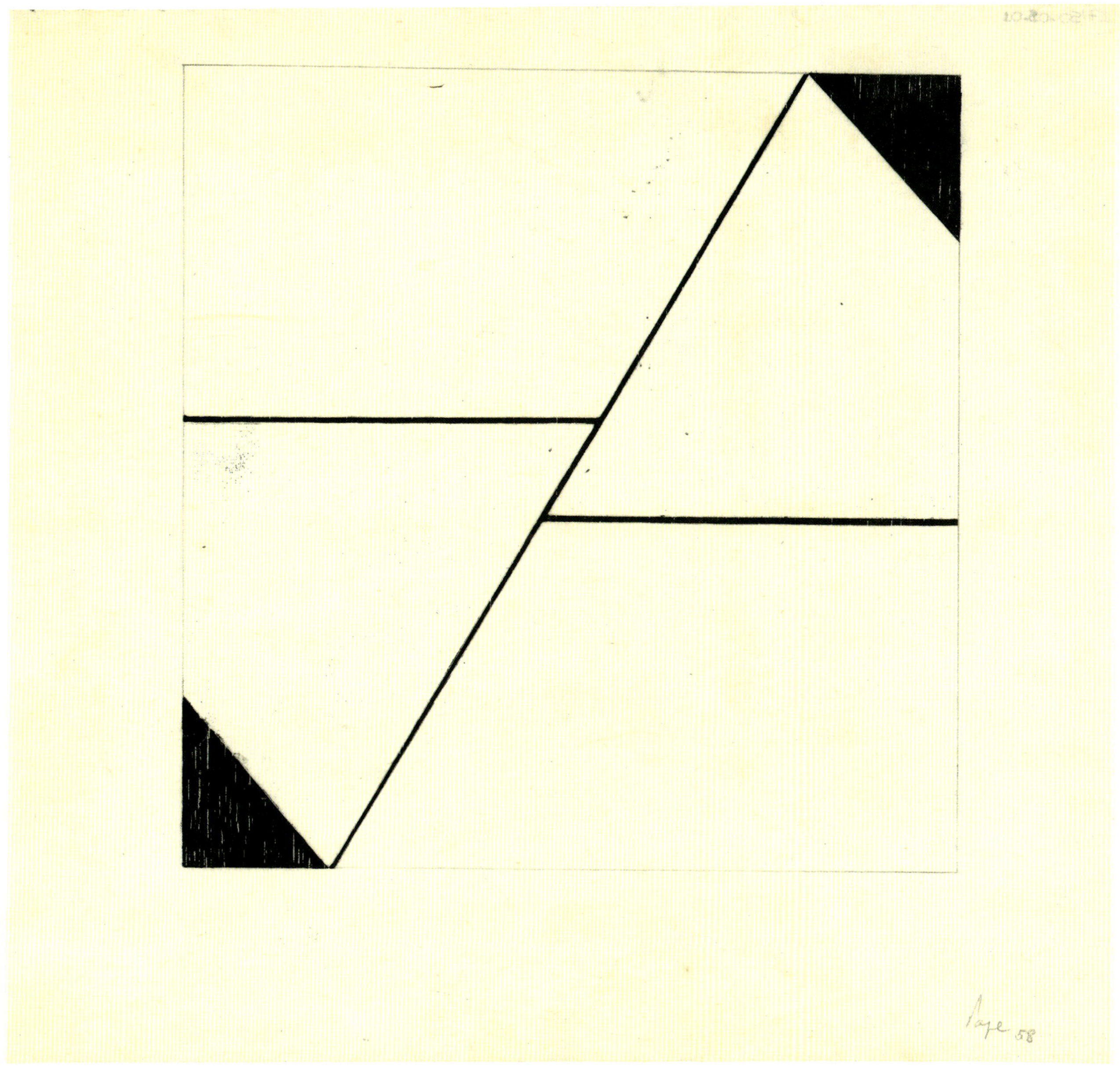

76 *TECELAR* (WEAVING), 1958

77 *TECELAR* (WEAVING), 1958

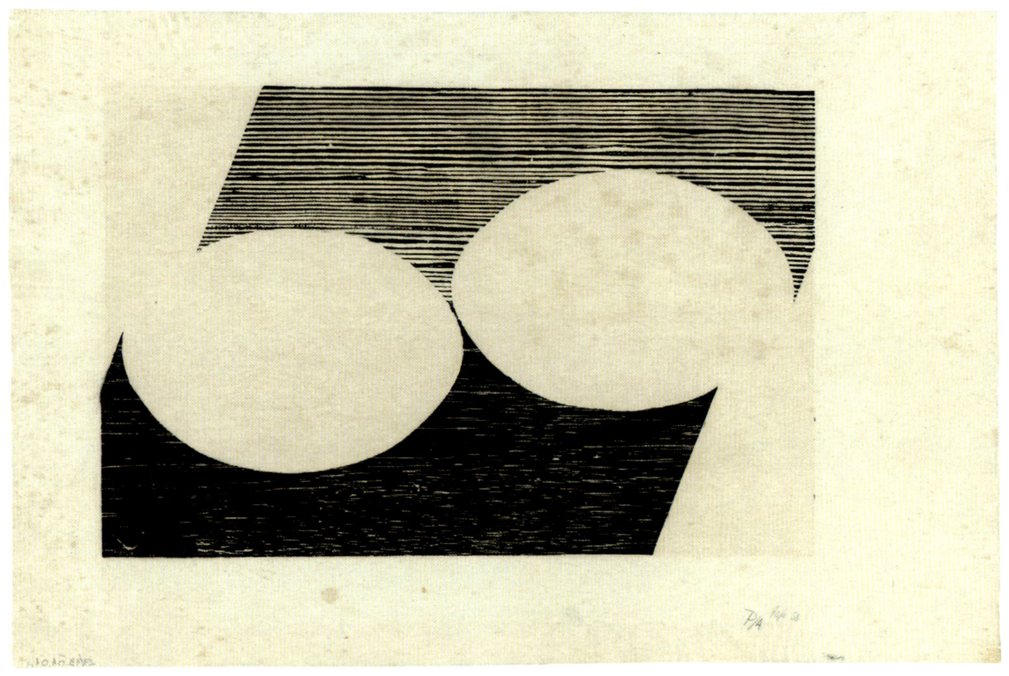

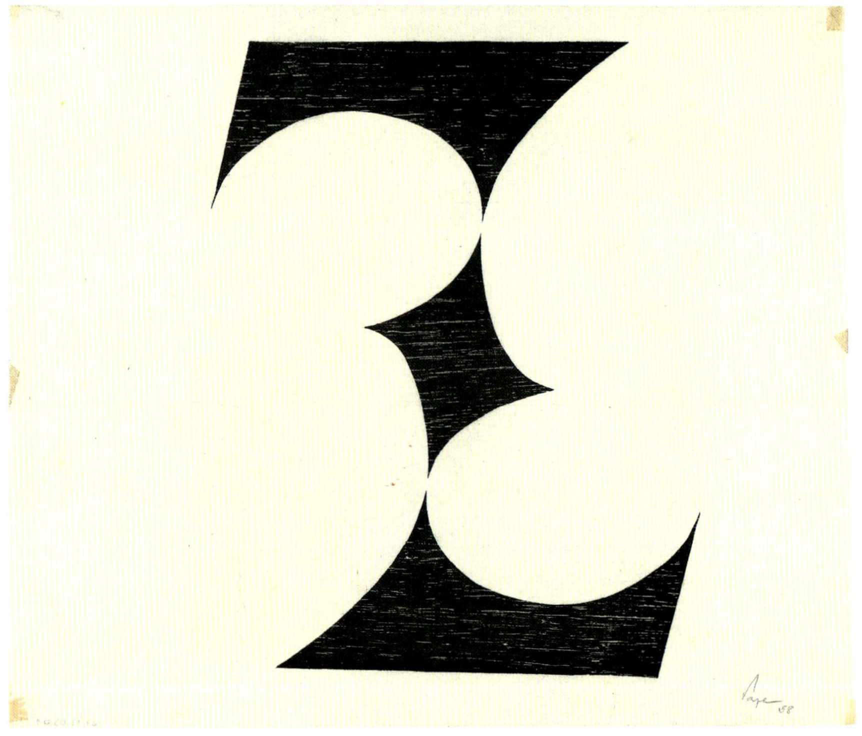

78 *TECELAR* (WEAVING), 1958

79 *TECELAR* (WEAVING), 1958

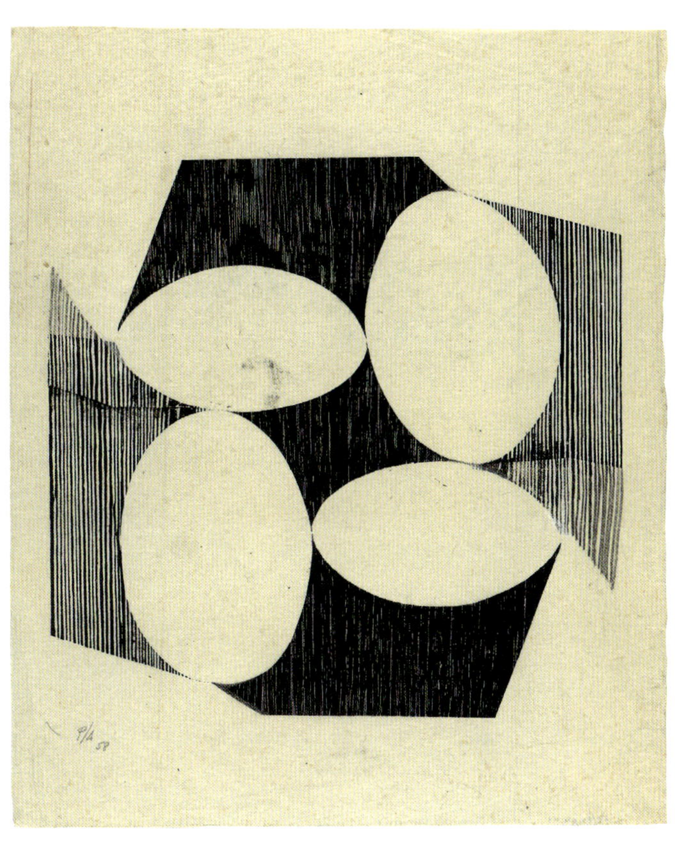

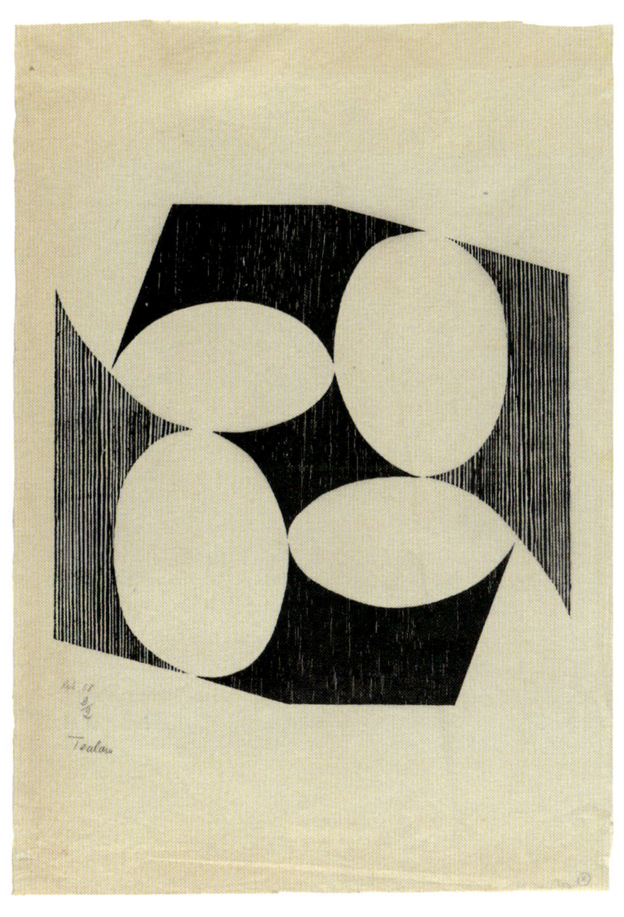

80 *TECELAR* (WEAVING), 1959

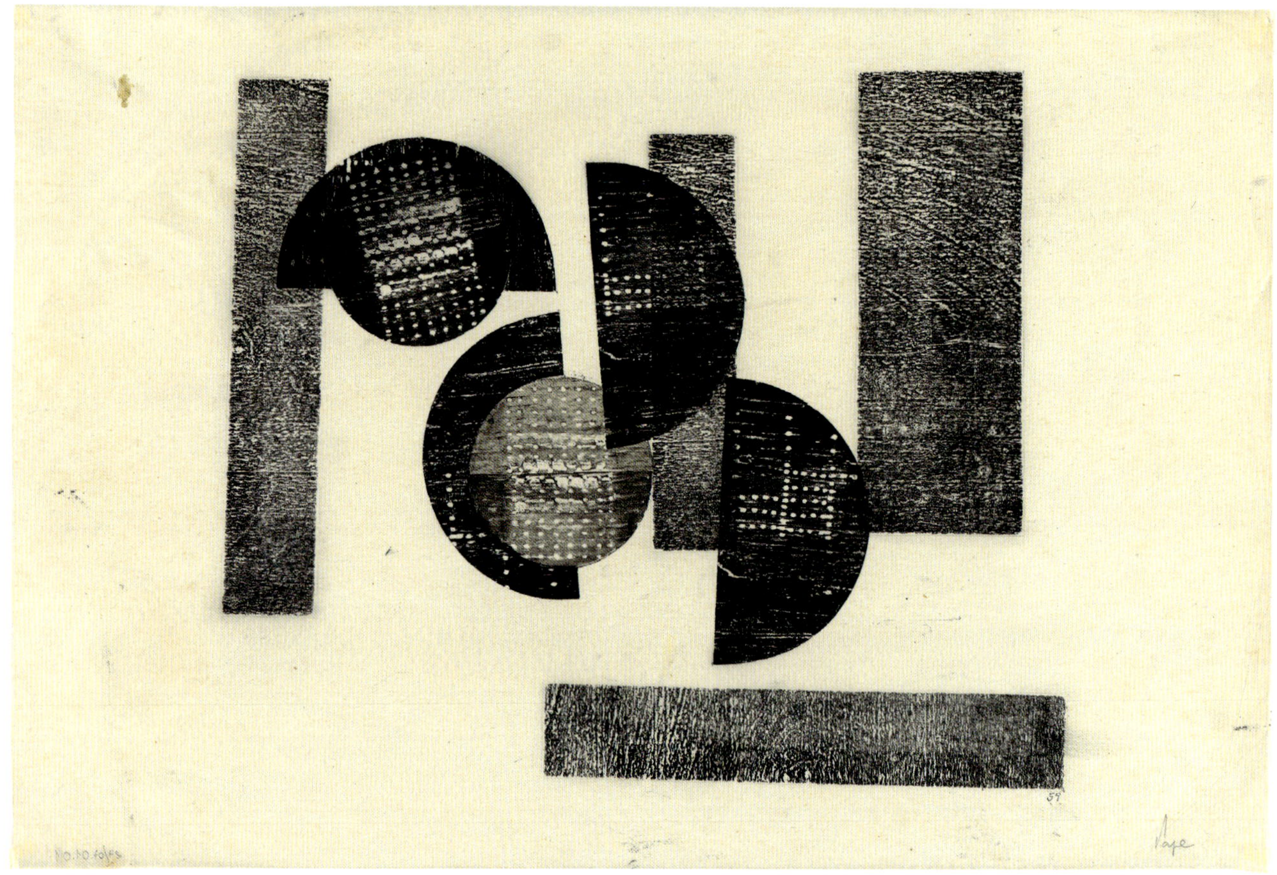

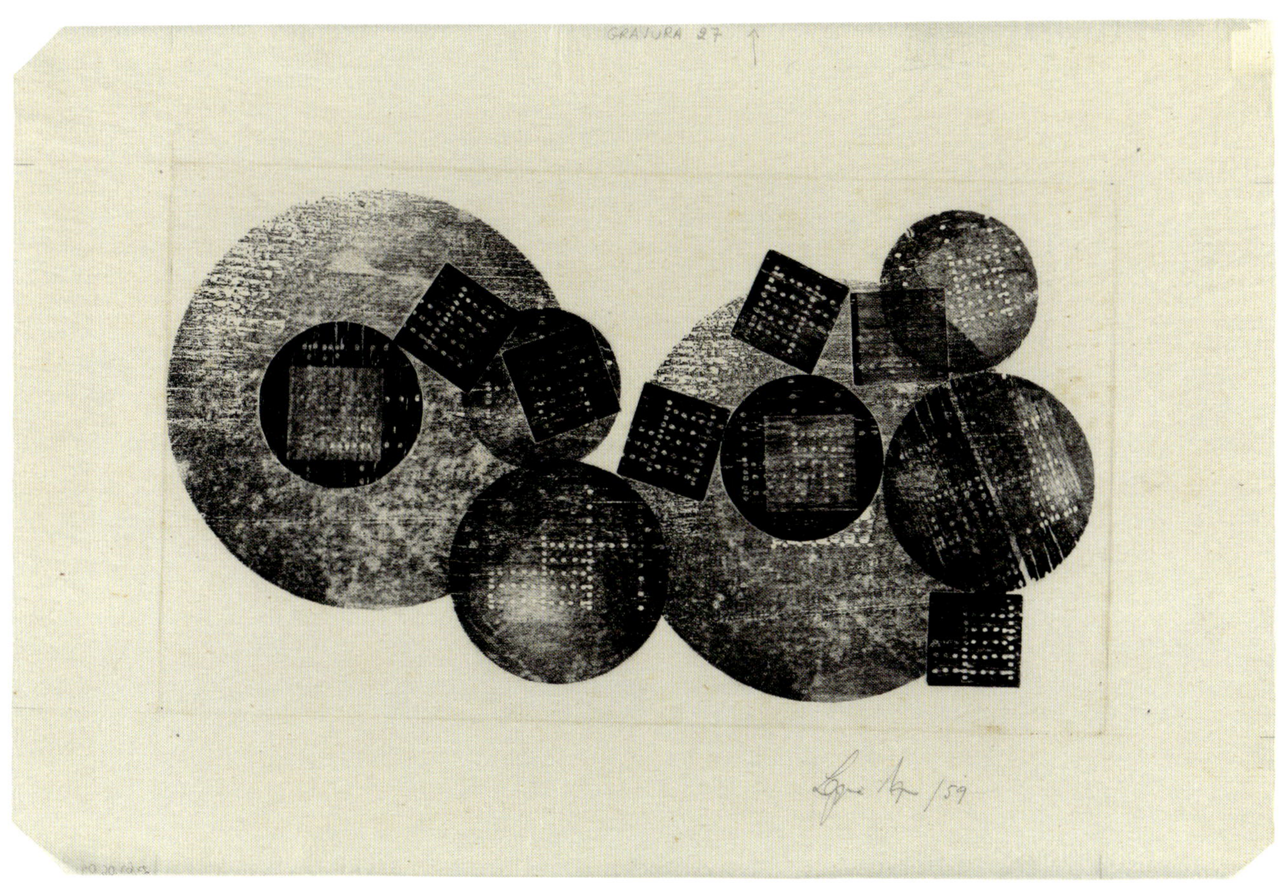
GRAVURA 27

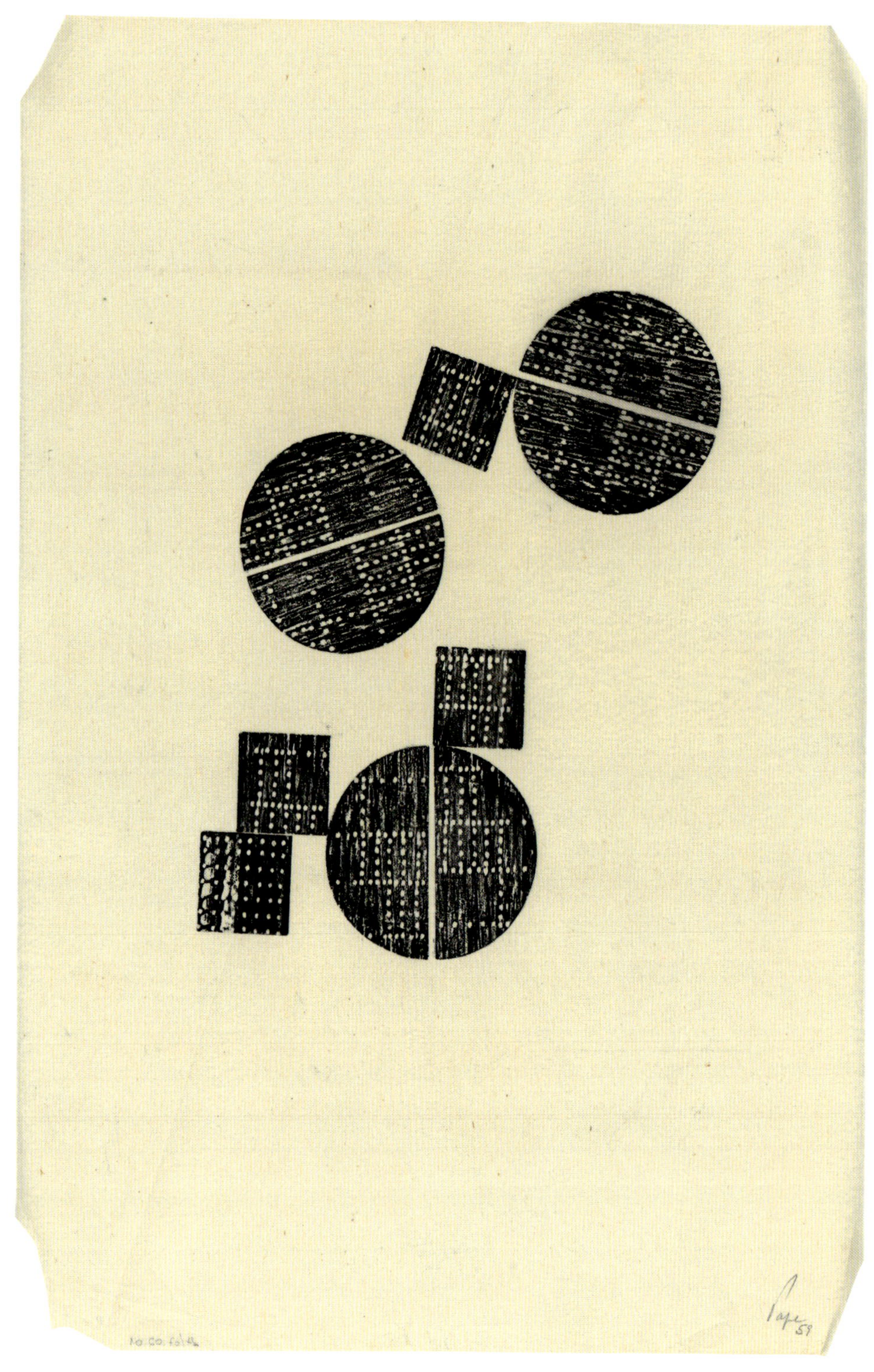

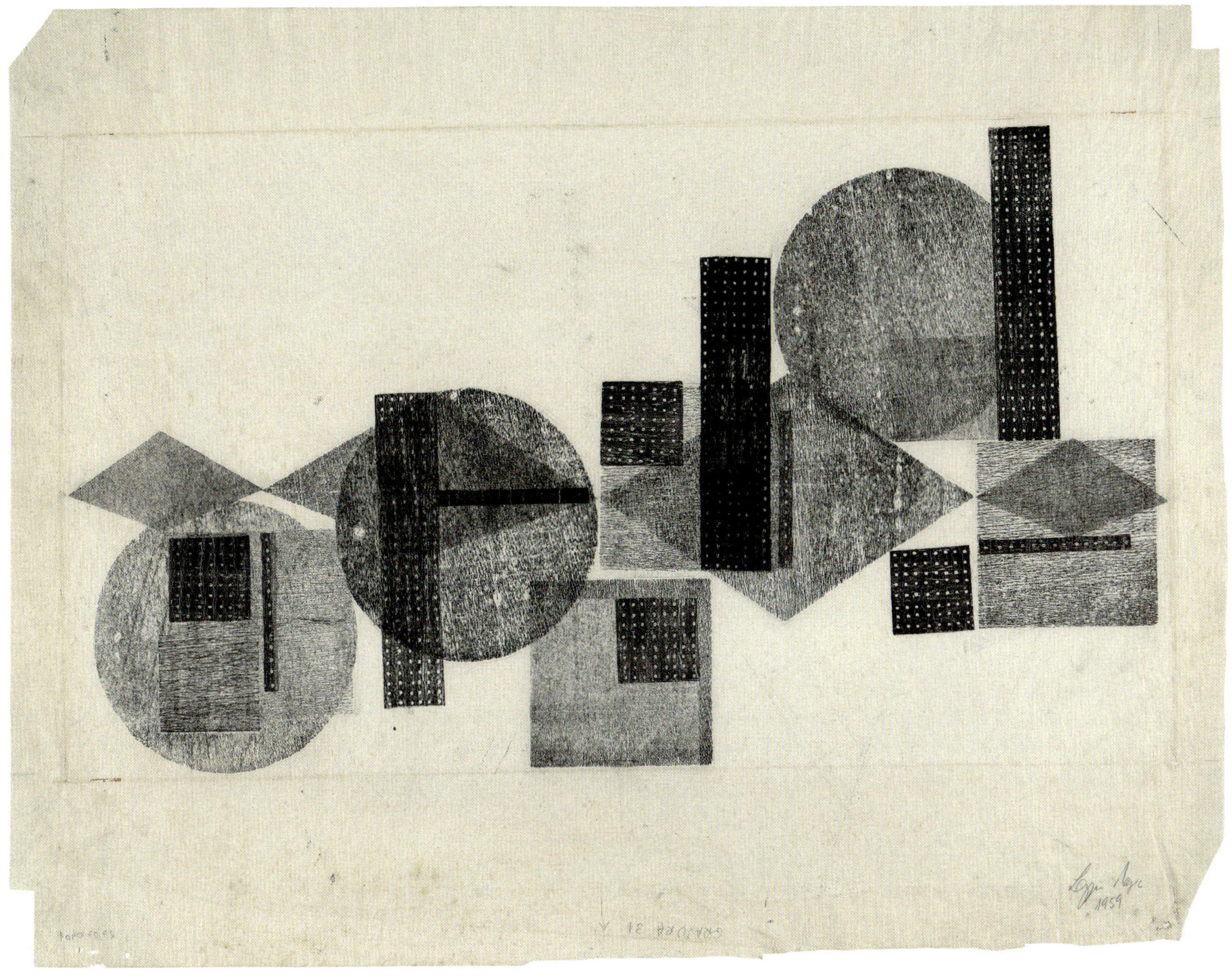

84 *TECELAR* (WEAVING), 1959

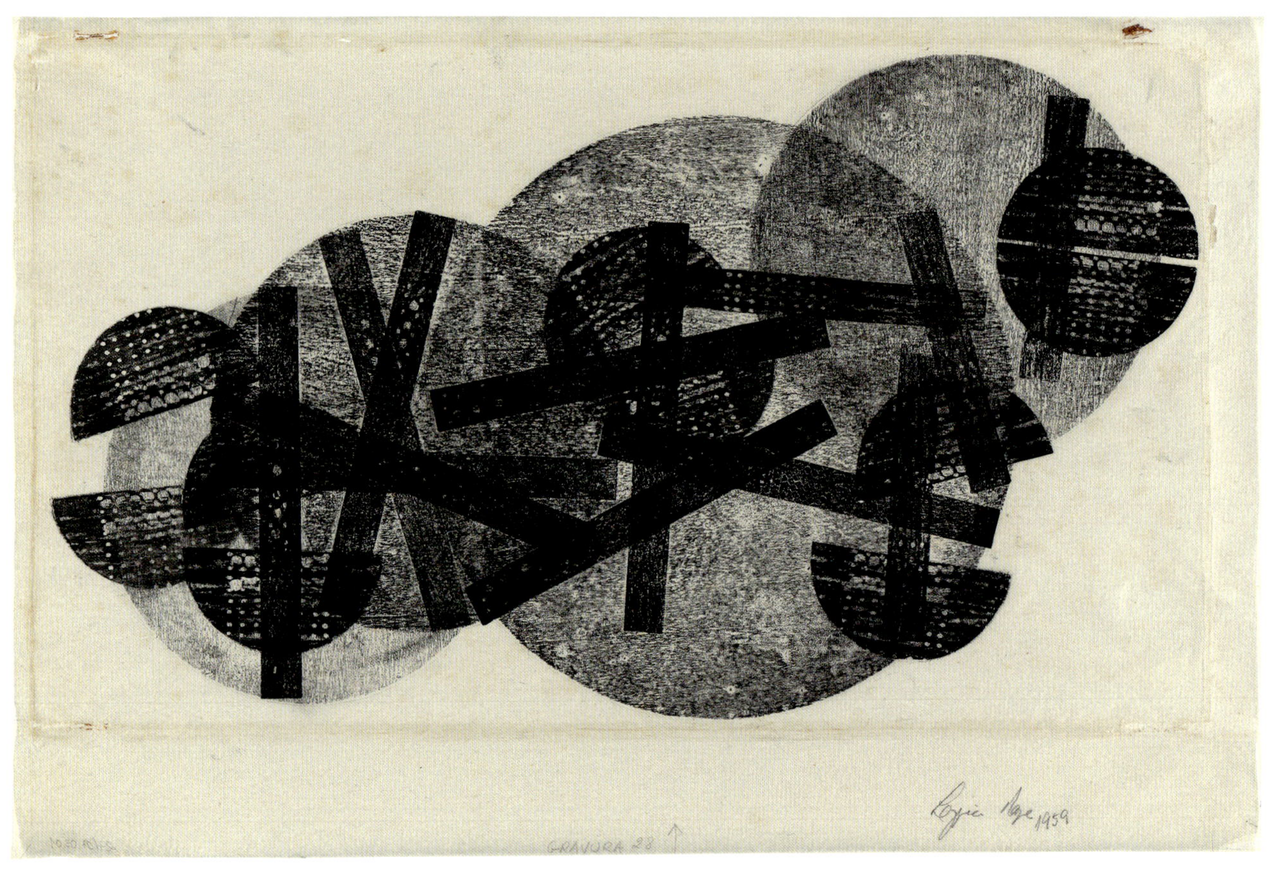

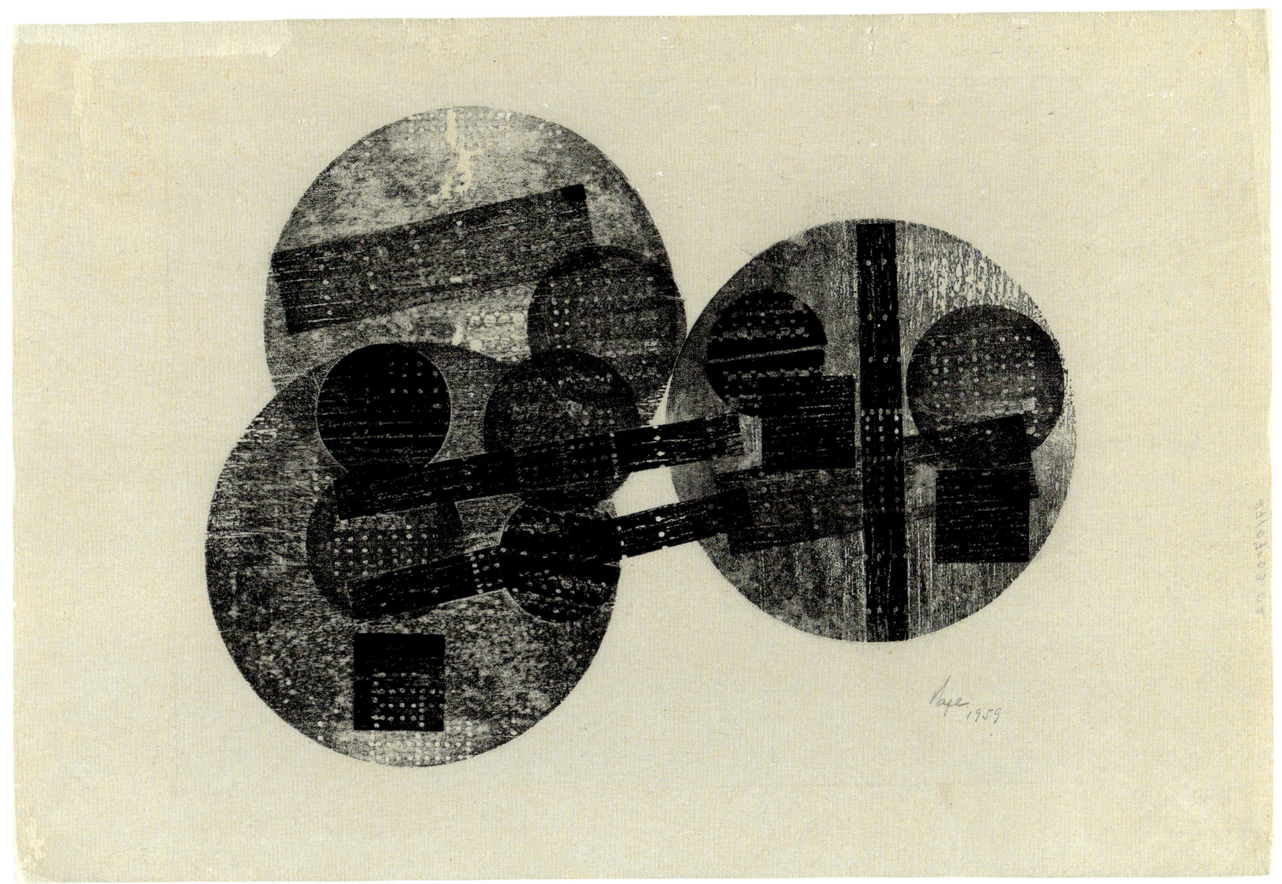

86 WOOD BLOCK FOR CAT. 87, 1959

87 *TECELAR* (WEAVING), 1959

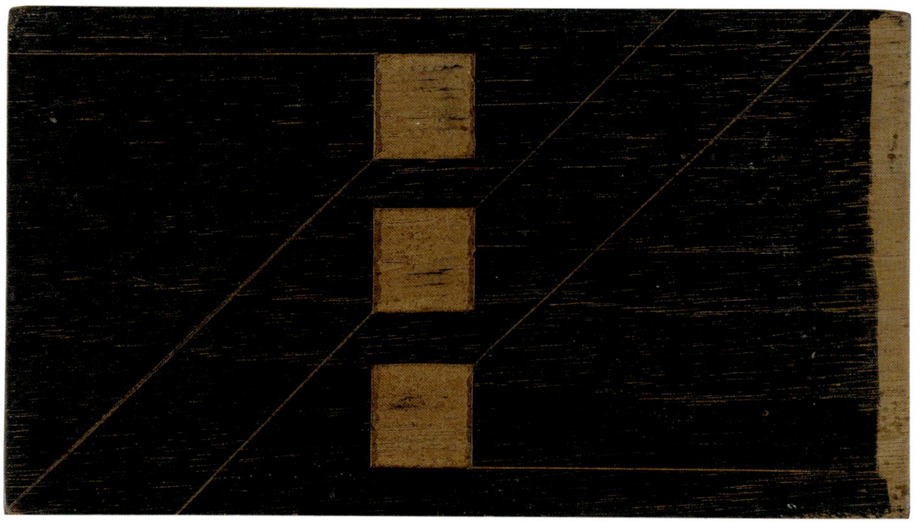

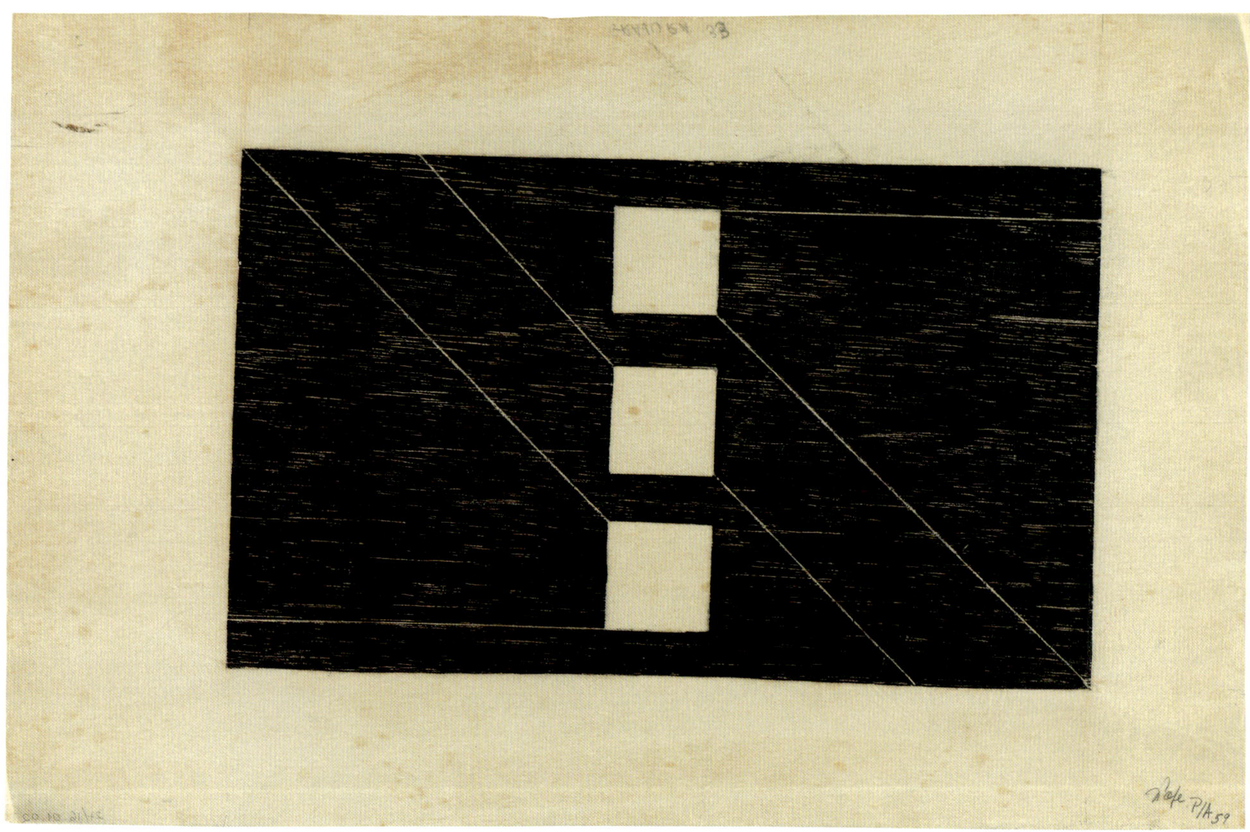

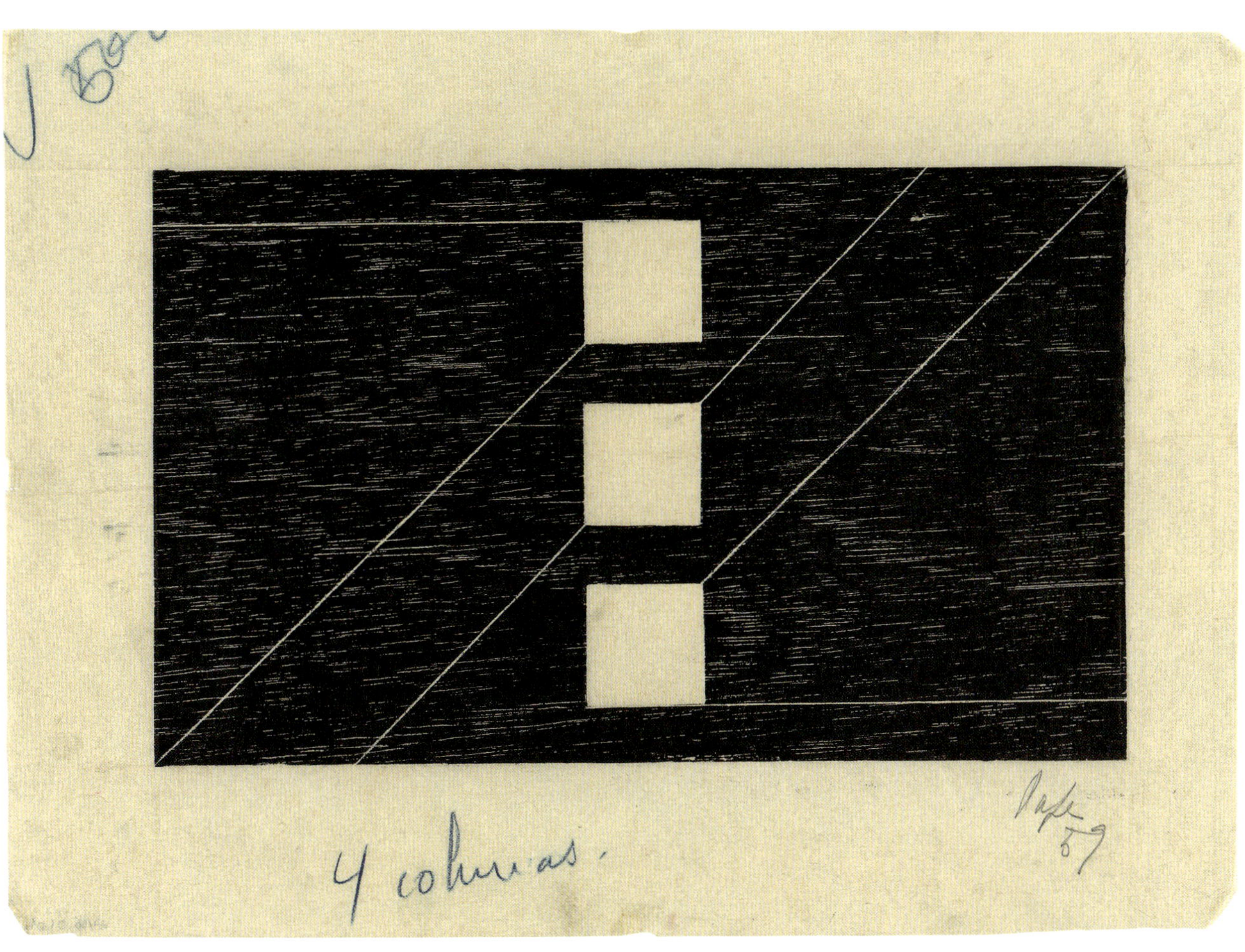
4 colunas.

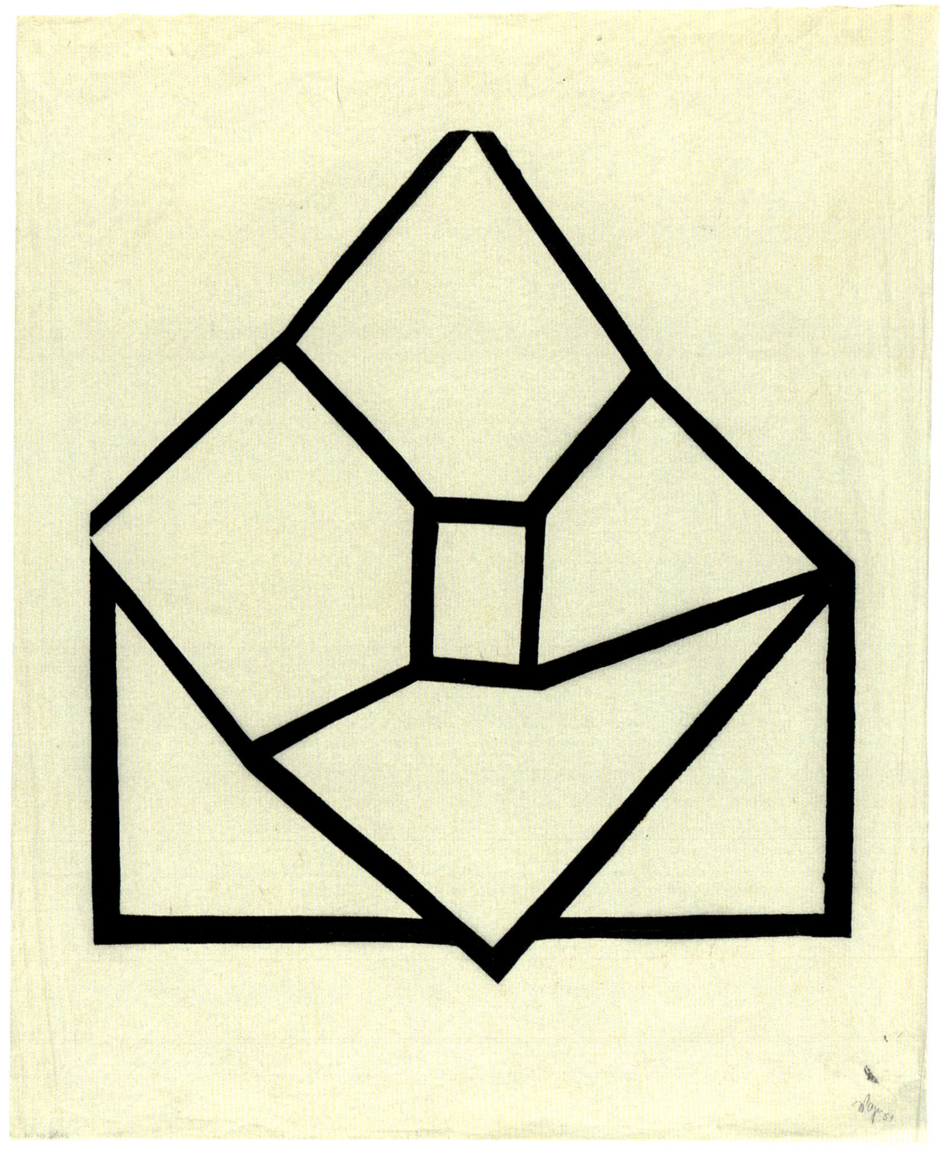

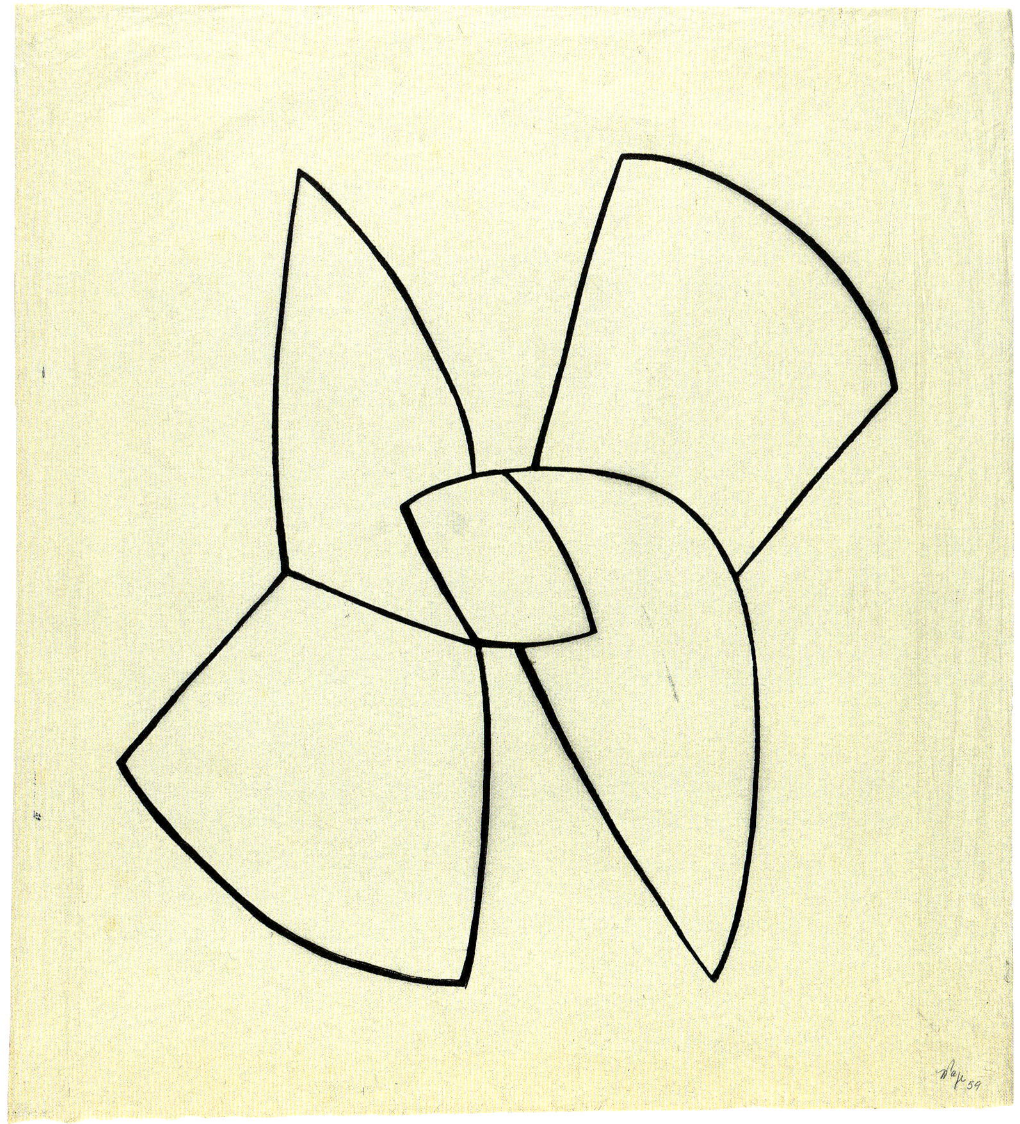

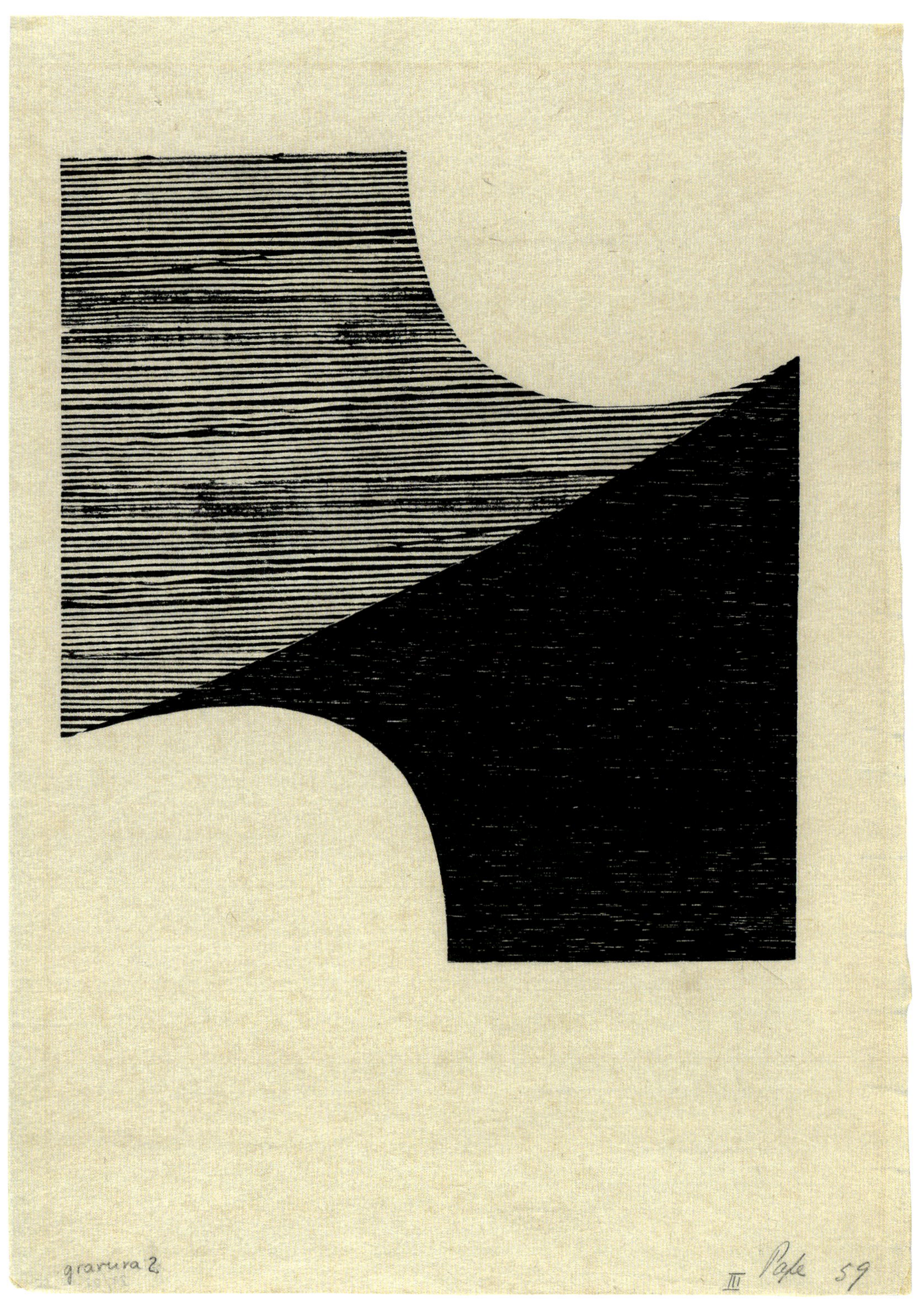
gravura 2
III Pape 59

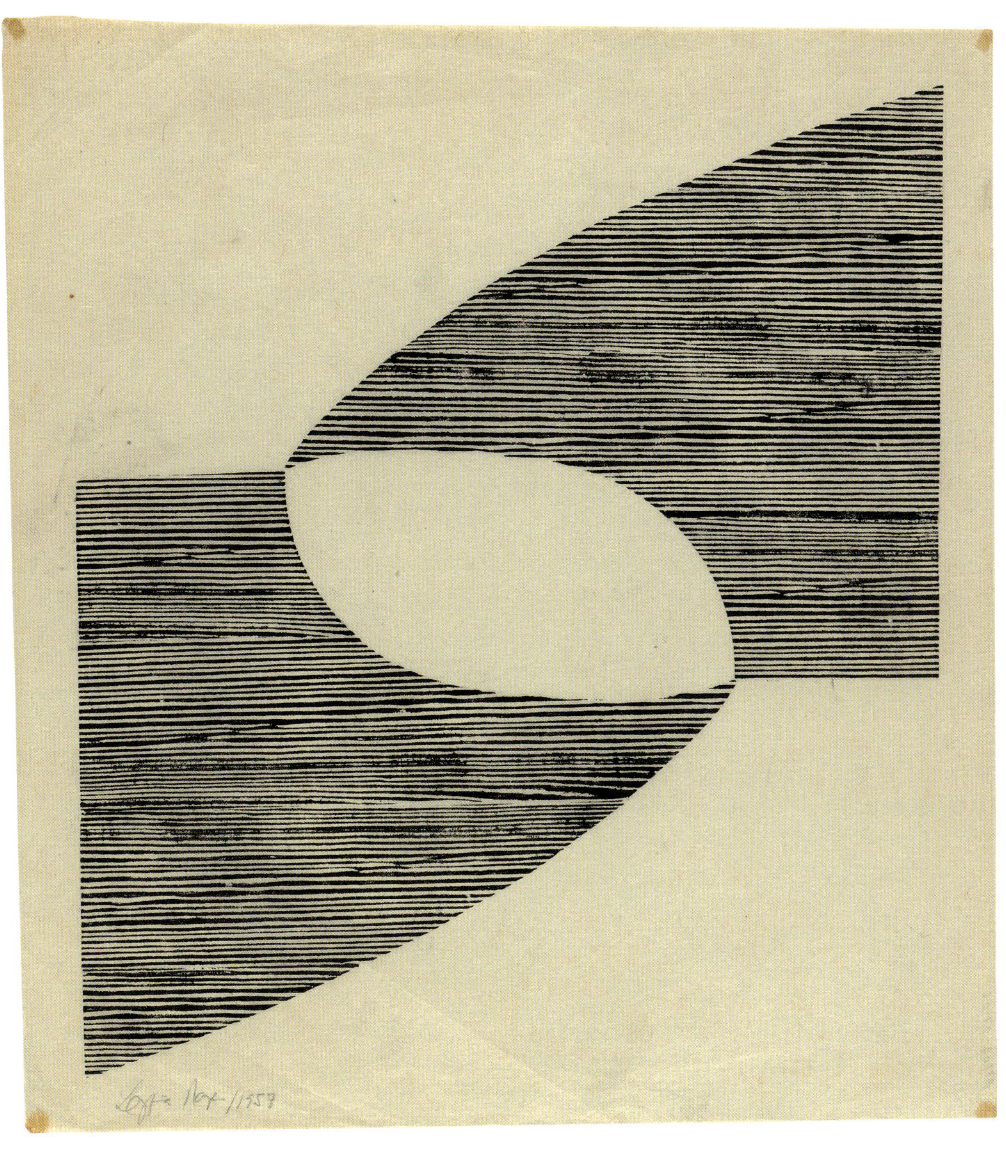

93 *TECELAR* (WEAVING), 1959

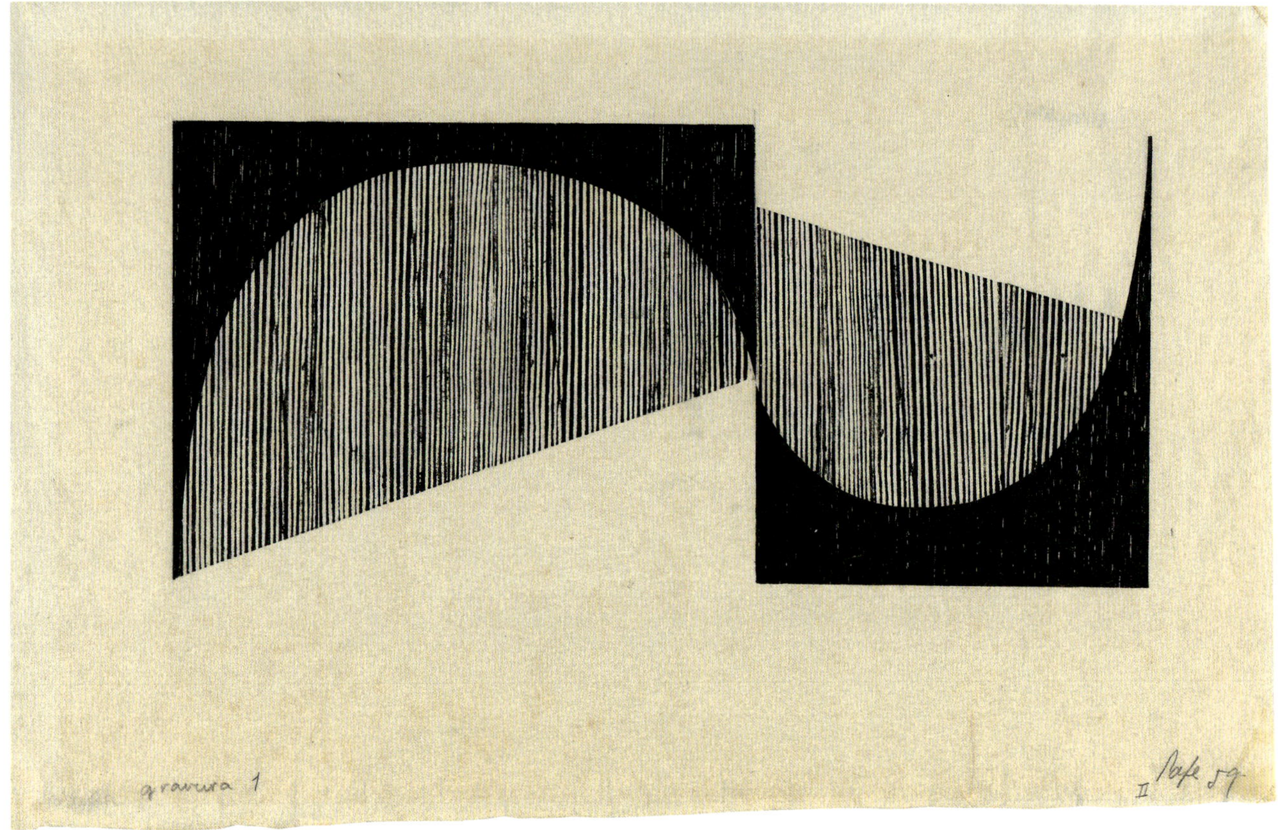

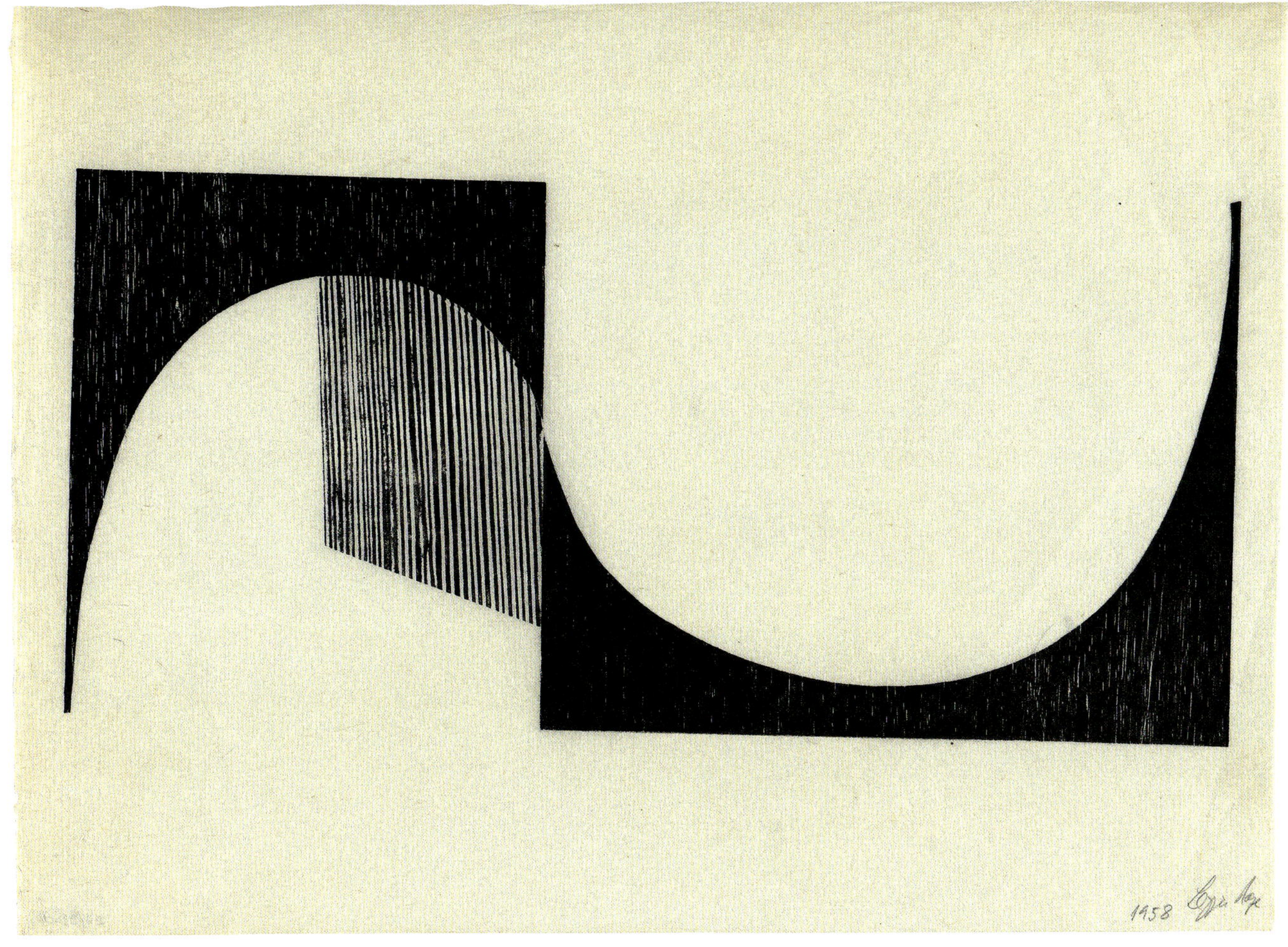

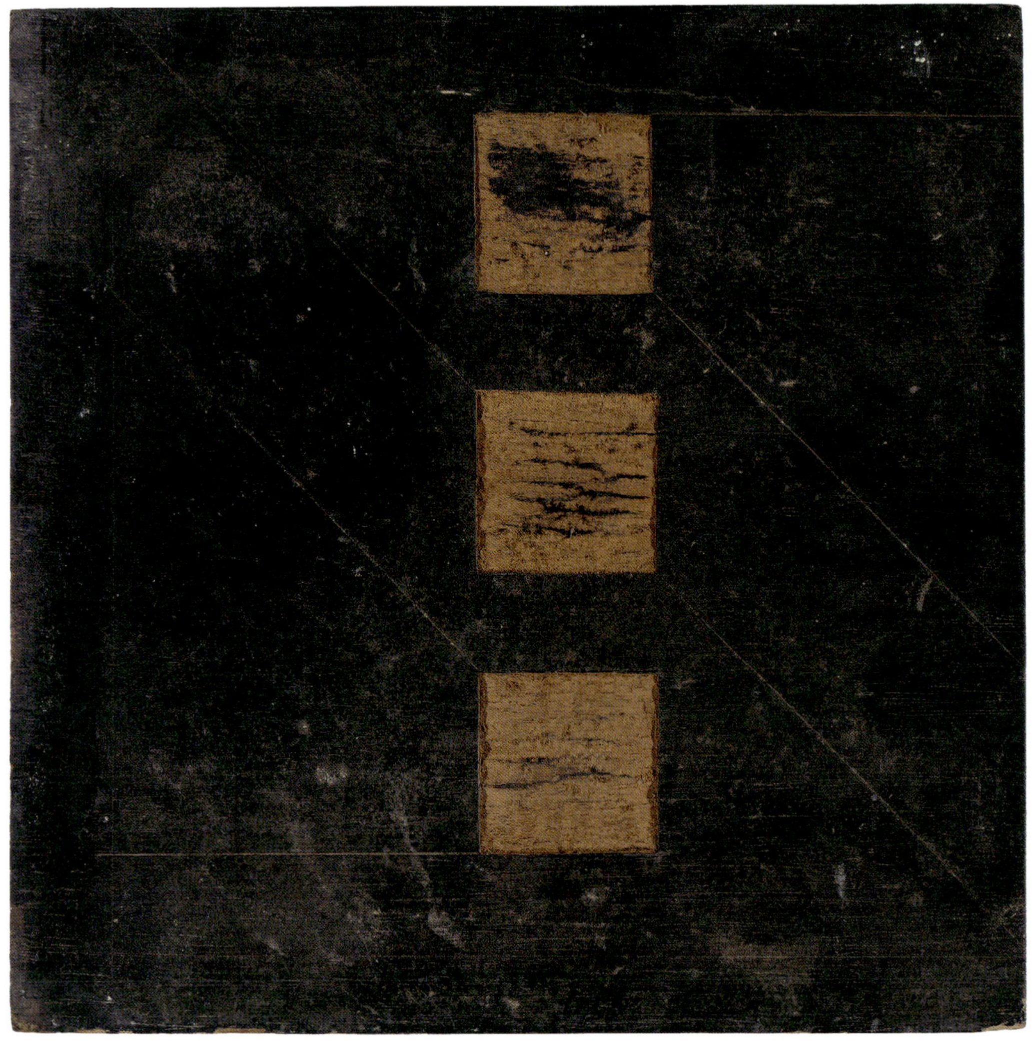

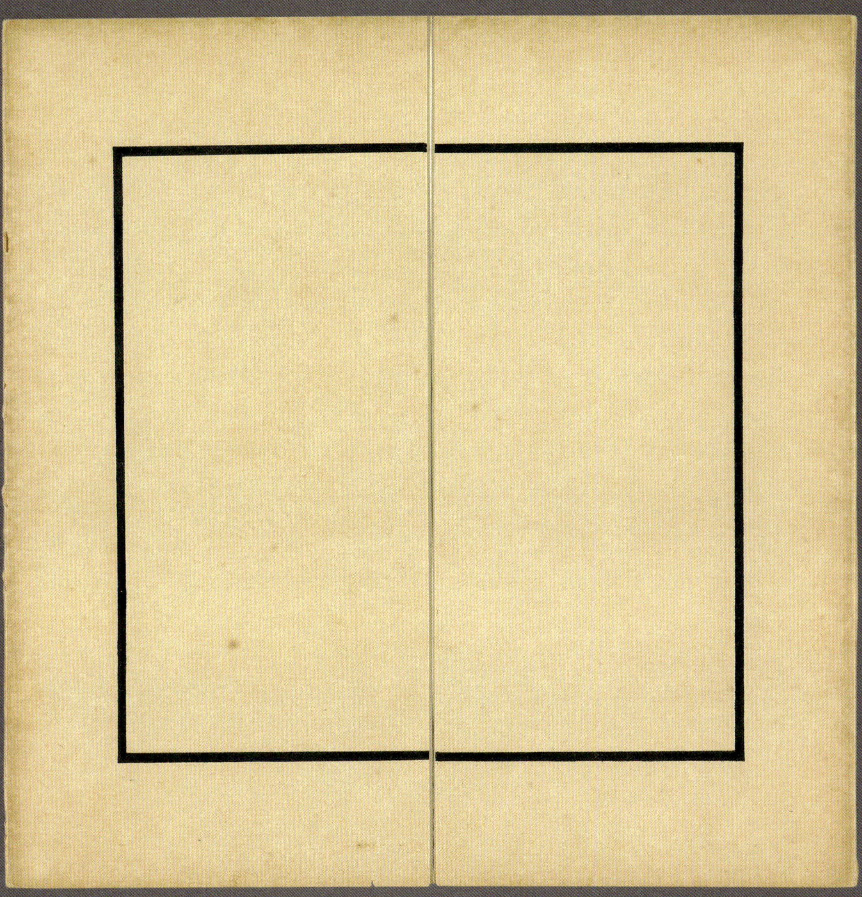

em quebra
em quebra
revela

em
brado

campo

em
claro

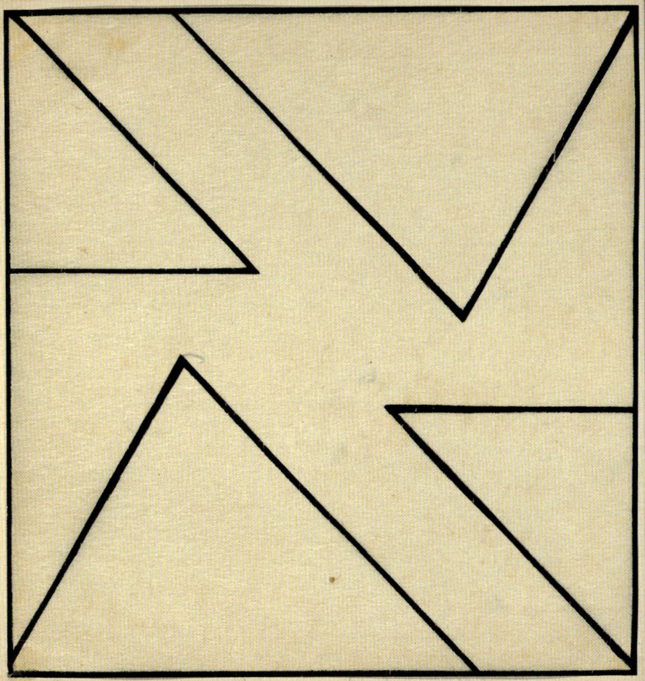

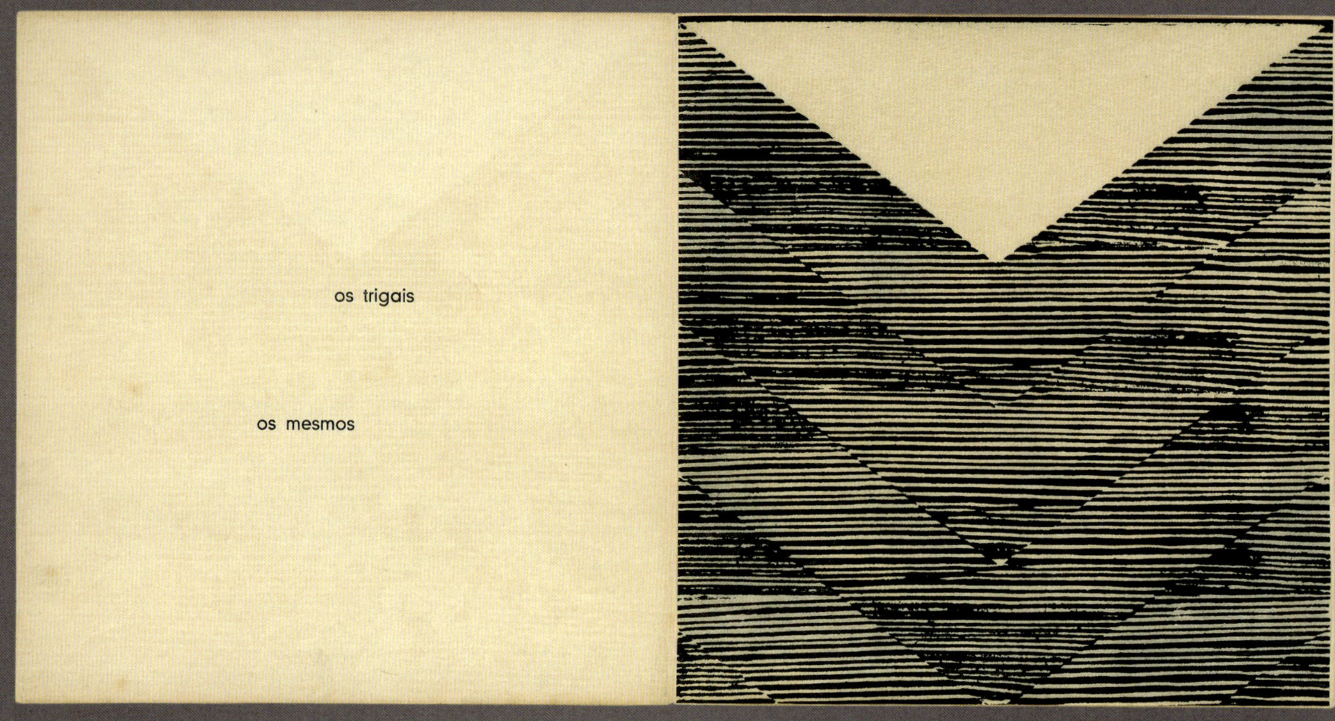
os trigais
os mesmos

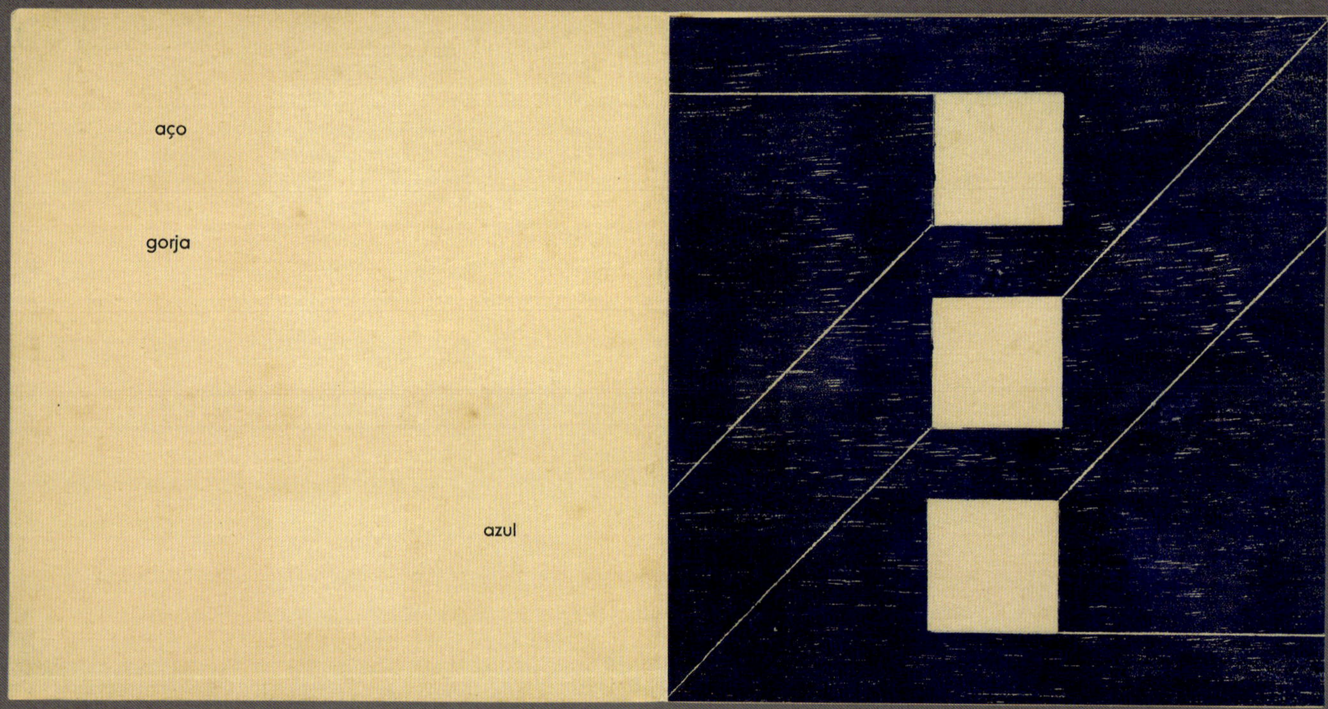
aço
gorja
azul

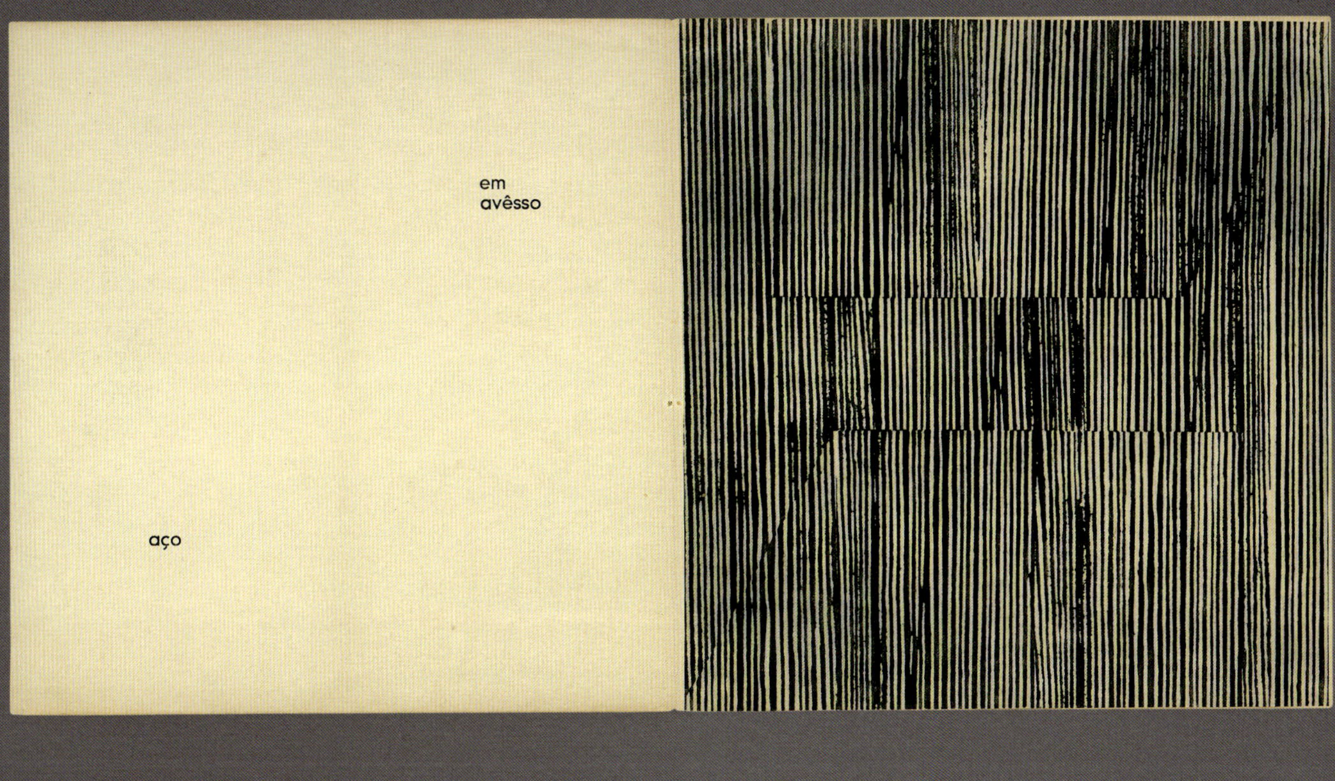
em
avêsso
aço

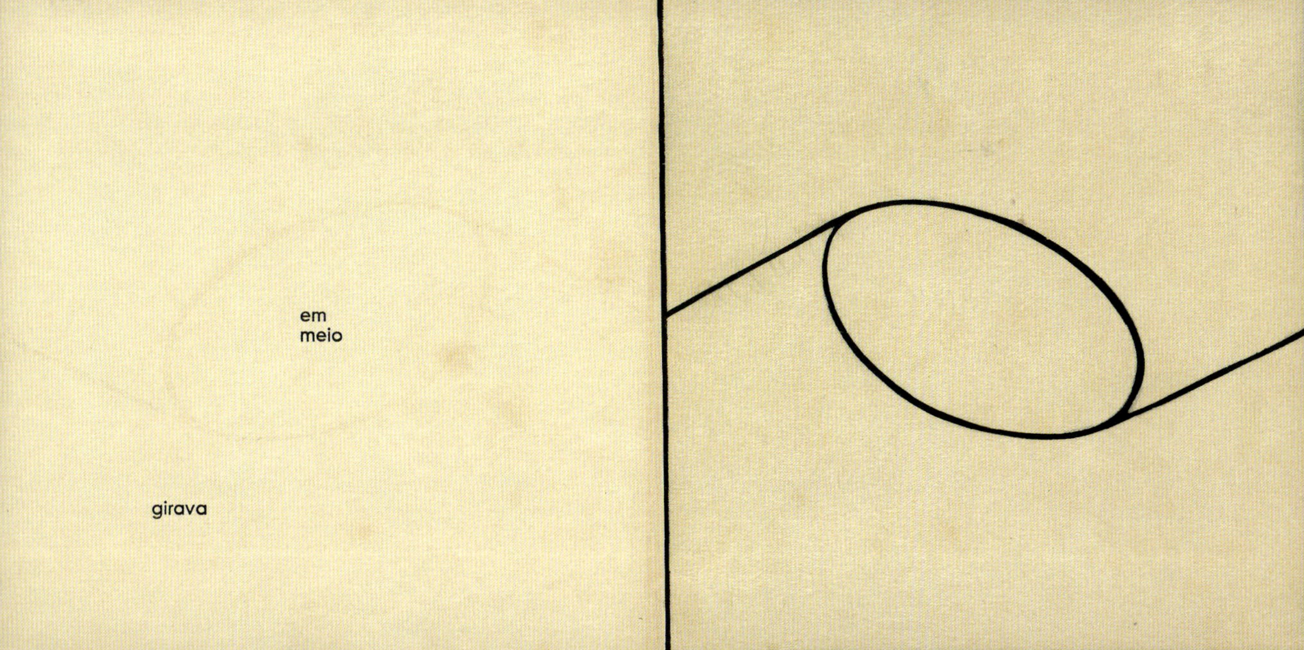
em
meio
girava

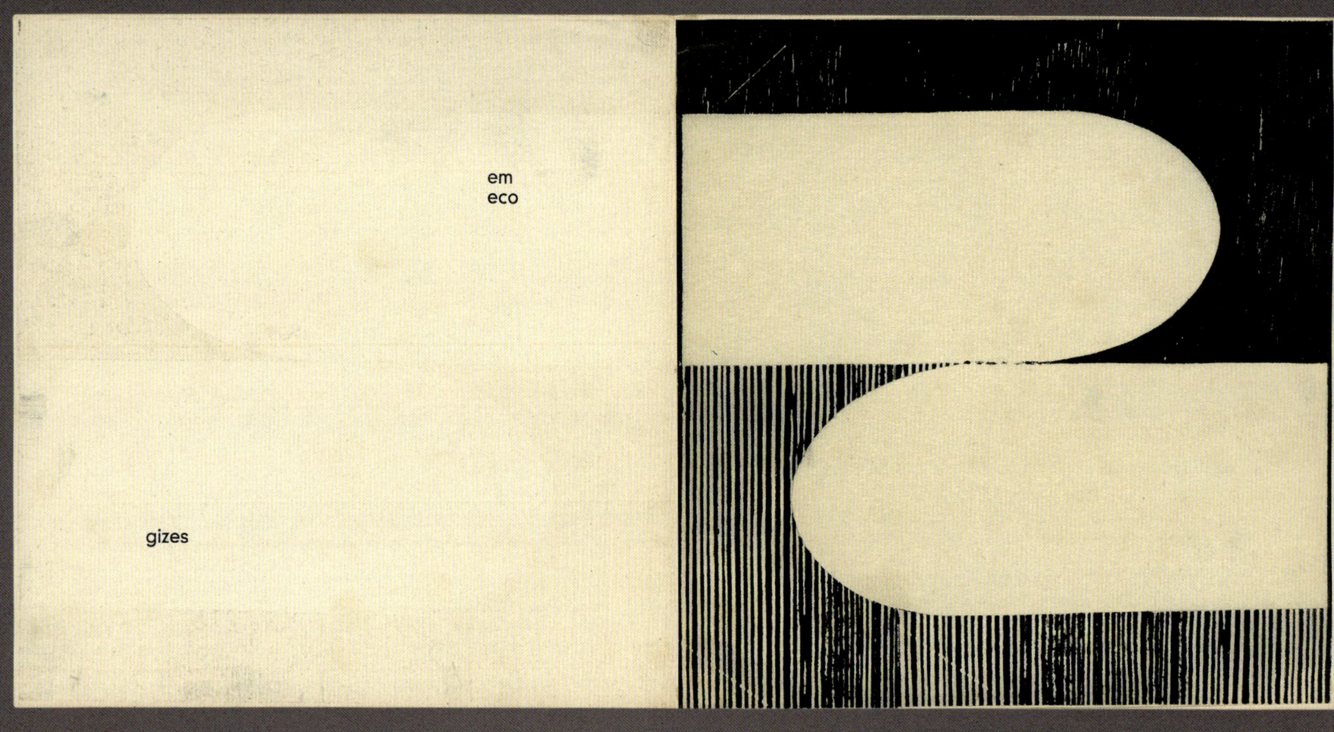
em
eco
gizes

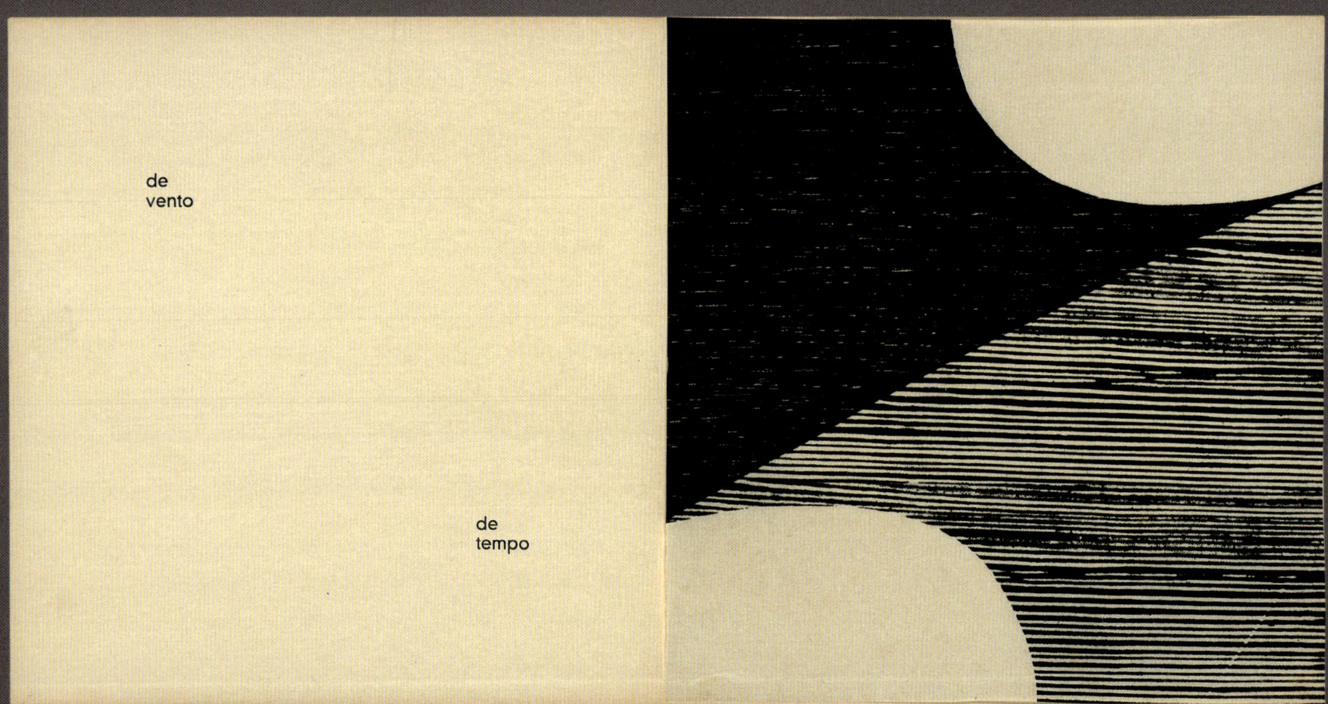
de
vento
de
tempo

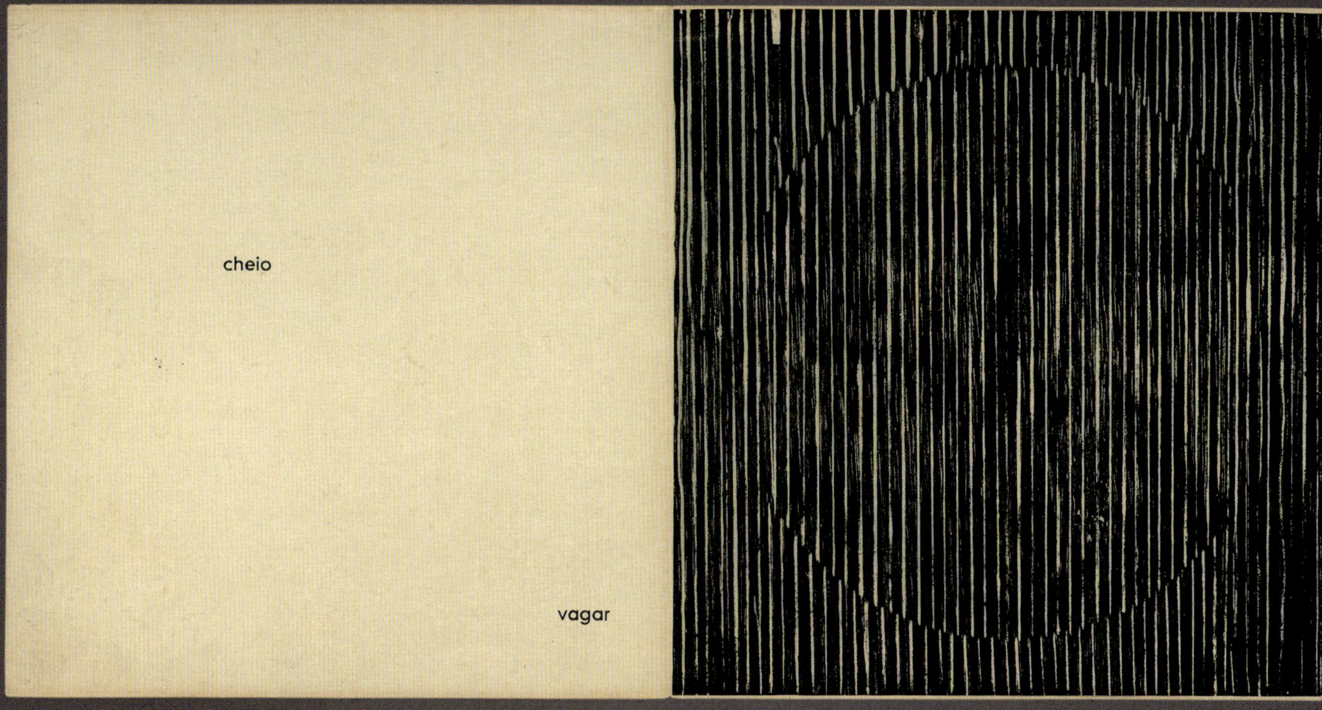
cheio
vagar

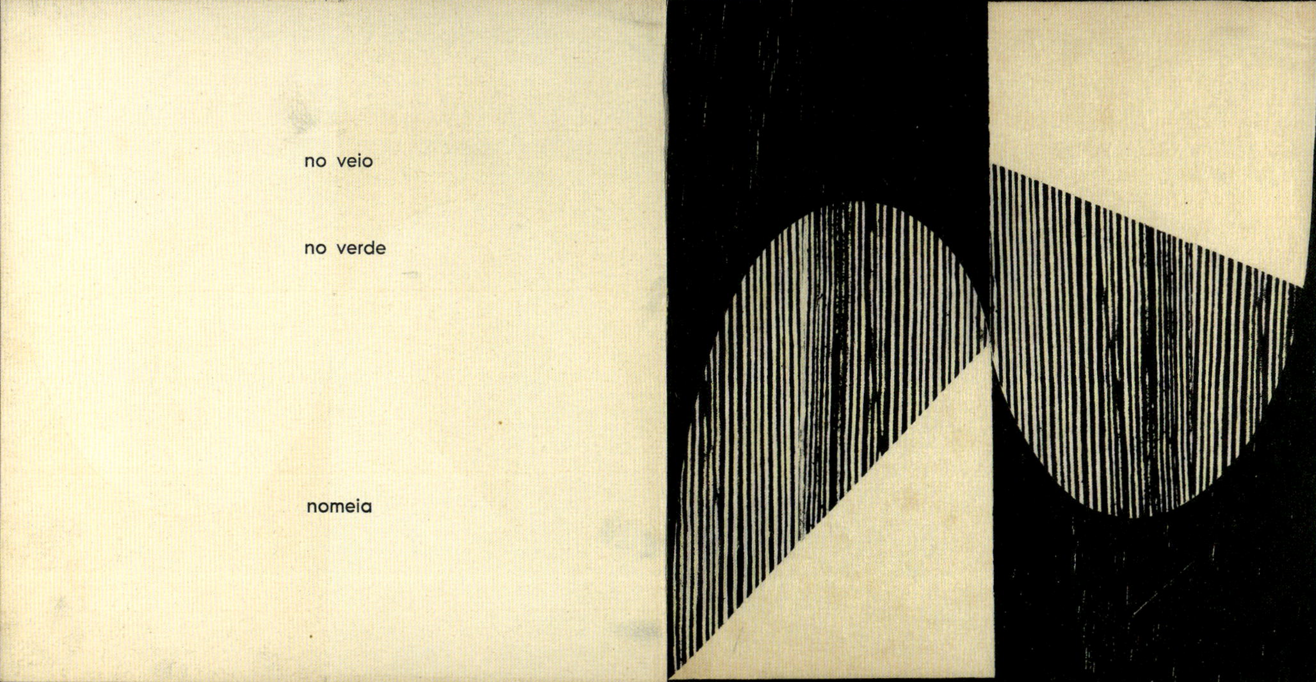
no veio
no verde
nomeia

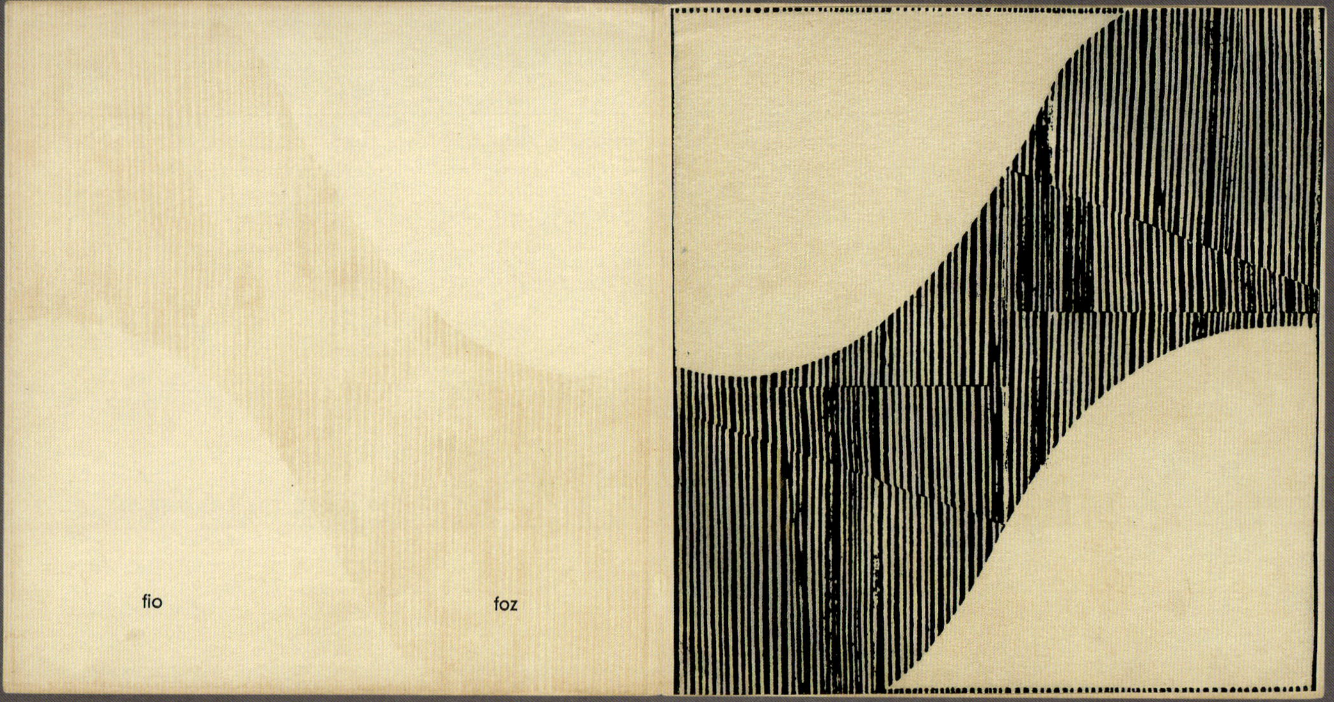
fio
foz

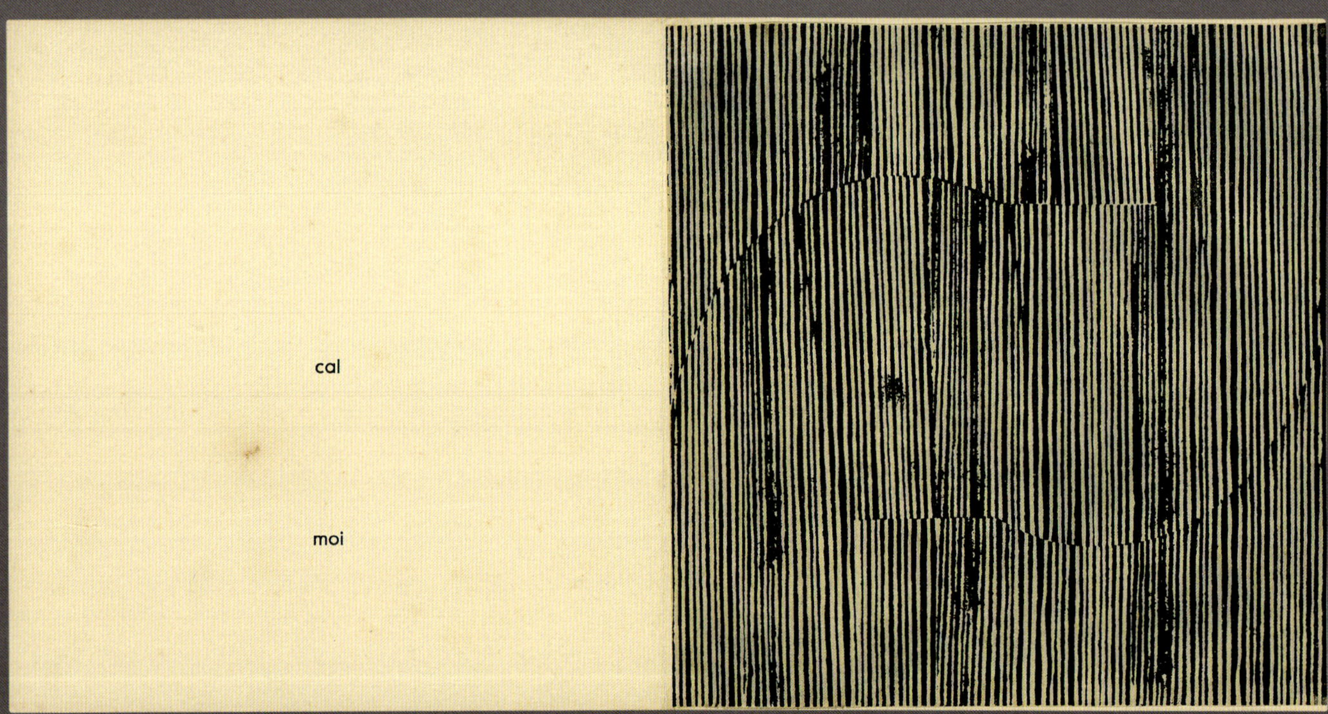
cal
moi

em
brado

campo

em
claro

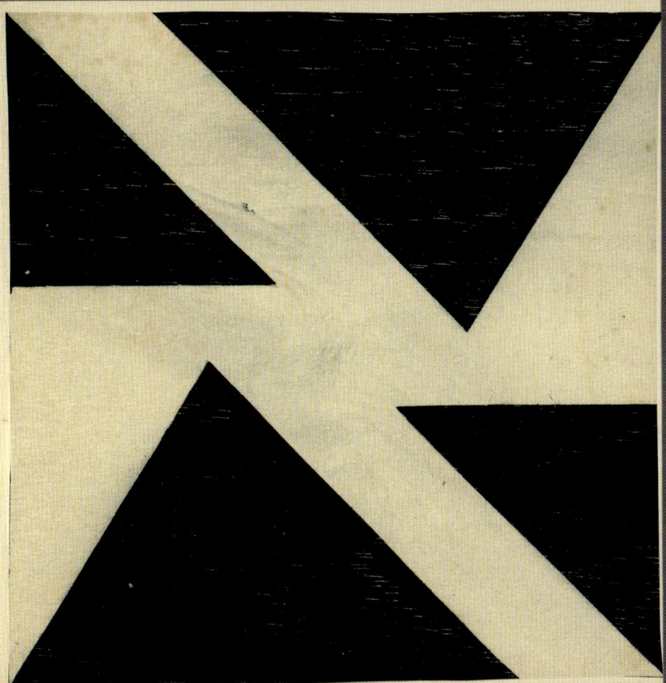

poemas

xilogravuras

Lygia Pape

lygia pape

coleção espaço 5 rio de janeiro maio 1960

98 PERFORMANCE OF *BALLET NEOCONCRETO*, 2000

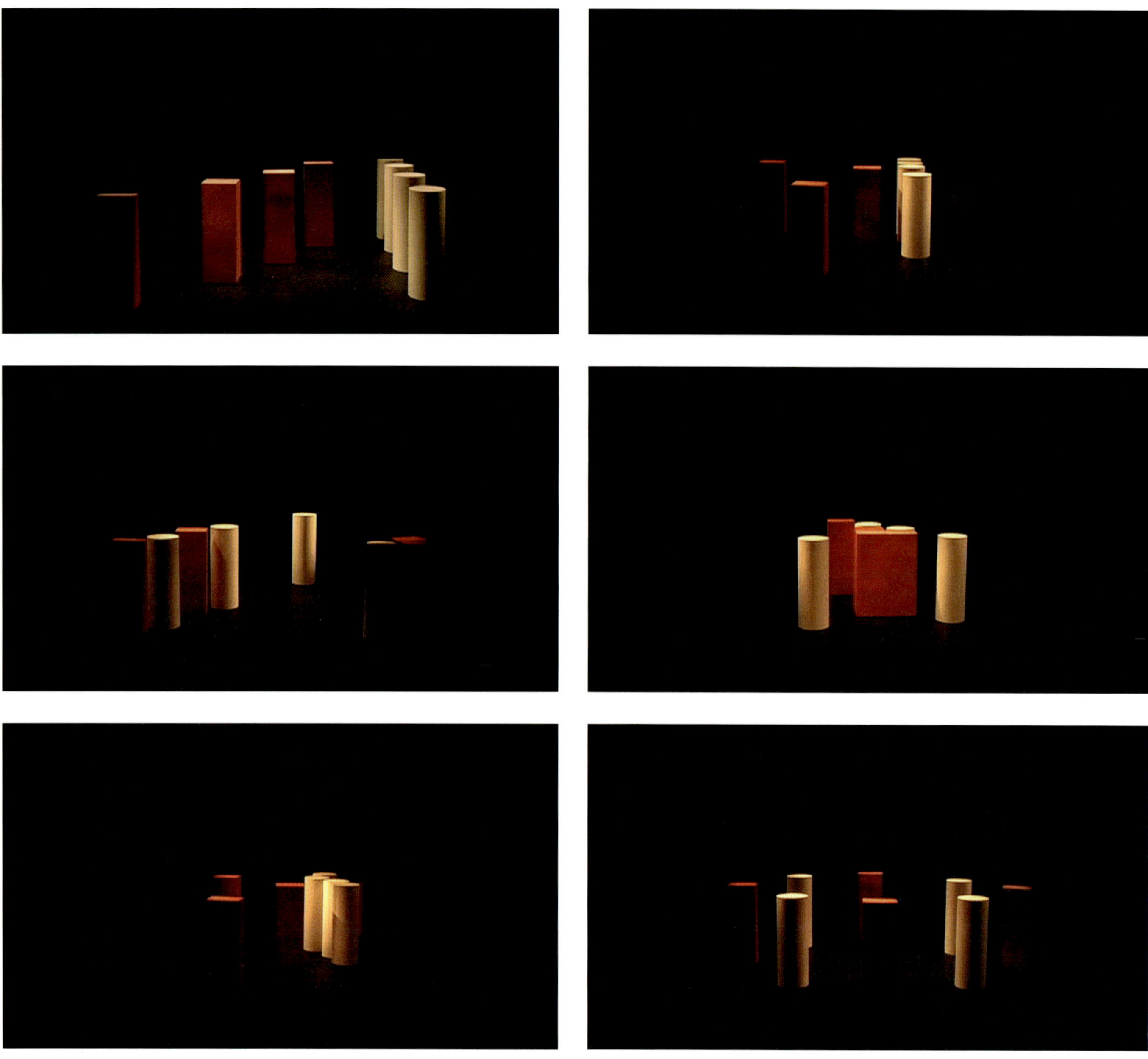

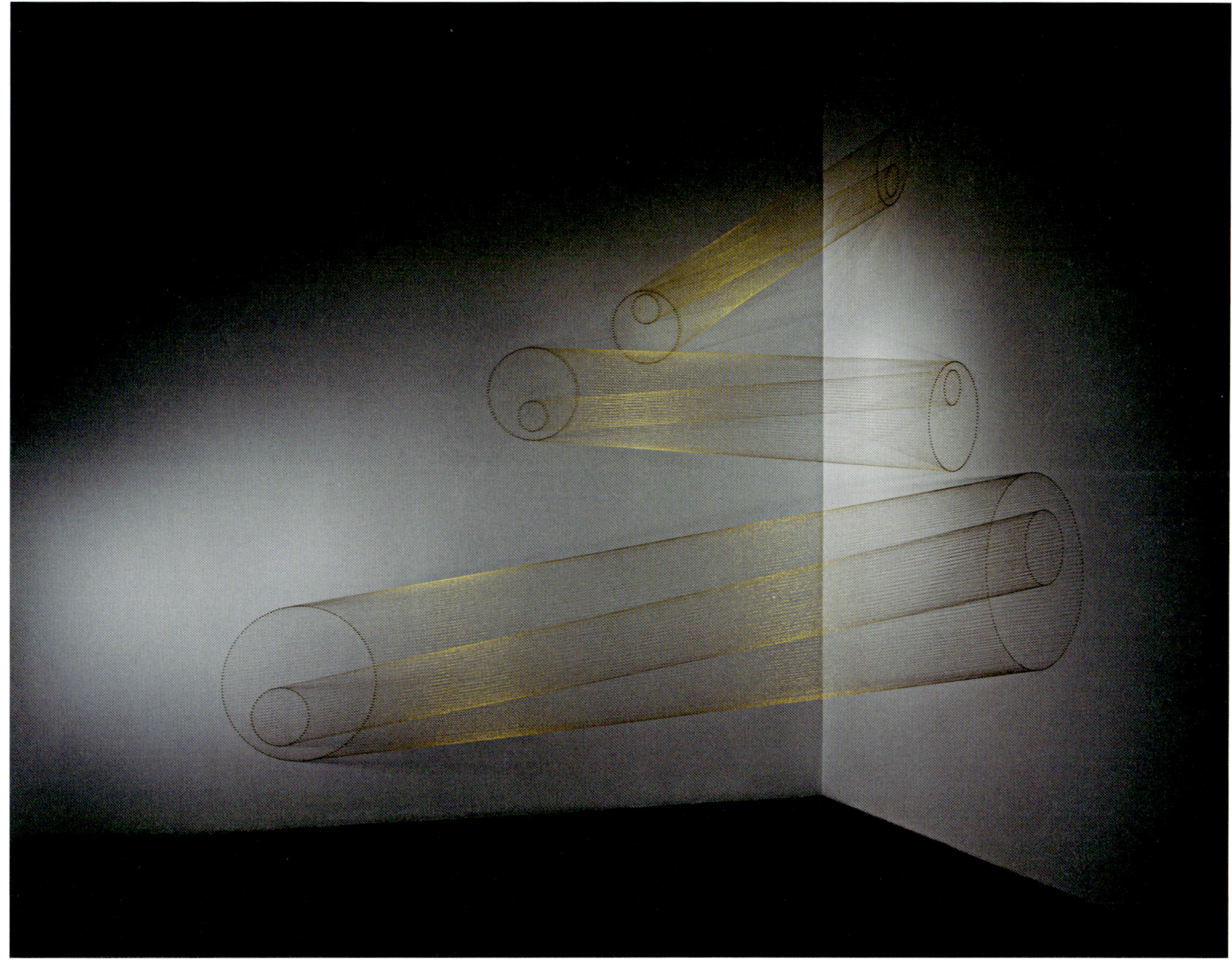

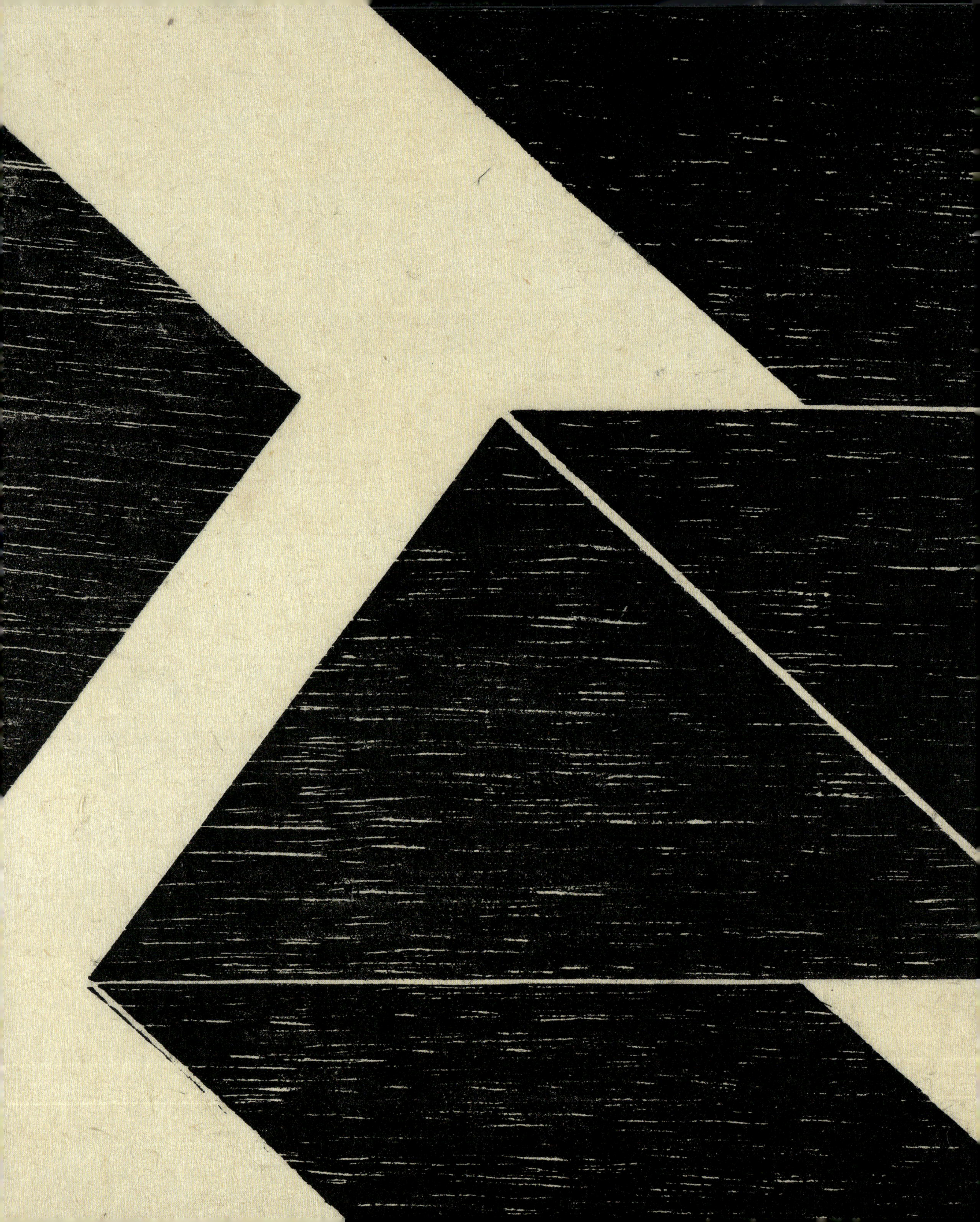

CHECKLIST OF THE EXHIBITION

All works are courtesy of the Projeto Lygia Pape unless otherwise noted. Late in her career, Pape designated her earlier body of print works collectively as *Tecelares*. The term, which she invented, translates loosely to *Weavings*. The singular form is given as the title for individual prints here. They are listed by year, with a few exceptions to show stylistic relationships between works. Pape often signed and dated prints some time after she made them. The dates listed here occasionally differ from those written on the object, but they are based on the best available knowledge of her practice. Because the paper rarely retains plate marks and the wood blocks are in most cases not extant, measurements for the Tecelares refer to the sheet rather than the image.

1 *Tecelar* (Weaving)
1952
Linocut on Japanese paper
23.1 × 30.5 cm (9 × 12 in.)

2 *Tecelar* (Weaving)
1952
Linocut on Japanese paper
32.6 × 44.6 cm ($12\frac{7}{8}$ × $17\frac{1}{2}$ in.)

3 *Tecelar* (Weaving)
1952
Color woodcut on Japanese paper
32.5 × 44.6 cm ($12\frac{3}{4}$ × $17\frac{5}{8}$ in.)

4 *Tecelar* (Weaving)
1952
Color woodcut on Japanese paper
44.7 × 32.7 cm ($17\frac{1}{2}$ × $12\frac{3}{4}$ in.)

5 *Tecelar* (Weaving)
1952
Woodcut with pastel on Japanese paper
30.1 × 48.6 cm ($11\frac{7}{8}$ × $19\frac{1}{8}$ in.)

6 *Tecelar* (Weaving)
1952
Woodcut on Japanese paper
32.8 × 44.4 cm (13 × $17\frac{1}{2}$ in.)

7 *Tecelar* (Weaving)
1952
Color woodcut on Japanese paper
32.8 × 44.8 cm ($12\frac{7}{8}$ × $17\frac{5}{8}$ in.)

8 *Tecelar* (Weaving)
1952
Woodcut on Japanese paper
63.7 × 47.8 cm ($25\frac{1}{8}$ × $18\frac{7}{8}$ in.)

9 *Tecelar* (Weaving)
1952
Woodcut on Japanese paper
63.4 × 47.9 cm (25 × $18\frac{7}{8}$ in.)

10 *Tecelar* (Weaving)
1952
Woodcut on Japanese paper
51.1 × 34.5 cm ($20\frac{1}{8}$ × $13\frac{1}{2}$ in.)

11 *Tecelar* (Weaving)
1953
Color woodcut on Japanese paper
32.7 × 44.6 cm ($12\frac{7}{8}$ × $17\frac{9}{16}$ in.)

12 *Tecelar* (Weaving)
1953
Color woodcut on Japanese paper
32.6 × 44.7 cm ($12\frac{7}{8}$ × $17\frac{5}{8}$ in.)

13 *Tecelar* (Weaving)
1953
Color woodcut, with woodcut collage element, on Japanese paper
32.7 × 44.9 cm ($12\frac{7}{8}$ × $17\frac{5}{8}$ in.)

14 *Tecelar* (Weaving)
1953
Color woodcut on Japanese paper
44.4 × 32.6 cm ($17\frac{3}{8}$ × $12\frac{3}{4}$ in.)

15 *Tecelar* (Weaving)
1953
Color woodcut on Japanese paper
30.5 × 23 cm (12 × 9 in.)

16 *Tecelar* (Weaving)
1953
Color woodcut on Japanese paper
22.9 × 30.2 cm (9 × $12\frac{1}{16}$ in.)

17 *Tecelar* (Weaving)
1953
Color woodcut on Japanese paper
44.6 × 25.7 cm ($17\frac{9}{16}$ × $10\frac{1}{8}$ in.)

18 *Tecelar* (Weaving)
1953
Color woodcut on Japanese paper
44.9 × 32.9 cm ($17\frac{5}{8}$ × $12\frac{7}{8}$ in.)

19 *Tecelar* (Weaving)
1953
Color woodcut on Japanese paper
44.9 × 32.6 cm ($17\frac{3}{4}$ × $12\frac{3}{4}$ in.)

20 *Tecelar* (Weaving)
1953
Color woodcut on Japanese paper
32.8 × 44.7 cm ($12\frac{7}{8}$ × $17\frac{5}{8}$ in.)

21 *Tecelar* (Weaving)
1953
Woodcut on Japanese paper
32.4 × 43.3 cm ($12\frac{3}{4}$ × $17\frac{1}{4}$ in.)

22 *Tecelar* (Weaving)
1953
Woodcut on Japanese paper
30.8 × 45.6 cm ($12\frac{1}{8}$ × $17\frac{15}{16}$ in.)
The Art Institute of Chicago, Harry B. and Bessie K. Braude Memorial Fund, 2018.197

23 *Tecelar* (Weaving)
1954
Color woodcut on Japanese paper
44.6 × 34.5 cm ($17\frac{1}{2}$ × $13\frac{5}{8}$ in.)

24 *Tecelar* (Weaving)
1954
Woodcut on Japanese paper
47.8 × 38.5 cm ($18\frac{7}{8}$ × $15\frac{1}{8}$ in.)

25 *Tecelar* (Weaving)
1955
Woodcut with ruling lines in graphite on Japanese paper
Folded: 27.2 × 47.3 cm ($10\frac{11}{16}$ × $18\frac{5}{8}$ in.); sheet: 45.8 × 60.9 cm (18 × 24 in.)

26 *Tecelar* (Weaving)
1955
Woodcut with ruling lines in graphite on Japanese paper
51 × 52 cm (20 ⅛ × 20 ⅜ in.)

27 *Tecelar* (Weaving)
1955
Woodcut with ruling lines in graphite on Japanese paper
46.4 × 60 cm (18 ¼ × 23 ⅝ in.)

28 *Tecelar* (Weaving)
1955
Woodcut on Japanese paper
49.6 × 61.1 cm (19 ½ × 24 in.)

29 *Tecelar* (Weaving)
1955
Woodcut with ruling lines in graphite on Japanese paper
61 × 50.7 cm (24 × 20 in.)

30 *Tecelar* (Weaving)
1956
Woodcut on Japanese paper
44.7 × 32.6 cm (17 ½ × 12 ⅞ in.)

31 *Tecelar* (Weaving)
1956
Woodcut on Japanese paper
26.7 × 31.5 cm (10 ½ × 12 ⅜ in.)

32 Wood Block for Cat. 33
1957
Wood block
50.1 × 49.8 × 3 cm (19 11/16 × 19 ⅝ × 1 3/16 in.)

33 *Tecelar* (Weaving)
1957
Woodcut on Japanese paper
65.7 × 89.3 cm (25 ⅞ × 35 in.)

34 Wood Block for Cats. 35 and 36
1957
Wood block
50.1 × 49.8 × 3 cm (19 11/16 × 19 ⅝ × 1 3/16 in.)

35 *Tecelar* (Weaving)
1957
Woodcut on Japanese paper
89.5 × 65.2 cm (35 ¼ × 25 ¾ in.)

36 *Tecelar* (Weaving)
1957
Woodcut on Japanese paper
89.3 × 65.3 cm (35 ¼ × 25 ¾ in.)

37 *Tecelar* (Weaving)
1957
Woodcut on Japanese paper
35 × 48 cm (13 ¾ × 18 ⅞ in.)

38 *Tecelar* (Weaving)
1957
Woodcut on Japanese paper
30.3 × 44.6 cm (11 ⅞ × 17 ⅝ in.)

39 *Tecelar* (Weaving)
1957
Woodcut on Japanese paper
44.8 × 32.8 cm (17 ⅝ × 12 15/16 in.)

40 *Tecelar* (Weaving)
1957
Woodcut on Japanese paper
44.6 × 32.7 cm (17 9/16 × 12 ⅞ in.)

41 *Tecelar* (Weaving)
1957
Woodcut with registration marks in graphite on Japanese paper
44.7 × 32.6 cm (17 ⅝ × 12 ⅞ in.)

42 *Tecelar* (Weaving)
1957
Woodcut on Japanese paper
44.5 × 32.6 cm (17 ½ × 12 ⅞ in.)

43 *Tecelar* (Weaving)
1957
Woodcut on Japanese paper
38.2 × 45.9 cm (15 1/16 × 18 ⅛ in.)

44 *Tecelar* (Weaving)
1957
Woodcut with registration marks in graphite on Japanese paper
32.5 × 44.7 cm (12 ¾ × 17 ⅝ in.)

45 *Tecelar* (Weaving)
1957
Woodcut on Japanese paper
27.6 × 44.6 cm (10 ⅞ × 17 ½ in.)

46 *Tecelar* (Weaving)
1957
Woodcut with registration marks in graphite on Japanese paper
30.7 × 46.4 cm (12 ⅛ × 18 ⅜ in.)

47 *Tecelar* (Weaving)
1957
Woodcut on Japanese paper
32.5 × 47 cm (12 ¾ × 18 ½ in.)

48 *Tecelar* (Weaving)
1957
Woodcut on Japanese paper
32.6 × 43.9 cm (12 ⅞ × 17 5/16 in.)

49 *Tecelar* (Weaving)
1957
Woodcut on Japanese paper
45 × 32.3 cm (17 ¾ × 12 ¾ in.)

50 *Tecelar* (Weaving)
1957
Woodcut on Japanese paper
32.5 × 44.1 cm (12 13/16 × 17 ⅜ in.)

51 *Tecelar* (Weaving)
1957
Woodcut on Japanese paper
32.3 × 24.3 cm (12 ¾ × 9 ½ in.)

52 *Tecelar* (Weaving)
1957
Woodcut on Japanese paper
44.8 × 35.5 cm (17 ⅝ × 13 ⅞ in.)

53 *Tecelar* (Weaving)
1957
Woodcut on Japanese paper
20.9 × 21 cm (8 ¼ × 8 ¼ in.)

54 *Tecelar* (Weaving)
1957
Woodcut with graphite on Japanese paper
21 × 20.9 cm (8 ¼ × 8 ¼ in.)

55 *Tecelar* (Weaving)
1957
Woodcut on Japanese paper
29.9 × 29.9 cm (11 13/16 × 11 13/16 in.)

56 *Tecelar* (Weaving)
1957
Woodcut on Japanese paper
30.1 × 30 cm (11 ⅞ × 11 ¾ in.)

57 *Tecelar* (Weaving)
1958
Woodcut on Japanese paper
62.8 × 92.4 cm (24 ⅝ × 36 ½ in.)

58 *Tecelar* (Weaving)
1958
Woodcut on Japanese paper
29.9 × 30 cm (11 ¾ × 11 ¾ in.)

59 *Tecelar* (Weaving)
1958
Woodcut on Japanese paper
46.2 × 44.7 cm (18 ¼ × 17 ⅝ in.)

60 *Tecelar* (Weaving)
1958
Woodcut on Japanese paper
32.7 × 48.1 cm (12 ⅞ × 19 in.)

61 *Tecelar* (Weaving)
1958
Woodcut on Japanese paper
30.2 × 44.9 cm (11 ⅞ × 17 ⅝ in.)

62 *Tecelar* (Weaving)
1958
Woodcut on Japanese paper
25.6 × 29.4 cm (10 1/16 × 11 9/16 in.)

63 *Tecelar* (Weaving)
1959
Woodcut on Japanese paper
34 × 64.3 cm (13⅜ × 25¼ in.)

64 *Tecelar* (Weaving)
1958
Woodcut on Japanese paper
29.9 × 65.2 cm (11¾ × 25¾ in.)

65 *Tecelar* (Weaving)
1958
Woodcut on Japanese paper
30 × 64.5 cm (11 13/16 × 25½ in.)

66 *Tecelar* (Weaving)
1958
Woodcut on Japanese paper
42.3 × 56.9 cm (16⅝ × 23⅜ in.)

67 *Tecelar* (Weaving)
1958
Woodcut on Japanese paper
65.2 × 27.5 cm (25¾ × 10⅞ in.)

68 *Tecelar* (Weaving)
1958
Woodcut on Japanese paper
27.3 × 63.3 cm (10⅞ × 24⅞ in.)

69 *Tecelar* (Weaving)
1958
Woodcut on Japanese paper
21.6 × 39.5 cm (8½ × 15½ in.)

70 *Tecelar* (Weaving)
1958
Woodcut on Japanese paper
32.2 × 52.2 cm (12⅝ × 20½ in.)

71 *Tecelar* (Weaving)
1958
Woodcut on Japanese paper
46.2 × 64.7 cm (18¼ × 25½ in.)

72 *Tecelar* (Weaving)
1958
Woodcut on Japanese paper
40.8 × 45 cm (16 1/16 × 17¾ in.)

73 *Tecelar* (Weaving)
1958
Woodcut on Japanese paper
30.5 × 33 cm (12 × 13 in.)

74 *Tecelar* (Weaving)
1958
Woodcut on Japanese paper
22.9 × 22.8 cm (9 × 9 in.)

75 *Tecelar* (Weaving)
1960
Woodcut collage on Japanese paper
21 × 20.1 cm (8¼ × 8⅛ in.)

76 *Tecelar* (Weaving)
1958
Woodcut on Japanese paper
28.3 × 44.2 cm (11¼ × 17 7/16 in.)

77 *Tecelar* (Weaving)
1958
Woodcut on Japanese paper
37.1 × 45.1 cm (14⅝ × 17¾ in.)

78 *Tecelar* (Weaving)
1958
Woodcut with graphite and traces of white pastel on Japanese paper
44.6 × 37.8 cm (17½ × 14⅞ in.)

79 *Tecelar* (Weaving)
1958
Woodcut on Japanese paper
53.8 × 38.9 cm (21¼ × 15¼ in.)

80 *Tecelar* (Weaving)
1959
Woodcut on Japanese paper
30.2 × 45.7 cm (11⅞ × 18 in.)

81 *Tecelar* (Weaving)
1959
Woodcut on Japanese paper
30.1 × 45.8 cm (11⅞ × 18 in.)

82 *Tecelar* (Weaving)
1959
Woodcut on Japanese paper
45.8 × 30.3 cm (18 × 11 15/16 in.)

83 *Tecelar* (Weaving)
1959
Woodcut on Japanese paper
45.7 × 60 cm (18 × 23½ in.)

84 *Tecelar* (Weaving)
1959
Woodcut on Japanese paper
29.8 × 45.7 cm (11¾ × 18 in.)

85 *Tecelar* (Weaving)
1959
Woodcut on Japanese paper
30.3 × 45.8 cm (12 × 18 1/16 in.)

86 Wood Block for Cat. 87
1959
Wood block
19.6 × 36 × 2.2 cm (7 11/16 × 14 3/16 × ⅞ in.)

87 *Tecelar* (Weaving)
1959
Woodcut on Japanese paper
30.4 × 47.8 cm (11⅞ × 18⅞ in.)

88 *Tecelar* (Weaving)
1959
Woodcut on Japanese paper
29.9 × 42.3 cm (11¾ × 16⅝ in.)

89 *Tecelar* (Weaving)
1959
Woodcut on Japanese paper
66.2 × 55.2 cm (26 × 21¾ in.)

90 *Tecelar* (Weaving)
1959
Woodcut on Japanese paper
65.8 × 61.2 cm (25⅞ × 24 in.)

91 *Tecelar* (Weaving)
1959
Woodcut on Japanese paper
44.6 × 32.7 cm (17½ × 12⅞ in.)

92 *Tecelar* (Weaving)
1959
Woodcut on Japanese paper
40.9 × 37.4 cm (16⅛ × 14¾ in.)

93 *Tecelar* (Weaving)
1959
Woodcut on Japanese paper
31.2 × 49.5 cm (12 5/16 × 19½ in.)

94 *Tecelar* (Weaving)
1959
Woodcut on Japanese paper
29.6 × 41.9 cm (11⅝ × 16½ in.)

95 Wood Block for Cat. 97 ("*Aço / Gorja / Azul*")
1960
Wood block
22.4 × 23 × 1.8 cm (8 13/16 × 9 1/16 × 11/16 in.)

96 Wood Block for Cat. 97 ("*Em Avêsso / Aço*")
1960
Photo-relief-etched metal sheet adhered to wood
21.9 × 21.8 × 2.1 cm (8 9/16 × 8⅜ × 13/16 in.)

97 *Poemas–Xilogravuras* (Poems–Woodcuts)
1960
Unbound book of 17 woodcuts and photomechanical metal relief prints on Japanese paper, tipped on letterpress-printed wove paper
Cover (unfolded): 21 × 43.5 cm (8¼ × 17⅛ in.); folios (unfolded): 21 × 41.3 cm (8¼ × 16¼ in.)

98 Performance of *Ballet Neoconcreto* at the Museu de Arte Contemporânea de Serralves, Porto, Portugal
2000
Color digital video, sound; 19 min. 43 sec.

99 *Ttéia 1, B*
2002–22
Gold nylon thread, nails, and light
440 × 430 × 210 cm (173¼ × 169 5/16 × 82 11/16 in.)

CONTRIBUTORS

Adele Nelson is Assistant Professor in the Department of Art and Art History at the University of Texas at Austin, where she also serves as Associate Director of the Center for Latin American Visual Studies. She is the author of *Forming Abstraction: Art and Institutions in Postwar Brazil* (2022) and co-organizer of the exhibition *Social Fabric: Art and Activism in Contemporary Brazil* (Visual Arts Center at UT Austin, 2022), which received the Andy Warhol Foundation for the Visual Arts Grant. Her writing has appeared in international magazines and academic journals, and she has contributed to numerous museum publications, among them *Lygia Clark: Painting as an Experimental Field, 1948–1958* (2020), *Mário Pedrosa: De la naturaleza afectiva de la forma* (2017), and *Hélio Oiticica: To Organize Delirium* (2016).

Mark Pascale has been active in the Chicago art world for forty years, as a curator, printmaker, professor, and researcher. He is the Janet and Craig Duchossois Curator, Prints and Drawings, at the Art Institute of Chicago, and concurrently Senior Lecturer of Art in Print Media at the School of the Art Institute of Chicago. He has edited or organized numerous publications and exhibitions, including *Joseph E. Yoakum: What I Saw* (2021), *Hairy Who? 1966–1969* (2018), *Along the Lines: Selected Drawings by Saul Steinberg* (2017), and *Martin Puryear: Multiple Dimensions* (2015). He is currently working on an exhibition focused on the work of Christina Ramberg.

María Cristina Rivera Ramos is Assistant Conservator of Paper in Conservation and Science at the Art Institute of Chicago. Since joining the museum in 2016, she has cared for its broad range of paper-based artwork, with a special emphasis on the Arts of Asia and Architecture and Design collections. She has worked on several exhibitions at the Art Institute, including *Senju's "Waterfall" for Chicago* (2021), *Noda Tetsuya: My Life in Print* (2020), *Everyone's Art Gallery: Posters of the London Underground* (2019), and *Rubens, Rembrandt, and Drawing in the Golden Age* (2019).

INDEX

Page numbers in *italics* refer to illustrations.

R

S

T

PHOTOGRAPHY CREDITS

Unless otherwise noted, photographs of artworks in the collection of the Art Institute of Chicago are by Imaging, the Art Institute of Chicago, and are copyrighted by the Art Institute of Chicago. Photographs of artworks by Lygia Pape are by Imaging, the Art Institute of Chicago, unless otherwise noted, and are copyrighted by the Projeto Lygia Pape, Rio de Janeiro and Lisbon.

Every effort has been made to identify, contact, and acknowledge copyright holders for all reproductions; additional rights holders are encouraged to contact the Art Institute of Chicago. The following credits apply to all images in this book for which separate acknowledgment is due.

Front cover: *Tecelar* (Weaving), 1958 (cat. 73)
Back cover: *Tecelar* (Weaving), 1956 (cat. 30)
Details: p. 2: *Tecelar* (Weaving), 1957 (cat. 35); p. 4: *Tecelar* (Weaving), 1959 (cat. 80); p. 6: *Tecelar* (Weaving), 1959 (cat. 75); p. 10: *Tecelar* (Weaving), 1957 (cat. 56); pp. 12–13: *Tecelar* (Weaving), 1953 (cat. 13); p. 14: *Tecelar* (Weaving), 1958 (cat. 58); p. 23: *Tecelar* (Weaving), 1957 (cat. 49); p. 24: *Tecelar* (Weaving), 1958 (cat. 78); p. 43: *Tecelar* (Weaving), 1956 (cat. 30); p. 44: *Tecelar* (Weaving), 1955 (cat. 25); p. 55: *Tecelar* (Weaving), 1957 (cat. 52); p. 56: *Tecelar* (Weaving), 1957 (cat. 38); p. 164: *Tecelar* (Weaving), 1958 (cat. 69)

P. 8; pp. 18–19, fig. 5; p. 30, fig. 4; p. 162, pl. 98; p. 163, pl. 99: Photo by the Projeto Lygia Pape

P. 17, fig. 3: Image used in accordance with the regulations of the Goeldi Project, www.oswaldogoeldi.org.br, São Paulo

P. 18, fig. 4: © 2022 Josef Albers / Artists Rights Society (ARS), New York

P. 21, fig. 7: Photo by Jamie Stukenberg; © 2022 Josef Albers / Artists Rights Society (ARS), New York

P. 21, fig. 8; p. 32, fig. 7: Photo by Günther Pape; © Projeto Lygia Pape

P. 28, fig. 2; p. 36, fig. 10: Digital image © The Museum of Modern Art / Licensed by SCALA / Art Resource, NY

P. 31, fig. 6: Arquivo Nacional, Rio de Janeiro

P. 33, fig. 8: Fundação Bienal de São Paulo / Arquivo Histórico Wanda Svevo

P. 34, fig. 9; p. 38, fig. 11: Jornal do Brasil, Rio de Janeiro

P. 39, fig. 12: Fundo Willys de Castro–Acervo Instituto de Arte Contemporânea, São Paulo

Lygia Pape: Tecelares was published in conjunction with an exhibition of the same title organized by the Art Institute of Chicago, held from February 11 to June 5, 2023.

Support for *Lygia Pape: Tecelares* is generously provided by The Diane & Bruce Halle Foundation.

First edition
Printed in Spain

ISBN: 978-0-300-26973-4 (hardcover)
Library of Congress Control Number: 2022948610

Published by
The Art Institute of Chicago
111 South Michigan Avenue
Chicago, IL 60603-6404
artic.edu

Distributed by
Yale University Press
302 Temple Street
P. O. Box 209040
New Haven, CT 06520-9040
yalebooks.com/art

Publishing, the Art Institute of Chicago
Lisa Meyerowitz, Editorial Director
Joseph Mohan, Director of Production
Lauren Makholm, Associate Director of Production and Manager of Digital Initiatives

Edited by Kit Shields
Production by Lauren Makholm and Ben Bertin
Photography research by Josephine Yanasak-Leszczynski
Proofreading by Sarah E. Robinson
Indexing by Jane Friedman

Imaging, the Art Institute of Chicago
Bonnie Rosenberg, Director of Imaging
Nathan Keay, Associate Director of Photography
Photography by Craig Stillwell
Postproduction by Hayley Hinsberger
Preproduction and coordination by Elyse Allen

Design and typesetting by Beverly Joel, pulp, ink.
Separations by Professional Graphics, Rockford, IL
Printing and binding by Brizzolis, arte en gráficas, Madrid

This book was made using paper and materials certified by the Forest Stewardship Council, which ensures responsible forest management.

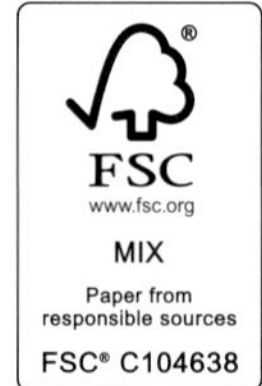